Natural Theology and the Problem of Evil

Natural Theology and the Problem of Evil

STEVEN R. LEWIS

WIPF & STOCK · Eugene, Oregon

NATURAL THEOLOGY AND THE PROBLEM OF EVIL

Wipf & Stock
An Imprint of Wipf and Stock Publishers
199 W. 8th Ave., Suite 3
Eugene, OR 97401

www.wipfandstock.com

PAPERBACK ISBN: 979-8-3852-6282-3
HARDCOVER ISBN: 979-8-3852-6283-0
EBOOK ISBN: 979-8-3852-6284-7

VERSION NUMBER 03/10/26

To Rachel, my wife.

Contents

Introduction

AMONG PHILOSOPHICAL ARGUMENTS POSED against the existence of God, the problem of evil is perhaps the most prominent. In its logical form, the argument poses a set of facts (given theism) that appear to contain a contradiction—specifically that the God of classical theism (if he exists) is necessarily omnipotent, omniscient, and perfectly good—and yet evil exists. Put simply, the problem of evil means to show that God (given the sort of divine nature and attributes he is said to possess) cannot exist in a universe that contains evil. Such an argument is not new to theistic philosophy. Thomas Aquinas, for example, describes a similar argument, writing from the thirteenth century, "It seems that God does not exist; because if one of two contraries be infinite, the other would be altogether destroyed. But the word 'God' means that he is infinite goodness. If, therefore, God existed, there would be no evil discoverable; but there is evil in the world. Therefore God does not exist."[1] Such an argument holds that God's infinite goodness simply precludes the possibility of evil in the world.

Theists have offered a range of responses to the logical problem of evil—including a slate of what are known as *theodicies* and *defenses*—in order to demonstrate how God could in fact exist in a world filled with evil. As such, the argument from evil has evolved to acknowledge and incorporate these theistic criticisms into a new approach known as the *evidential problem of evil*. The evidential argument rejects a position of strong logical certainty in favor of a more inductive approach that takes the evil in the world as *evidence* that appears to favor non-theism over theism—thus, God's existence is said to be unlikely, given the sheer quantity and severity of evil found in the world. Of particular interest to this approach is what is often referred to as *gratuitous* evil—evil with no

1. Aquinas, *Summa Theologiae*, I.2.3.

apparent greater good associated with it that may justify its existence in a theistic universe. Though theists have critiqued the evidential form of the problem of evil in various ways, some philosophers of religion have argued that "the evidential argument from gratuitous evil is now widely considered the most formidable objection to theistic belief."[2]

However, despite the prevalence of the evidential argument in the recent philosophical literature, it seems to me that the argument contains an illicit category mistake that undermines its potency as an argument against the existence of God. Put simply, the evidential problem of evil holds that God's existence is unlikely given the evidence of evil in the universe, and this is argued on the basis that God—given his infinite power and perfect goodness—should and would always prevent evil from occurring whenever it would be possible for him to do so. The critical factor here for evidential arguments is specifically the nature of God's goodness and what this goodness necessarily entails in terms of divine action (or inaction) in relation to some world God may choose to create. This expectation of divine behavior (on account of God's goodness) many hold to be akin to what humans recognize and describe as "moral obligations" to the overall benefit of created beings. If God is morally obliged to employ his power and wisdom toward the overall good of creatures to the best of his ability, then it would be surprising in a world created by God to find evidence of gratuitous evil and suffering. Thus, it is critical for the evidential problem of evil that God's goodness entails a set of divine moral obligations, given what can be reasonably predicated of God in accord with his divine attributes.

In this regard, a careful analysis of God's existence and attributes plays an important role in an evaluation of the problem of evil, and I believe that such an analysis from the position of natural theology reveals that God's infinite goodness does not in fact entail the sort of moral obligations commonly attributed to created moral beings. Therefore, I believe that the univocal attribution of moral obligation to God in any way similar to the moral obligations often found in sentient creatures is an illicit category mistake and cannot be established from a position of natural theology. God's divine goodness as applied to the created world only "constrains" him to act toward that world in a purely suppositional sense, given the sort of world he chooses to create, and there is no reason to think that there does or should exist some "macro-obligation" for

2. Peterson, *God and Evil*, 85.

God to create any particular possible world over another. In short, if God has chosen to create a world populated with beings and things that are subject to privation (like the actual one), then the presence of privation in such a world cannot possibly constitute a coherent argument against the existence of its creator. If this is so, then any evidence or example of gratuitous evil in the world would hold no contradiction to the existence of God.

While I believe that my approach does sufficiently resolve the evidential problem of evil, I also believe that a new argument from evil is possible from such an analysis that relies on what I will call *inexplicable evil*—evil which appears by all accounts to be devoid of explanation as an aspect of a theistic universe. Thus, even if evil need not be *morally justified* for the theist, it must still be *sufficiently explained* in terms of its causal relationships and privative nature. Also, since the evidential argument from evil is an argument directed largely against the human belief and confidence in the existence of God (rather than the logical possibility of God's existence), then the human experience and perception of evil is a critical element in the discussion. Therefore, while it may not be true that some instance of evil necessarily contradicts God's existence, it may yet undermine one's own confidence in God and his divine goodness as a matter of human belief.

Such is the pursuit of the "why" question of evil—that which seeks an explanation as to why evil may be found in the world if God does in fact exist. Even if evil presents no real contradiction against God's existence, one may ask, then why does evil yet exist? As Bruce Little argues, "It is the human experience that begs for some answer, some meaningful clarification. It is the pervasiveness of evil and the personal affliction from evil that causes the heart to cry: 'God, why this evil?'"[3] In light of evil which seems largely *unexplained* in this regard, I seek to offer a possible response for the theist which preserves both a reasoned understanding of God and his classical attributes from an adroit natural theology and a reasonable confidence and trust in God and his divine goodness in light of the evil apparent in the universe. While my approach admittedly stops short of providing direct answers to the "why" question, it nevertheless affirms that these answers necessarily exist, given what is known of God and his attributes from natural theology, and thus any actual evil in the world is always necessarily explained in a theistic universe. As such, the

3. Little, *God, Why This Evil?*, 11.

burden of proof shifts to the non-theist, who must henceforth argue that there is in fact no *possible* explanation of some apparent instance of evil in the world in order to establish the soundness of the new evidential problem that I will propose.

In chapter one, I will present a brief synopsis of the foundations and development of the modern problem of evil, beginning with its stronger logical form in the works of philosophers such as David Hume and J. L. Mackie. I will follow with an analysis of a shift in the argument resulting from certain criticisms of the logical problem—particularly from Alvin Plantinga's "free will" defense—toward a new *evidential* argument from evil as proposed by philosophers such as William Rowe and Paul Draper. Finally, I will conclude with a brief survey of various ways that theists have attempted to resolve the evidential problem by attacking its premises.

In chapter two, I will present an argument from natural theology (following a largely Thomistic vein) as a means to establish a foundational understanding of God and his attributes from which to further evaluate the inherent claims and assumptions of the evidential problem of evil. I intend to demonstrate how certain divine attributes critical to the problem of evil emerge naturally from a basic understanding of God's existence, as deduced from the *intellectus essentiae* argument for God's existence, which allows the theist to proceed to a comprehensive view of God's nature and attributes without relying on any *ad hoc* assertions or unfounded assumptions in the classical view of God. I will finish by considering a few possible objections to this approach to natural theology and how the argument I present avoids these objections.

In chapter three, I will proceed with a more focused and nuanced examination of God's omniscience, as considered from a position of natural theology with particular relevance to the problem of evil. I will largely limit my analysis of this divine attribute to what can be deduced from the understanding of God as *ipsum esse subsistens* (as revealed from the *intellectus essentiae* argument). I will also evaluate and critique two major objections often levied against God's omniscience (that of "freedom and foreknowledge" and the problem of "tensed truths") and show how the analysis of God's omniscience from a Thomistic natural theology resolves these objections.

In chapter four, like the previous chapter, I will offer a more focused and nuanced examination of God's omnipotence, once again as considered from a position of a Thomistic natural theology. I will evaluate and critique two paradoxical objections to God's omnipotence (the "paradox of the stone" and the "paradox of sin") and show how my approach to natural theology resolves these objections and preserves the classical meaning of this divine attribute.

In chapter five, I will turn to an analysis of God's perfect goodness as a critical divine attribute in consideration of the problem of evil. I will consider how God can be properly said to be "good" and what that goodness necessarily entails as an aspect of the divine essence. I will show that God's perfect goodness does not imply or require a "perfect moral goodness" in the same way that creatures are said to be morally good, and thus it is a category mistake to ascribe moral duties and obligations to God. I will then consider various ways that moral categories are often applied to God in analogical ways, whether these are consistent with the understanding of God as *ipsum esse subsistens*, and whether such distinctions bear direct relevance to the problem of evil. I will conclude that God is not a "moral being" in the same way that creatures are, and the understanding of God as perfectly good from a position of a Thomistic natural theology does not and should not entail any moral obligation on God's part toward creatures in the face of evil.

In chapter six, I will turn to a detailed analysis of the nature of evil itself and what sort of form or nature evil can be said to possess when it occurs in the context of the natural world. Toward this end, I will argue that evil *per se* has no nature independent from the things in which it inhabits or infects. Evil, therefore, is not a force in the universe or a thing in itself but rather a *privation of the good* in real existing things with no existence of its own. As such, evil cannot be said to be directly caused by God (whether moral or natural evil), though it can be caused by created things in a teleological pursuit of the good—even if those things sometimes fail to achieve the good they seek on account of a corruption of the acting agent or the act itself. I will conclude with a direct comparison of the nature of God and the nature of evil with the intent to demonstrate that the existence of God is fully compatible with the existence of evil in a universe created by God.

In chapter seven, I will explore the origin and explanation of evil in the universe with a particular focus on various arguments and responses often proposed by theists in response to the problem of evil. I will first consider what it means for God to be necessarily obliged to create only the "best of all possible worlds" and whether such a concept (whatever it may entail) is legitimate given the understanding of God as *ipsum esse subsistens.* I will conclude that *any* possible world that does not contain a contradiction remains a possible world for God to create regardless of the amount of good or evil it may contain, and any response to the problem of evil must remain grounded in the only possible world apparent to human observers—the present one. I will then examine a few of the most widely disseminated theodicies and defenses typically posed in response to the question of gratuitous evil and consider whether these have merit in terms of the problem of evil in light of the view of God I have defended. I will conclude with an analysis of God and gratuitous evil specifically, and I will show that gratuitous evil can exist in a theistic universe and that the evidential arguments from both William Rowe and Paul Draper are fully resolved on this basis.

In chapter eight, I will consider a renewed evidential argument from evil akin to the "why" question that seeks an *explanation* rather than a *justification* of evil. I will first consider the proper perspective of evil that leads to the "why" question in the first place, with an eye on the facts of theism as discovered by natural theology as a basis for moving toward a resolution of this question. I will then consider whether it can be said that God has "reasons" for what he does and does not do, and I will argue that while God cannot act for reasons in the same way that humans do, it is nevertheless reasonable to conclude that God does act toward ends that always coincide (and are in fact identical) with his own divine nature and attributes. I will then present a new evidential argument from evil that takes these considerations into account—one that both accepts the possibility of gratuitous evil as an aspect of a theistic universe while also considering the explanation of evil as resulting from good causes that are in turn ordered toward (or produced by) something that is inherently good as created by God.

In chapter nine, the final chapter, I will expound on the this new evidential argument—one that focuses on good and evil as understood from a human perspective. Toward a resolution of this new argument, I will propose a solution grounded in a reasoned *belief and trust in God* in the face of evil employed toward a resolution of the "why" question of evil and grounded in a foundation of natural theology. I will consider this proposed solution and how the evidence for God's existence from the perspective of a Thomistic natural theology offers the theist a reasonable basis to conclude that all evil (however gratuitous or inexplicable it may seem) can be and necessarily is fully explained in a theistic universe—even if the actual causal factors at play cannot be directly observed or known from a human perspective. I will follow with a consideration of God's goodness in the face of evil and examine various ways in which the good can at times be seen, in its causal relationships, related to the evil in the world, which plays an important role for the theist in understanding how evil can be properly explained in a theistic universe and how God's perfect goodness can be seen throughout a creation otherwise permeated with evil and suffering. I will conclude by considering a few possible objections to this approach. I will argue that apparent gratuitous or excessive evil does not provide a sufficient reason to reject a belief in God and that those who maintain a committed belief and trust in God have good reason to deny that any evil in existence is or can possibly be truly inexplicable.

I will conclude with an overall summary of my arguments and conclusions. I intend to show that evidential arguments from evil (such as those proposed by William Rowe and Paul Draper) simply do not arise in a theistic universe as understood from the position of a Thomistic natural theology, because God (as properly considered) does not hold any real moral obligation to prevent or exclude gratuitous evil from the effects of his creation. Further, even if the argument from evil is adjusted to appeal specifically to the "why" question of evil that survives this analysis on the basis of inexplicable evil (at least from a human perspective), the theist retains a reasonable response in a committed faith in God in the face of evil, given what is known of God and his attributes from a position of natural theology. Thus, a committed belief and trust in God's existence and divine attributes cannot be undermined by the evidential problem of evil.

1

The Problem of Evil

God exists. God is good. Evil exists. These three simple truths have been universally affirmed by theists since antiquity, yet there seems to be something about these three simple statements that does not quite fit together. If God exists, and he is good, then why would there be any evil or suffering in a world created by him? Why would a good God allow (or even perhaps *cause*) evil and suffering? Questions like these lead to what is often called the "problem of evil," which suggests that the existence of a good God (or at least a rational basis for belief in God) is somehow undermined by the evil that seems so readily apparent in the created world.

When properly considered, the problem of evil either succeeds or fails on how its premises are determined, defined, and defended. What do we mean by "God," and what reasons do we have to think that he exists? If God exists, what does it mean to say that he is good, and what reasons do we have to think that he is good? What exactly is evil, and what do we mean when we say that evil "exists" in the world? Does the goodness of God necessarily preclude the existence of evil *per se,* or is there a rational explanation as to why evil may exist in a world created by God? Depending on how these questions are answered and defended, the problem of evil either presents a real problem for theistic belief, or it is perhaps no real problem at all.

Before proceeding to an analysis of the problem of evil, it is important to note that there are two distinct problems that arise from an awareness or experience of evil and suffering in the world: the *philosophical* problem of evil and the *pastoral* problem of evil. The philosophical problem of evil is what I have described above—a logical or evidential argument against rational belief in God from a certain set of premises involving God's existence, his nature, and the severity and prevalence of evil in the world. This sort of problem is a rational and intellectual one that must be addressed and answered with sober philosophical arguments and evidence. It is a very *cold* argument in that respect as a strictly intellectual endeavor. What is at stake here is purely the *rationality* of theistic belief.

The pastoral problem of evil, however, is of a different sort. This problem deals with one's own personal or emotional struggle with some instance or experience of evil and suffering. Perhaps a close friend or family member has been diagnosed with cancer, or perhaps a child has been victimized or abused, or perhaps there is a brutal terrorist attack or a devastating tsunami that kills countless innocent victims. This sort of challenge presents a very *warm* argument with a certain degree of personal impact. The emotional weight of the evil one encounters in life can create a potent individual challenge to theistic belief, and such a challenge certainly cries out for answers. This distinction is important here because the answers to each of these problems can be very different. Intellectual problems of evil require sober intellectual answers, while pastoral problems of evil require empathetic pastoral care. While I believe the answers to both of these problems do hold a significant degree of overlap, in this work I intend to focus largely on the *philosophical* problem of evil, and thus my arguments and conclusions may seem to be of a particularly cold intellectual and rational nature. A sufficient answer to the *pastoral* problem of evil would require a different approach that would constitute a work in itself.

Finally, it is important to note that I am an evangelical Christian, and I believe that the Bible is the inerrant, inspired word of God. However, for the sake of my argument here, I have not presupposed theism, Christianity, or the truth of the Bible in developing a response to the problem of evil. To be clear, I do believe that both the Bible and the historic Christian faith have a great deal to say about both the philosophical and pastoral problems of evil—in fact, I believe the unique and poignant answers they provide are of themselves sufficient to overcome the entire philosophical category of arguments from evil altogether. However, the nature of the problem in the first place is one that calls into question God's very existence, and it is a bit sloppy and uncouth to simply assume for the sake of argument the very thing that is being argued. A more effective response, therefore, must draw on common human knowledge and commonly held beliefs about the world and its operations as a basis for developing a cogent response. Since the problem of evil calls into question the rationality of theistic belief on the basis of our experience and knowledge of the world, I shall propose a solution to the problem of evil also drawing on what can be properly known of God, his nature, and evil solely on account of our experience and knowledge of the world—in other words, *natural theology*. As such, I will argue for God's existence and nature from what can be known of him from the effects of his creation and the machinations of the natural world. With this said, it is also important to note that the target of these sorts of arguments from evil is most often directed at the God of Christianity. Many anti-theists who promote the problem of evil argue against the God of the Bible as a particularly egregious example of what they deem to be a capricious deity who appears either complicit or ambivalent to all of the evil and suffering in his creation. As such, I may at times introduce some biblical examples in my arguments here and there primarily for illustrative purposes. Though I believe an argument from natural theology—without any reference to a particular theistic tradition such as Christianity—is sufficient to fully resolve the problem of evil, I do also believe that no theistic tradition better embodies the God revealed by natural theology than the biblical God of Christianity.

It is now prudent to examine the problem of evil and the basic structure and premises of the argument. In philosophical circles, the problem of evil is often segregated into two distinct categories—the *logical* problem of evil and the *evidential* problem of evil. The logical problem holds that certain claims about God and evil pose a necessary logical contradiction, and thus the existence of evil serves as a basis for a deductive logical proof against the existence of God. The evidential problem holds that evil only serves as inductive evidence that God does not exist, though it is not enough to necessitate a logical proof. Thus, as the evidential problem asserts, the prevalence of evil and suffering in the world makes God's non-existence more likely or *evident* to the believer, and a denial of God's existence becomes the most reasonable response when the amount and severity of evil in the world is properly considered. Though many iterations of both logical and evidential arguments have been proposed, I will focus here on two landmark examples: those of J. L. Mackie and William Rowe.

MACKIE'S LOGICAL PROBLEM OF EVIL

Though the philosophical problem of evil in its traditional form dates back at least as far as the ancient Greek philosopher Epicurus (341–270

BC), the early origin of the modern logical form of the argument is most widely attributed to J. L. Mackie (1917–81), who himself draws from Scottish philosopher David Hume (1711–76). In his highly influential work *Dialogues Concerning Natural Religion*, Hume gives us an imagined dialogue between two fictional characters: Philo and Cleanthes. In their ongoing back-and-forth, Philo and Cleanthes eventually settle on certain philosophical difficulties that seem to arise about the nature and attributes of God, which leads them to Epicurus's own ancient argument. In Hume's dialogue, Philo makes the argument as follows: "Epicurus' old questions are yet unanswered. Is [God] willing to prevent evil, but not able? Then he is impotent. Is he able, but not willing? Then he is malevolent. Is he both able and willing? Whence then is evil?"[1]

Though the picture of God presented by Hume's *Dialogues* (and defended by Cleanthes) is a very anthropomorphic one that assumes God should be expected to act and behave much like a human, the challenge he presents is nevertheless poignant and significant. If God is both powerful enough to prevent evil and good enough to desire a world without evil, then why is there any evil at all? Expanding on Hume, philosopher J. L. Mackie presents a similar argument:

> In its simplest form the problem is this: God is omnipotent; God is wholly good; and yet evil exists. There seems to be some contradiction between these three propositions, so that if any two of them were true the third would be false. But at the same time all three are essential parts of most theological positions: the theologian, it seems, at once *must* adhere and *cannot consistently* adhere to all three.[2]

Here, Mackie draws out what he believes to be a logical contradiction between three basic truths, all to which any theist is inevitably committed: "God is omnipotent; God is wholly good; and yet evil exists." Mackie himself admits that these three premises do not constitute a contradiction by themselves, and thus he offers additional arguments centered around what it means for God to be "good" and what one might expect from God on account of his divine goodness.

> These additional principles are that good is opposed to evil, in such a way that a good thing always eliminates evil as far as it can, and that there are no limits to what an omnipotent thing

1. Hume, *Dialogues Concerning Natural Religion*, 74.
2. Mackie, "Evil and Omnipotence," 200; emphasis in original.

> can do. From these it follows that a good omnipotent thing eliminates evil completely, and then the propositions that a good omnipotent thing exists, and that evil exists, are incompatible.[3]

In other words, as Mackie explains, anything "good" stands in a natural opposition to anything "evil" and must necessarily eliminate evil whenever and however it is able to do so. If this is granted as the definition of God's infinite, perfect goodness, then there does seem to be a contradiction of sorts, when one discovers some instance of evil in the world, that an omnipotent being could easily have been prevented. In order to resolve the argument in favor of theism, according to Mackie, the theist is left in the uncomfortable position to deny one of two basic tenets of classical theism: God's omnipotence or God's perfect goodness.

This form of the argument from evil is often called the *logical* problem of evil, as it purports to demonstrate a logical contradiction between a set of premises to which the theist is necessarily committed, and as such, this argument is presented as a logical denial of theism. Admit that God cannot stop evil, and you admit that he is impotent. Admit that God is unwilling to stop evil, and you admit that he is not good. Deny that evil exists or occurs, and you deny a basic fundamental fact about the universe that seems abundantly obvious to every observer—the fact that evil does exist. Given such a potent challenge, what is the theist to do?

Some have pointed out that Mackie misses a critical detail in his argument—specifically that God could very well have *good reasons* to allow at least some evil to permeate an otherwise-good universe. Perhaps a world with at least some evil is better in some respect than a world with no evil at all, because some higher goods may just require at least the *possibility* (or even perhaps the *actuality*) of evil and suffering. Alvin Plantinga, for example, lays out what he calls a "defense" against Mackie's logical problem of evil that suggests a *possible* (though not necessarily *actual*) reason for God's permission of evil in the world—that of *free will.* For Plantinga, God's goodness can be successfully defended in the face of evil so long as the evil in question makes possible some higher good. Plantinga then proposes "free will" as just such a higher good that requires at least the possibility of evil.

> A world containing creatures who are sometimes significantly free (and freely perform more good than evil actions) is more valuable, all else being equal, than a world containing no free

3. Mackie, "Evil and Omnipotence," 201.

> creatures at all. Now God can create free creatures, but he cannot cause or determine them to do only what is right. For if he does so, then they are not significantly free after all; they do not do what is right *freely*. To create creatures capable of *moral good*, therefore, he must create creatures capable of moral evil; and he cannot leave these creatures *free* to perform evil and at the same time prevent them from doing so. . . . The fact that these free creatures sometimes go wrong, however, counts neither against God's omnipotence nor against his goodness; for he could have forestalled the occurrence of moral evil only by excising the possibility of moral good.[4]

According to Plantinga, therefore, it would not be within the power of God (as a logical impossibility) to create free moral agents without at least the *possibility* of moral evil, and a world with free moral agents is more valuable than one without; thus, "free will" constitutes a greater good that justifies moral evil. Hence, for Plantinga, God could not have created a world of free agents without allowing at least the possibility (and eventual actuality) of at least some evil resulting from the outcome of their free choices.

As a result of Plantinga's defense, logical arguments from evil (such as Mackie's) have been largely abandoned in the philosophical sphere. Philosopher Brian Leftow speaks to Plantinga's success: "But if you think that evil currently provides any very strong argument against the existence of God, you have not been paying attention. The deductive ('logical') versions of the problem of evil are very widely conceded to be 'dead,' killed off by Plantinga's free-will defense."[5] Hence it is now widely accepted that Plantinga has successfully proven that the logical problem of evil does not necessitate a denial of theism.

Putting Plantinga's defense aside for the moment, it seems to me that Mackie's logical argument has yet another critical flaw that does not require the theist to produce a theodicy or defense in an attempt to explain God's moral justification for evil. Significantly, Mackie does not explain what evil actually is (in respect to how it comes to exist and the operative causes that bring it about), how the existence and nature of God is known, why God is said to be "good" in the first place and what his divine goodness necessarily entails, and more specifically why a perfectly good being would be somehow obliged to eliminate or prevent evil in

4. Plantinga, *Nature of Necessity*, 166–67; emphasis in original.

5. Leftow, *God and Necessity*, 547.

every possible world. These all seem to involve an unstated set of assumptions about God, his nature, and evil that are just presumed without argument by Mackie (and others). To be clear, it is not necessarily a flaw in a philosophical argument to avoid page after page justifying every term or concept used when making an argument—which would be otherwise grossly impractical (if not practically impossible). It is common for those like Mackie to simply assume agreement on basic concepts and proceed from that basis, and Mackie should not be faulted for this *per se*. However, it is possible that the resolution of an argument such as Mackie's lies within those unstated assumptions of agreement. If the initial assumptions about who God is, what his nature entails, what evil is, and what constitutes God's relationship to evil are flawed in some way, then it is possible that the argument itself is either unsound or even incoherent. This is precisely where I believe that Mackie's argument suffers its greatest challenge, and while I will engage with those foundational assumptions later in greater detail, I will here briefly outline one such problem that arises from Mackie's formulation of the argument.

The image of God presented by Mackie smuggles in certain anthropomorphic ideas about God that would not necessarily apply to an infinite divine being who actively causes the existence of all things. One such concept is that of God's own duties and obligations toward a creation that he himself designed, initiated, and sustains. It may be self-evident to me, for example, that if I had the means and ability to stop a criminal from assaulting a helpless bystander, then I would be morally obliged to do so. But if both criminal and the victim exist and operate within the bounds of a universe of free creatures, acting and suffering according to the laws and operations of that very universe—as designed and created by a divine, rational being—then it would seem odd to suppose that their Creator would be of a type of moral character (analogous to humans) such that he must override or supersede the very universe he has made in order to rescue the bystander from the criminal. In other words, I should help the stranger if I am able because I have a moral duty to do so on account of my position as a human moral creature with a moral nature inside a moral universe, but God is no such creature, has no such obligatory nature that determines his actions, and is the very designer and sustainer of the world inhabited by the parties involved. In short, given the sort of God that is revealed to us by a basic natural theology, for example, there seems to be no reason to think that a good God would be somehow unable to create a good world where bad things happen (so long as the ends toward which nature and the moral will are directed are always good—but more on that later). For now, suffice to say, it is a reasonable time to move beyond Mackie's argument and examine a further development in the problem of evil.

ROWE'S EVIDENTIAL PROBLEM OF EVIL

In an attempt to avoid some of the traditional pitfalls of Mackie's logical argument, philosopher William Rowe (1931–2015) has offered a modified argument—what has become known as the *evidential* problem of evil. Instead of a logical syllogism designed to establish the impossibility of God's existence given evil, Rowe proposes a weaker thesis: that evil simply serves as *evidence* for God's non-existence, though it may not by itself guarantee or prove that God does not exist. Per Rowe, one must take the sum of evil in the world as evidence of God's non-existence and weigh it out in a sort of "probability calculus" against any other evidence for God's existence. Such an argument shifts from the deductive certainty of a logical syllogism to a case of inductive probability. Given the amount and severity of evil that is evident in the world, the argument claims that it is simply *unlikely* or *improbable* (though not *impossible*) that God exists, and thus a denial of God's existence becomes a rational and reasonable position to hold on that basis. The sort of evil in question that is meant to serve as evidence of God's non-existence is often referred to as *gratuitous* evil, which describes any case of evil in the world that God could have prevented without losing some greater good or unleashing some greater evil.

Rowe's argument, therefore, centers on the incompatibility of God and gratuitous evil (taking *God* to be an "omnipotent, wholly good being" and *gratuitous evil* to be any instance of evil in the world that God could have prevented without forfeiting some greater good or unleashing some greater evil).[6] His argument can be summarized as follows:

(1) Gratuitous evil exists that God could have prevented.

(2) God would prevent any gratuitous evil he could.

(3) Therefore, God does not exist.

6. Rowe, "Problem of Evil and Some Varieties of Atheism," 336.

Though expressed here as a valid logical argument, Rowe does not believe that anyone can conclusively prove (1) to be true. Rowe argues that gratuitous evil seems to be readily apparent throughout the world as far as we know, but he admits that "it would seem to require something like omniscience on our part before we could lay claim to *knowing* that there is no greater good connected to" some apparent instance of gratuitous suffering.[7] Rowe relies instead on establishing rational grounds to believe that (1) is true, which he argues is achieved by recognizing the quantity and severity of evil that is apparent throughout the world. It would seem to be entirely rational, per Rowe, to conclude that God could have likely prevented at least some of this evil without forfeiting some greater good or unleashing some greater evil, even if one cannot know for certain that this is true. With the vast evidence of apparently gratuitous evil in mind, therefore, Rowe argues that (1) should be accepted as a rational belief. Rowe further argues that (2) is so universally obvious and affirmed by theists that it requires little or no defense. Therefore, Rowe concludes that it is at least a rational belief that God *most likely* does not exist. As Rowe argues: "I'm sure it strikes most of us as just plain reasonable to think that if there were an omnipotent, omniscient being, then a bit more activity on his part would have made the world somewhat better."[8]

Attempts at countering Rowe's evidential argument for the non-existence of God vary widely among theists—most of which tend to focus on what Rowe considers to be the most controversial premise (1). Some argue that God could not have prevented certain evils that appear to be gratuitous on account of some connected goods that might be hidden to an observer for one reason or another, such as the good of moral virtue or a world of meaningful moral interaction. Others argue that humans are just not in a position to know or recognize the goods associated with the evils we encounter in the world; such goods lie within the nigh-omnipotent purview of God alone and are simply beyond our ken. However, unlike Mackie's logical argument, the evidential argument from evil enjoys a number of prominent defenders today, and no conclusive theistic response has garnered widespread support in the way that Plantinga's free will defense has for the logical argument.

The question of Rowe's evidential argument centers on whether or not the evidence or examples of evil and suffering in the world constitute

7. Rowe, "Problem of Evil and Some Varieties of Atheism," 337; emphasis in original.

8. Rowe, "Ruminations About Evil," 74.

prima facie evidence against God's existence. If evil stands in some sort of opposition or rebellion to God's design for the universe and its otherwise-good operations, then it would seem that one's rational belief in the existence of God would in fact reduce to some sort of probability calculus. Whether or not theism is a rational belief, therefore, would be determined by the sum of evidence either for or against God's existence. In this calculus, Rowe is convinced that the evidence favors atheism, and even more so that this evidence, he believes, abundantly dwarfs the opposing evidence for theism. However, like Mackie, Rowe's argument suffers from the same sort of problems, with the slate of unstated assumptions that undergird Rowe's own premises. Some relevant questions and considerations, for example, would be what evil is and how it may fit into a theistic universe. After all, if evil in the world (even of the gratuitous sort) is not at all surprising given theism for some reason or another, then Rowe's evidence simply disappears.

Along these lines, a problem exists for Rowe in his second premise. Despite Rowe's insistence on the widespread and obvious acceptance of premise (2), it is not immediately obvious that God would necessarily prevent any gratuitous evil he could. Perhaps gratuitous evil is simply the natural byproduct of a good universe, or perhaps it is the result of the free actions of the agents of that universe, or perhaps it is simply altogether unexplained (at least from a finite human perspective). The most relevant question remains: What is it about gratuitous evil that is inherently *by definition* opposed to God's existence? This is in fact where I believe the greatest weakness in Rowe's argument truly lies. As my examination of natural theology will reveal, God's existence and nature are both apparent and knowable to the observer of the natural world, and what is revealed about God through natural philosophy simply and defensibly precludes any attempt to compel certain acts on God's part in response to evil and suffering in the world—even evil that may be genuinely gratuitous (i.e., without any associated greater good sufficient to morally justify its existence in a theistic world). So long as the world operates according to God's design (toward a *telos* that is itself ultimately good, of course), then there is no reason whatever to assume that God must override or contradict that very world on account of something that naturally follows from it, including evil. Furthermore, the creation of such a world where evil is either likely or inevitable is not evidence against God's goodness or perfection so long as the world itself is good and teleologically directed toward the good (though such ends may fail on account of the limited agents that operate within it). As such, it is of value here to proceed to an examination of God's being and essence as revealed by natural theology.

2

The Existence and Nature of God

The evidential argument from evil relies heavily on the experience and perception of various evils in the world (particularly those that appear to be *gratuitous* or without any morally justifying reason for God to allow those evils to occur) to make its case for God's non-existence. However, the evidential argument also requires certain premises or assumptions about the character and nature of God that are necessary for the argument to succeed, and as far as I have seen, it is rare that any such argument is explicit toward justifying those premises. The character and nature of God in most cases is simply stated (or parroted from classical theistic claims), and agreement on these points is simply assumed. In this way, God is often stated to be "omnipotent, omniscient, and perfectly good" as a matter of mutual agreement, and it is assumed that these attributes necessarily commit God to acting or behaving in a certain manner in relation to his creation—namely, preventing or minimizing evil as much as he can for the good of the universe itself. But what is the argument to support these ideas? Do we have any good reason to think that God in fact has all of these attributes and the sort of character or moral obligations one would expect him to have? Is it reasonable to consider God as a sort of "moral agent writ large," so to speak, who must act in defense of creatures' well-being against the natural operations of the world? We turn now to evaluate exactly what others have said about God and his attributes before examining for ourselves what natural theology reveals about the divine being and essence.

William Rowe offers this concise definition of God and his attributes: "The dominant idea of God in western civilization, then, is the idea of a supremely good being, creator of but separate from and independent of the world, all-powerful (omnipotent), all-knowing (omniscient), eternal, and self-existent."[1] Rowe gives this basis for a definition of God without argument, and he bases this assertion on the historic claims of the monotheistic faiths, though he then clarifies the importance of evaluating the specific meaning and export of these divine descriptors as well. "Of course, this list of the major elements in this idea of God will be illuminating to us only insofar as the elements themselves are understood."[2] Thus, as Rowe here explains, it is of value before proceeding to a full evaluation of the evidential problem of evil to first investigate the nature and attributes of God and what such a concept itself entails. Such an evaluation will need to include a certain degree of nuance and specificity so that an accurate appraisal of evil in the world (and God's responsibility in the face of evil) can reasonably follow.

Just as the evidential argument begins with what we can and do know of the evils we witness and experience in the world, there is a great deal of knowledge and understanding that even finite creatures can reasonably conclude about God and his nature from the effects of the world around us and the sorts of things it contains. This is what is known as *natural theology* or what is known about God and his nature from the powers of human reason and the evidence seen in the natural world. As Maurice Holloway explains, "In natural theology, which is the crowning point and supreme moment in the science of metaphysics, we want to know what is the truth about God, insofar as that truth can be grasped by the human intellect reflecting upon the data of existing things."[3] Thus, for Holloway, it is precisely in our experience and knowledge of the things that exist that one is able to reason to truths about the causes of those things. "God is not found among the beings of our experience. If he does exist, that existence must somehow be inferred, be concluded to by a careful reflection upon the beings that do fall within our immediate experience."[4] The goal in such an approach is to demonstrate a foundational argument for God's existence from which to draw important conclusions about God's nature and attributes that rely neither on ecclesiastical doctrine, ungrounded presuppositions, nor *ad hoc* assertions. The advantage of such an approach is that the reasoning process employed presents an objective

1. Rowe, *Philosophy of Religion*, 6.
2. Rowe, *Philosophy of Religion*, 6.
3. Holloway, *Introduction to Natural Theology*, xiii.
4. Holloway, *Introduction to Natural Theology*, 43.

framework for investigating specific claims about God and his nature. Per Thomistic philosopher Brian Davies, "We can think of [natural theology] as the attempt to show that belief in God's existence can be (even if it does not *have* to be) defended by reason or argument which ought to be acceptable to anyone, not simply to those who already believe in God."[5] With an eye on the universal appeal of such an approach, I will in this chapter present a case for attaining and discussing knowledge of God from a position of natural theology, beginning with an argument for God's existence and proceeding to an evaluation of God's nature and attributes on the basis of that argument. The specificity and nuance provided by this approach, I believe, is a necessary step in considering and evaluating the evidential problem of evil.

THE EXISTENCE OF GOD

Many arguments have been proposed for the existence of God. Among those are many valid and compelling theistic arguments that incorporate ideas such as the causes and origins of things such as life or the universe itself, the apparent intelligence required to achieve such a specific combination of universal constants and natural laws necessary to sustain a world of relative stability and the formation of complex organisms, the universality and predictability of the world and its operations, the necessary grounding of a universal sense of value judgments such as good and evil (notwithstanding moral categories and obligations held by human moral agents), and a number of other things specific to universal, objective human experience such as beauty, desire, knowledge, and purpose. My goal here is not to promote or negate any particular argument such as those mentioned here, nor does my overall argument in this work necessarily depend on any particular argument for God's existence. To be clear, a great deal of nuance and understanding about God and his nature can be appropriately gleaned from many of these myriad arguments—either taken individually or cumulatively. For the sake of illustration and simplicity, however, I will focus my present attention on one particular theistic argument from which one may build a full-throated and nuanced view of God's nature and attributes. My aim is to show that theists not only have reason to believe that God exists, given a basic observation and experience of the natural world, but theists also have good reason

5. Davies, *Introduction to the Philosophy of Religion*, 41.

to attribute to God all of the classical attributes most often ascribed to him, such as those that are integral to an evaluation of the problem of evil—omnipotence, omniscience, and perfect goodness.

Before proceeding with the argument in question, it is important to note that such an approach to natural theology must not begin with any preconceived, full-formed ideas about God and his nature (which would invariably beg the question) but rather with a natural knowledge of sensible things. Without such an approach, any response to the problem of evil on the basis of unfounded claims regarding God's nature and attributes, as I intend to present, would be vulnerable to the criticism of either special pleading or an appeal to *ad hoc* propositions meant only to circumvent or resolve the problem. Thus, the starting point for such an investigation should contain as few assumptions about God as possible (or even none at all). In the example of natural theology that I intend to present, I shall begin only with a concept of being that signifies an important and obvious aspect of all existing things. This does not in itself guarantee God's existence without further argument (which would be begging the question); it simply identifies that which is common to all of sensible reality from which to philosophically investigate the concept of existence and being itself.

The argument I shall put forth is adapted from the medieval philosopher and theologian Thomas Aquinas (1225–74) and has come to be known as the *intellectus essentiae* (translated "knowledge of the essence") argument, or the argument from being and essence. This argument, if sound, establishes not only the existence of God but also certain details about his divine nature and attributes that become relevant in an evaluation of the problem of evil.[6] While many theistic arguments would invariably reach the same or similar conclusions about God and his nature, I will offer the *intellectus essentiae* argument as a concise starting point from which to demonstrate a nuanced natural theology sufficient for our purposes here.

6. As already stated, my overall response to the problem of evil does not depend solely on the success of the *intellectus essentiae* argument, and thus I intend to avoid the time and space required for a full-throated defense of this argument here. However, for an excellent defense of this argument in full. See Kerr, *Aquinas's Way to God*.

The Essence and Existence Distinction

Beginning from the things we experience in the world, it is apparent that all sensible things necessarily have both *essential properties* and *non-essential* properties. Humans, for example, have essential properties such as a physical body and a rational mind, and they have a number of non-essential properties such as brown eyes or freckles. The essential properties of a thing are what is usually defined as its *essence* or *nature*—in short, *what* the thing is. For example, my Christmas tree has the *essential* aspect of being a tree (or "treeness," so to speak) including wood, bark, pine needles, or leaves, and so on. Anything that lacked these essential properties as an aspect of its nature could not be properly considered a "tree" in any rational sense. However, my Christmas tree also has the *non-essential* property of being in a pot in my living room. While a tree can still be a tree while it is in a pot, it is not *essential* that it be in a pot in order to be a tree. The essence or nature, therefore, describes *what a thing is* divested from its accidental properties and characteristics, and its essence is precisely how it can be known as the sort of thing that it is. All human knowledge and language (at least when applied to reality) relies on this basic aspect of all existing things as being true. Thus, it is universally apparent and non-controversial as all knowledge, thought, and language depends on things having a real nature or essence that can be accessed and abstracted from that which is known and known by intelligent agents in some way.

Another universal aspect of everything observed in sensible reality is its *existence* or its "act of being" so to speak—what Aquinas calls the *esse.*[7] This concept of being simply describes that which all real things have in common—namely, that they exist in reality. In short, while the essence of a thing describes *what* it is, the *esse* of a thing describes *that* it is. This observation appears to be necessarily and certainly true of all things that are, and like all other aspects of sensible things (as discussed above), the act of being must be either *accidental* or *essential* to the thing itself. In other words, the act of being—considered as a definable and real aspect of anything—must be something that is part of the essence of the thing or something accidental to it. In other words, the very fact that a thing

7. The term *esse* is the Latin infinitive of the verb "is" and literally means "to be." Though often translated into English as "being," this can be deceptive due to the dual manner in which the word "being" is used in English (both as a verb and a noun, for example). Thus, many philosophers choose to retain the word *esse* in its original Latin form to preserve the idea that the word refers to a substance (noun) that exists.

exists is either essential to the thing itself, or it is not. Once this distinction is understood, it is immediately difficult to see how a sensible thing's act of existence could possibly be essential to the thing itself, for there is nothing in the essence of a tree, for example, that guarantees or necessitates that there are actually any trees at all—or that any tree whatsoever actually exists. From this, it seems obvious upon reflection that whether or not something exists must depend not on its own essence (as an inherent aspect of its nature) but on something distinct from the thing itself.

To illustrate this, it is clear that the essence of a thing can be easily understood apart from its own act of existence, even if the thing in question does not actually exist. In all likelihood, I do not right now (as you read this) actually have a Christmas tree in my living room, though it is not difficult to understand the essence of such a tree even if it does not exist. In other words, you can know about Christmas trees even though it may not be the season for Christmas trees and there are no Christmas trees at all anywhere in the world; the essence or nature of a Christmas tree does not depend on whether or not it exists. Maurice Holloway offers a similar explanation as to how the real distinction follows from this conceptual difference:

> To the answer to the question, what a thing is, corresponds the essence of that existing thing. To the answer to the question, whether the thing is, corresponds the existence of the thing. And since we have seen that these two principles cannot be the same in the thing, it follows that there is a real distinction in the thing between the essence and the act of that essence—existence. Or to put it positively, there is in the thing an actual composition between essence and existence.[8]

As Holloway here explains, because essence and existence in sensible things are distinct and cannot account for one another, a real distinction follows. If this is true, then it follows necessarily that the cause of existence in any existing thing must be something other than itself.

A Being Whose Essence Is Existence

If essence and existence do in fact comprise a real distinction in a thing (and it is difficult to see how this could be otherwise), the second step of the *intellectus essentiae* argument is to note that the existence of a thing

8. Holloway, *Introduction to Natural Theology*, 157.

must come from something other than itself. In other words, if a thing cannot account for its own present act of existence, then something else must account for it instead and serve as the present "cause" of that act of being. In his *De Ente et Essentia*, Thomas Aquinas (in a discussion about angels) argues that even as beings divested of matter, angels are still composed of essence and existence because there is nothing in the essence of an angel that guarantees its act of existence. Aquinas then proceeds to an explanation of the causal necessity that is entailed by such a composition of even immaterial beings:

> It is therefore necessary that every such thing, the existence of which is other than its nature, have its existence from some other thing. And because everything which exists by virtue of another is led back, as to its first cause, to that which exists by virtue of itself, it is necessary that there be something which is the cause of the existence of all things because it is existence alone. Otherwise, there would be an infinite regress among causes, since everything which is not existence alone has a cause of its existence, as has been said. It is clear, therefore, that an [angel] is form and existence, and that it has existence from the First Being, which is existence alone. And this is the First Cause, which is God.[9]

Here, Aquinas takes nothing more than the fact that creatures are composed of essence and existence to demonstrate that the ultimate cause of such a composition must be a being which is necessarily "existence alone"—in other words, a being whose essence *is* its own existence (*esse*). It is clear that such a being is not something discoverable in sensible reality, and it is also clear that there can be only one such being, as stated previously by the argument from multiplicity. Further, such a being is necessarily the cause of all other beings composed of essence and existence, which makes such a being the continuous existing cause of all of reality itself. This being, per Aquinas's argument, is necessarily the "First Cause, which is God."

But why must a being whose essence just is its own act of existence be anything like what theists hold to as God—or even a divine being at all? Is there any good reason to think that such a being contains the sort of attributes that are typically attributed to God? In fact there is. Such a being who essence is its own *esse* is what Gavin Kerr refers to as *esse tantum* ("existence alone"), which Aquinas has argued is the proper

9. Aquinas, *De Ente et Essentia*, 80.

causal terminus of all composite beings (beings composed of essence and existence); such a being simply lacks this sort of composition. "Causing *esse* through itself, such a cause of *esse* is not an essence-*esse* composite, but is simply *esse* itself or *esse tantum*. Thus, the primary cause of *esse* is *esse tantum*, and this is what we understand God to be."[10] Such a definition of God goes beyond the typical path of negative theology by saying something positive about God—that God is "subsistent being itself" or *ipsum esse subsistens*, which is shown to necessarily exist by reasoning from effect to cause. As Kerr explains, it is in fact precisely this causal relationship that has led to this conclusion:

> The conclusion that there exists a cause of the existence of all things has now been established, and in so existing such a cause does not merely have *esse*, but is *esse* itself or pure *esse* (*esse tantum*). That is, the cause of *esse* of things is not another one of the things that has *esse*, or in which essence and *esse* are distinct, things that motivated the causal regress in the first place; rather, it is a cause that is such that it terminates the regress of causes of *esse* in *esse* itself.[11]

Thus, for Kerr, having established a real distinction between essence and *esse*, Aquinas has shown that such a being whose essence and *esse* are identical is necessarily the cause of all *esse*. Without such a being, *esse* for anything would be simply impossible, and nothing at all could exist. Such a being, therefore, does not *have esse*; such a being *is esse*. Such a being is literally the necessary explanation of why there is something rather than nothing.

This result also yields other important facts about such a being, as Holloway further explains: "Our conclusion, then, becomes clear. Existence as an effect can be proportioned or proper only to that being whose very nature is existence, where, therefore, existence is limited by nothing but itself, that is to say, where it has no limits whatsoever. Such a being must be pure act, subsistent existence. And this Being we call God."[12] Thus, per Holloway, certain aspects or attributes follow from such a being whose essence is its existence, including that such a being is necessarily limitless, devoid of potency ("pure act"), and subsistent being itself (*ipsum esse subsistens*). These distinctive characteristics follow logically and

10. Kerr, *Aquinas's Way to God*, 146.
11. Kerr, *Aquinas's Way to God*, 147.
12. Holloway, *Introduction to Natural Theology*, 159.

necessarily from what has thus far been demonstrated, and from these follow all of the divine attributes identified and understood by classical theology. As such, one need only accept this argument as at least plausible, and not only God's existence but also all of his classically understood divine attributes become plausible (and necessary) as well.

One may find it surprising that I have chosen a particular Thomistic argument for God's existence that Aquinas himself omitted from his "Five Ways" in the opening sections of his *Summa Theologiae*. In fact, it is true that the *intellectus essentiae* argument appears early in Aquinas's body of work (*De Ente et Essentia* is widely considered one of Aquinas's earliest works), and it seems that Aquinas may have abandoned this argument later in favor of more direct proofs. However, Aquinas's *intellectus essentiae* argument is not isolated to his *De Ente* and appears (at least in part) in many of his other works,[13] and he nowhere attempts to discredit or retract the argument. As Steven A. Long explains, "As the premises yield a valid conclusion, and Thomas nowhere renounces this argument but seems everywhere to reason in ways consistent with it, we are better advised seriously to appropriate it than to avert our gaze as though the significance of a text were merely an index of the number of times it appears."[14] Thus, the *intellectus essentiae* argument should be treated as a valid argument among Aquinas's works so long as the premises yield valid conclusions. Taken as at least one philosophical argument for the existence of God that also necessarily entails certain details and facts about God's nature and attributes, I take this argument to be a helpful starting point in building a picture of natural theology from which to evaluate the problem of evil.

13. For example, see Aquinas, *Summa Contra Gentiles*, I.22.9; and Aquinas, *Quaestiones Disputatae de Potentia*, VII.2. Further, in his *Summa Theologiae*, I.3.4, Aquinas reasons to God as a being such that his existence and essence are unified. Though this is done after his proofs in the "Five Ways," the reasoning process offered is similar to what is seen in *De Ente* and arguably constitutes the same framework as the prior example. Also see Aquinas, *Summa Contra Gentiles*, II.52.2, where Aquinas argues to the uniqueness of any subsistent being—namely God, and that no other subsistent being is possible. Also see Aquinas, *De Spiritualibus Creaturis*, where Aquinas makes a similar argument equating God's essence with his existence as distinct from other created beings. Finally, see Aquinas, *Quaestiones Disputatae de Potentia*, III.5, where Aquinas argues that all beings that are not their own *esse* must receive their *esse* from another, and that there is of necessity a simple being of pure act from whom all other beings receive their *esse*.

14. Long, "On the Natural Knowledge of the Real Distinction," 96.

THE ATTRIBUTES OF GOD

Having considered God as *ipsum esse subsistens*—a being whose being and essence are identical—a number of conclusions can be drawn that yield a more comprehensive picture of the sort of being God must necessarily be. In fact, per Gavin Kerr, the sort of being that follows from such an analysis can be nothing less than the God of classical theism: "Conceiving of God as pure *esse* permits us to arrive at a God that has many of the characteristics of the God of classical theism; for example, such a God is the primary cause of all that is, without this God there is nothing, such a God is Lord of all things and all things stand under this God."[15] It is from this foundational position of natural theology that a number of divine attributes logically follow. For example, as Aquinas explains, such a being must be unique and immaterial:

> Now, if we posit a thing which is existence alone, such that this existence is subsistent, this existence will not receive the addition of a difference because it would no longer be existence alone, but existence plus some form. And much less will it receive the addition of matter because it would no longer be a subsistent existence, but a material existence. Whence it remains that such a thing, which is its own existence, cannot be but one.[16]

Per Aquinas, a being who is its own *esse* cannot be differentiated without the addition of some form apart from its own act of being, as are all sensible things. Thus, such a being is necessarily one. Also, such a being cannot be composed of matter and form because subsistent being cannot be composed unless its *esse* differs from its essence and is thus immaterial.

Another important conclusion that follows from the *intellectus essentiae* argument is that such a being cannot be divested of act and potency and is thus "pure act." As Kerr explains, "Given that pure *esse* is subsistent *esse* it depends on nothing. As dependent on nothing, *esse tantum* does not stand in potency to anything, in which case it is not perfectible by anything."[17] Therefore, because subsistent being does not depend on something else for its existence, it requires no "actualizing principle" to make it be and thus has no unactualized potency. Such a being always comprises the whole of its existence and essence perfectly and completely at every moment it exists. Further, as Owens explains,

15. Kerr, *Aquinas's Way to God*, 166–67.

16. Aquinas, *De Ente*, 78.

17. Kerr, *Aquinas's Way to God*, 154.

subsistent being is the sole act of being by which all other acts of being are actualized: "Since being is the act of all acts and the perfection of all perfections, where it subsists it will be perfection in the highest degree. There is no higher act that could make it more perfect. It has, accordingly, no potency to further perfection. This means that as subsistent it has no potency at all. It is pure act."[18] As a being of pure act, subsistent being is therefore the recipient of a host of other classical attributes including divine simplicity (because subsistent being cannot be composed in any way), absolute perfection (because a being of pure act is necessarily complete and unified in its being), immutability (because a being devoid of potency is incapable of change), eternality or atemporality (because a being devoid of change cannot be measured in time), infinity (because a being of pure act possesses all possible perfections and is thus infinite in nature), and so on.[19]

Considering those divine attributes that bear direct relevance to the problem of evil, it is important to note that subsistent being does in fact suggest certain conclusions about God's intellect, will, power, and goodness as well. What follows from such a concept is an argument for God's omniscience, omnipotence, and perfect goodness. I will now proceed with a more careful and directed examination of each of these three divine attributes, which are those most often addressed by the problem of evil. It is here that the importance of nuance arises in light of the task at hand. If one is unclear or mistaken about some aspect of God's nature and attributes, a cascade of possible error could quickly follow that may lead to confusion, paradox, contradiction, or incoherence. Here, I intend to present only what the foundational understanding of God as subsistent being itself (*ipsum esse subsistens*) allows. The result is intended to be a nuanced look at God's omniscience, omnipotence, and perfect goodness such that one is able to proceed to a discussion of God's relation to evil while remaining on the footing of a consistent natural theology. In

18. Owens, *Elementary Christian Metaphysics*, 83.

19. After reasoning to an identity of essence and existence in God in his *Summa Theologiae*, Aquinas proceeds to a discussion of each of these divine attributes (and more) on that basis. While space does not allow a full exposition on each of these attributes and how they follow from the *intellectus essentiae* argument, suffice to say that I believe it is apparent upon reflection that each of these characteristics naturally follows from such an analysis and becomes intuitively evident once *ipsum esse subsistens* is granted of God. For Aquinas's own detailed arguments for each, see Aquinas, *Summa Theologiae*, I.3, I.4, I.7, I.9, I.10, and I.11. Also see Owens, *Elementary Christian Metaphysics*, 353–64; and Holloway, *Introduction to Natural Theology*, 228–332.

the next two chapters, I will address specifically God's omniscience and omnipotence, as well as a few of the major objections to each and how the view of God as *ipsum esse subsistens* avoids those objections.

3

God's Omniscience

Given the understanding of God as detailed by the *intellectus essentiae* argument presented in the previous chapter, it is clear that a number of specific observations about God naturally emerge. Such a being as described by the argument (*ipsum esse subsistens*) is necessarily singular, simple, unified, complete, perfect, timeless, immaterial, and without limit. But what of the classical attributes of God most relevant to the problem of evil: omniscience, omnipotence, and perfect goodness? Are there any good reasons to think that these divine attributes can be understood from such a being? In this chapter, I will present an argument for God's divine omniscience and what this necessarily entails, given this understanding of the divine nature described above. I will also address a few of the most prevalent objections that often arise in relation to God's knowledge and show how this understanding of God either overcomes or evades those objections.

The concept of omniscience as applied to God is traditionally defined as God knowing all real things, knowing of all true propositions that they are true, or possessing all possible knowledge. Some questions remain, however, that bear on certain interpretations of the problem of evil in light of divine omniscience, and here it is helpful to identify precisely how it is that God knows anything at all, what the proper object of his knowledge must be, and whether God can know things like evil, substantially free choices, or future contingent events. Many questions arise surrounding God's knowledge that seem to carry certain implications about the problem of evil. For example, if God knows perfectly the devastation and destruction that might or will be caused by the natural operation of a world he chooses to create, then it would seem that God is necessarily the primary cause of all natural evil such a world may produce (e.g., hurricanes, tsunamis, earthquakes, forest fires, etc.). Furthermore, if God knows perfectly the outcome of every free choice any creature makes before those choices are made, then how is it that the will of creatures could possibly be free? Then if the will of creatures is not free, then that would seem to include even evil or wicked deeds that some created beings commit, and thus it would seem that God is also the author of all moral evil as well. Given what we know of God's perfect knowledge, then, it would seem that a reasonable person might expect that God could not allow the sorts of evil we see all around us both in the natural world and in the free choices of created moral beings. As such, it is of value to take a closer look at exactly what sort of knowledge God does and does not possess and consider whether a more careful and nuanced understanding of God's knowledge may help resolve these concerns in favor of theism.

It seems that God—as the present and ongoing cause of everything that exists—must necessarily possess knowledge in two distinct ways: that of his immateriality and causality. Aquinas, for example, explains the connection between God's knowledge and his immateriality in that a being is said to be intelligent (or possess knowledge) if it contains within itself not only its own form but the form of other things as well.

> In God there exists the most perfect knowledge. To prove this, we must note that intelligent beings are distinguished from non-intelligent beings in that the latter possess only their own form; whereas the intelligent being is naturally adapted to have also the form of some other thing; for the idea of the thing known is in the knower. . . Therefore it is clear that the immateriality of a thing is the reason why it is cognitive; and according to the mode of immateriality is the mode of knowledge. . . . Since therefore God is in the highest degree of immateriality as stated above, it follows that He occupies the highest place in knowledge.[1]

As Aquinas here explains, knowledge and ideas (like the forms they attain to) are an aspect of immateriality comprising the form of the thing known, and God being uncomposed and perfectly immaterial possesses all possible knowledge and ideas as an aspect of his very nature. In short, God existing as a being of the "highest immateriality" (or one completely uncomposed as a unity of being and essence) must necessarily possess

1. Aquinas, *Summa Theologiae*, I.14.1.

all possible knowledge. Furthermore, Aquinas explains that God knows things other than himself as a matter of his causal relationship with everything he creates and sustains in existence (or that which participates in his own *esse*).

> God necessarily knows things other than Himself. For it is manifest that He perfectly understands Himself; otherwise His existence would not be perfect, since His existence is His act of understanding. . . . Since therefore the divine power extends to other things by the very fact that it is the first effective cause of all things, as is clear from the aforesaid, God must necessarily know things other than Himself. . . . Hence whatever effects pre-exist in God, as in the first cause, must be in His act of understanding, and all things must be in Him according to an intelligible mode: for everything which is in another, is in it according to the mode of that in which it is.[2]

Here, Aquinas explains that through a perfect knowledge of himself and his own power, God also knows everything perfectly to which his power extends—namely all things in existence that are composed of essence and *esse*. Thus, God's knowledge does not depend in any way on somehow observing or discovering the existence or behavior of other things, but rather other things depend on him and his knowledge for their own form and act of being. Such is a remarkably distinct concept of God's act of knowing from that of all human knowledge, which is largely extracted or deduced from a process of reason stemming from our observations of the external world.

If Aquinas is right, as *ipsum esse subsistens* seems to suggest, then God's knowledge is not one of observation and extraction, but rather it is the very existence and natures of other things that depend on God and his own knowledge for their own acts of being. As such, the object of God's knowledge is not the things themselves that he perfectly knows; rather, the proper object of God's knowledge is his own infinite existence and divine nature, since God knows things through his own immateriality and causal relationship with everything that exists. The resulting knowledge of God is therefore knowledge with nothing other than himself as its proper object. "Just as God knows himself through his divine essence, so God knows all other things through that same essence. The intelligible species by which God knows creatures is his own essence. God

2. Aquinas, *Summa Theologiae*, I.14.5.

knows other things in themselves, but he knows them through himself."[3] God's object of knowledge, therefore, is always self-directed. Likewise, per Aquinas, "So we say that God sees Himself in Himself, because He sees Himself through His essence; and He sees other things not in themselves, but in Himself; inasmuch as His essence contains the similitude of things other than Himself."[4] Such describes an important facet of divine omniscience—that God knows not as an act of cognition received from other things but rather as a facet of his own nature by way of his causal activity behind everything that exists. "God knows Himself perfectly and He knows only Himself immediately. . . . But the divine power extends to other things than God himself, since he is the first efficient cause of all beings. It is therefore necessary that in knowing Himself God knows all the rest."[5] This understanding of divine omniscience follows directly from what is understood as a being whose essence is its existence, which follows from the argument for God presented in the previous chapter. As such, it would seem to follow that one would have good reason to hold God as knowing all things it is possible for one to know simply on the basis of natural theology.

Further, God knows not only all that exists but all possibilities as well, even that which is never actualized. As Aquinas explains,

> Now it is possible that things that are not absolutely, should be in a certain sense. For things absolutely are which are actual; whereas things which are not actual, are in the power either of God Himself or of a creature, whether in active power, or passive; whether in power of thought or of imagination, or of any other manner of meaning whatsoever. Whatever therefore can be made, or thought, or said by the creature, as also whatever He Himself can do, all are known to God, although they are not actual. And in so far it can be said that He has knowledge even of things that are not.[6]

Thus, for Aquinas, God knows not only what is but everything possible by his own power or the power of others, even if they "are not absolutely" (or are not actual). With this understanding of God's knowledge, it follows that God knows not only everything that is but also everything that could possibly be. In a similar vein, Aquinas also offers reason on

3. Holloway, *Introduction to Natural Theology*, 294–95.
4. Aquinas, *Summa Theologiae*, I.14.5.
5. Gilson, *Christian Philosophy of St. Thomas Aquinas*, 112.
6. Aquinas, *Summa Theologiae*, I.14.9.

this basis to consider God's perfect knowledge of the past and the future. Per Aquinas, God's knowledge not only extends to things that exist now (from a human perspective) but to all things that have ever existed before or will ever exist in the future.

> For though some of them may not be in act now, still they were, or they will be; and God is said to know all these with the knowledge of vision: for since God's act of understanding, which is His being, is measured by eternity; and since eternity is without succession, comprehending all time, the present glance of God extends over all time, and to all things which exist in any time, as to objects present to Him.[7]

Thus, when considered alongside God's atemporal, eternal existence, God's knowledge must necessarily encompass all things, actual and possible, for all time. Since God knows everything that exists—as well as their own operative causal relationships with everything else in existence—and God necessarily causes all things to exist at every moment of their existence, then God knows all there is to know for all time. If this is true and God is not a temporal being as *ipsum esse subsistens* suggests, then God knows all past, present, and future events.

Given this understanding of God's knowledge, it seems that God knows himself perfectly on account of the unity of his essence and existence, he knows all possible knowledge (including both what exists and what is possible but does not exist) on account of his perfect immateriality, and he knows all existing things and their own intermediate causal operations (such as created beings and their own free choices and effects) on account of his own causal operations as the first efficient cause of all that exists. Thus, God's knowledge encompasses perfectly his own divine essence and being, everything that is possible, everything that is, and everything that has ever been or ever will be (on account of his eternality and atemporality).

This brief survey of God's knowledge demonstrates how one may argue from the foundation of *ipsum esse subsistens* toward a comprehensive view of God's knowledge. Such a description explains how such a being necessarily possesses all knowledge—not just of himself but by way of himself to everything that exists. Further, God knows not only actual things as they are but also contingent things in their full range of potency and possibility—even if never actualized. He also knows all of this for all

7. Aquinas, *Summa Theologiae*, I.14.9.

time (as considered from a human perspective). In short, given the concept of the divine being yielded by *ipsum esse subsistens*, God necessarily possesses the classical attribute of omniscience as an aspect of his nature, and omniscience is attributed to God in this way, not as an *ad hoc* addition to a human concept of God but as a direct consequence of a specific path of natural theology reasoning from effect to cause.

OBJECTION: FREEDOM AND FOREKNOWLEDGE

Perfect divine omniscience is not without its detractors, and perhaps one of the most prevalent attacks on God's omniscience that has gained popularity in recent years (and has some significant bearing on the problem of evil) is that of the problem of human freedom and divine foreknowledge. Simply stated, if God infallibly knows the outcome of all human free choices before they happen, how is it that humans can be said to possess genuine freedom of the will such that they are morally responsible for their own good and evil choices? In the end, such an objection seems to identify God as the author of evil. Thomas Morris offers an example:

> But if he now knows, and always has known, how each and every one of us will act, in every detail, on every occasion in the future, how can we possibly be thought to be free in our actions, selecting among alternatives equally available to us? If God already knows exactly how we shall act, what else can we possibly do? We must act in that way. We cannot diverge from the path that he sees we shall take. We cannot prove God wrong.[8]

Some have used just such an objection as a means to discredit the classical understanding of divine omniscience, and the result has direct implications on the problem of evil. If divine omniscience precludes even the possibility of genuine human freedom, then it would seem that God is the primary cause of human moral evil—a claim in direct opposition to classical theism. For example, if God's foreknowledge of human sin somehow necessitates or determines the occurrence of that sin and its consequences, then it would seem reasonable to claim that God is responsible for that moral evil; however, if his foreknowledge does not necessitate that evil, then evil would seem to be something beyond the power or knowledge of God. Either way, the classical understanding of God is at stake.

8. Morris, *Our Idea of God*, 89.

The objection of the incompatibility of divine foreknowledge and human freedom is one with a rich and expansive philosophical history, dating back at least to Augustine in the fourth and fifth centuries.[9] For the sake of brevity, however, I will present only one such formulation of this objection as a benchmark example from Alvin Plantinga:

> For suppose in fact Paul will mow his lawn in 1995. Then the proposition God (eternally) knows that Paul mows in 1995 is now true. That proposition, furthermore, was true eighty years ago; the proposition God knows (eternally) that Paul mows in 1995 not only is true now, but was true then. Since what is past is necessary, it is now necessary that this proposition was true eighty years ago. But it is logically necessary that if this proposition was true eighty years ago, then Paul mows in 1995. Hence his mowing then is necessary in just the way the past is. But, then it neither now is nor in future will be within Paul's power to refrain from mowing.[10]

Here, Plantinga illustrates the force of this objection to divine omniscience in that such a proposition (as is typically included in claims about God's infallible knowledge) that "God knows Paul will mow" holds a definitive truth value even prior to Paul's own decision to mow, and this knowledge then necessarily precludes Paul from any power to act otherwise, however much Paul may think his own decision to mow is entirely free and undetermined. The argument, as presented by Plantinga, may be summarized as follows (let *K* stand for the fact that Paul does in fact choose to mow his lawn on some specific future date, as assumed by the argument):

9. Augustine presents the argument as, "For if God foreknows that someone is going to sin, you say, it is necessary that he sin; but if it is necessary, then there is no choice of the will in his sinning, but an unavoidable and fixed necessity instead." See Augustine, *On the Free Choice of the Will*, 76. In response, Augustine argued that the human will does in fact act by necessity due to God's foreknowledge but remains free because it is always within the power of the creature to will however it does. Augustine's solution, in my judgment, is problematic and will not be addressed further in the context of my own response. For a detailed analysis of Augustine's argument, see Rowe, "Augustine on Foreknowledge and Free Will," 356–63; and Gerald, *Freedom and Necessity*.

10. Alvin Plantinga, "On Ockham's Way Out," 239. Note that Plantinga is writing in 1986, and thus 1995 (as used in his argument) is future to him.

(1) Eighty years ago, God eternally knew *K*.

(2) It is now-necessary that 1 is true (because whatever is past is now-necessary).

(3) If 1 is true, then *K* is true (because God's knowledge is infallible).

(4) It is now-necessary that *K* is true (from 2 and 3).

(5) If *K* is now-necessary, then Paul cannot do other than *K* suggests (definition of what is meant by "now-necessary").

(6) If Paul cannot do otherwise, then what he does is not free (definition of freedom).

(7) Therefore, Paul does in fact eventually mow his lawn on some future date (as per *K*), though he does not do it freely (from 4, 5, and 6).

Arguments such as this have resulted in a modern exodus of philosophers from a classical view of divine eternality toward a type of "theistic personalism" that prefers a general univocity of terms regarding God and time such that God is said to stand in relation to time in much the same way creatures do.[11] However, such a position is not without alternatives.

One traditional response to this problem that does not require the abandonment of the more traditional view of divine eternality focuses on God's essential timelessness itself as the means toward a resolution. As such, God's knowledge is not "foreknowledge" *per se*, as temporal creatures may imagine, but it is a *transcendent* knowledge that cannot be properly tensed into past, present, and future in the way Plantinga's

11. William Hasker is one such philosopher who denies divine eternality and immutability in favor of a changing God who exists in time facing an "open future" in much the same way creatures do. Per Hasker, such a change in his philosophical position in this matter is a direct result of his commitment to the analytical tradition. As Hasker states, "But many of us have also found our philosophical home in the analytical tradition. And it is simply a fact that the habits of thought engendered by that tradition are not particularly congenial to the theory of divine timelessness. It is not so much that specific objections to or inconsistencies in the theory have been discovered . . . But the deeper problem is that the modes of thinking encouraged by our philosophical practice fail to nurture and sustain an outlook that comports well with eternalism." (Hasker, *God, Time, and Foreknowledge*, 181.) Hasker also admits an abandonment of divine eternalism on the basis of a personal preference for a more "relatable" deity: "And if in order to have immediate awareness of temporal facts, God must himself be temporal, then so be it. To make the other choice leaves too great a distance between the God who is affirmed theologically and the God who is known through Scripture and experience." (Hasker, *God, Time, and Knowledge*, 181.) Thus, Hasker's own views on this matter appear to be influenced not solely by rigorous philosophical work but also as a matter of personal preference.

argument requires. Boethius, for example, emphasizes a familiar resolution in his description of God's "eternal present":

> Since, then, every mode of judgment comprehends its objects conformably to its own nature, and since God abides forever in an eternal present, His knowledge, also transcending all movement of time, dwells in the simplicity of its own changeless present, and, embracing the whole infinite sweep of the past and of the future, contemplates all that falls within its simple cognition as if it were now taking place. And therefore, if thou wilt carefully consider that immediate presentment whereby it discriminates all things, thou wilt more rightly deem it not foreknowledge as of something future, but knowledge of a moment that never passes.[12]

Here, Boethius argues that the divine knowledge is temporally transcendent and encompasses all past and future in one simple, changeless instant. Taking up this approach and expanding further on Boethius, Aquinas argues in a similar way:

> Now God knows all contingent things not only as they are in their causes, but also as each one of them is actually in itself. And although contingent things become actual successively, nevertheless God knows contingent things not successively, as they are in their own being, as we do, but simultaneously. The reason is because His knowledge is measured by eternity, as is also His being; and eternity being simultaneously whole comprises all time, as said above. Hence all things that are in time are present to God from eternity, not only because He has the types of things present within Him, as some say; but because His glance is carried from eternity over all things as they are in their presentiality. Hence it is manifest that contingent things are infallibly known by God, inasmuch as they are subject to the divine sight in their presentiality; yet they are future contingent things in relation to their own causes.[13]

Like Boethius, Aquinas emphasizes God's eternality as a means toward resolving his knowledge of contingent things. Interpreting Aquinas here, Joseph Owens is helpful:

> Since God's being is eternal is the full sense of the notion, his knowledge is correspondingly eternal. Everything that happens

12. Boethius, *Consolation of Philosophy of Boethius*, V.6.

13. Aquinas, *Summa Theologiae*, I.14.13.

> in time, whether past, present, or future, is coincident with the eternal now of the divine being and knowledge. God's cognition of things that actually do happen in time is called his 'knowledge by vision,' in the sense that God is seeing them as present to him from all eternity. About the fact of God's knowledge from all eternity of free acts of man that actually will take place in time, there is consequently no special problem.[14]

Hence the solution to Augustine's classic problem of freedom and foreknowledge, per Boethius and Aquinas, is found in God's timeless nature. It makes little sense to speak of God knowing some fact about the future *before* it happens if there is no past or future to God. As Morris likewise explains,

> According to atemporal eternalism, God does not believe anything in advance of the occurrence of anything, because to hold a belief, or to do anything, prior to or in advance of anything else is to be a temporal being subject to time. So when the time arrives for me, or for you, to make a decision or to choose one avenue of action over another, God has not already held a belief concerning exactly what will be done, and so it seems that there is nothing in our temporal circumstances to prevent our having a real array of options equally available to us. Another way of putting this is to say that God's eternal knowledge of our actions is more like simultaneous knowledge than it is like advance knowledge.[15]

Thus, per Morris, God does not "hold beliefs" about some event "before" it occurs. If time is eternally present to God, then any aspect of his knowledge is present to him as well, and when God knows some fact that is future to humans, it is not because it is first somehow determined or necessary that it must happen as it does at some time prior to what is known (as per Plantinga's argument), but rather the thing known is eternally present to God and cannot be tensed in this fashion at all.

Notice, however, that Plantinga is not ignorant of this defense, and he structures his argument in just such a way as to avoid this solution by substituting "God eternally knows" some fact that is future to us as a proposition that is itself necessarily either true or false at any given time, even "eighty years ago" as Plantinga argues. Thus, per Plantinga, if the proposition "God eternally knows Paul mows on some future date" is

14. Owens, *Elementary Christian Metaphysics*, 358–59.

15. Morris, *Our Idea of God*, 97–98.

true in 1915, then it is "now-necessary" that this proposition is true (or at least suppositionally necessary in the same way the past is necessary). In this way, Plantinga avoids any need to "tense" God's knowledge into a temporal framework to make his case and substitutes a simple fact about God's eternal knowledge to circumvent Boethius's solution. However, I do not believe Plantinga has here successfully evaded the challenge presented by Boethius and Aquinas.

In order to successfully sustain his argument, Plantinga must still add a temporal component to God's eternal knowledge, which in fact commits an illicit category mistake. As Jerry Walls explains, "It seems to me that the problem we have reconciling human freedom and divine foreknowledge is due to a misleading mental picture we have when we consider this issue. This picture is formed when we slide from thinking of God as knowing our future to imagining that we do as well."[16] Plantinga does exactly this by converting the premise "God eternally knows *K*" to a related but very different "the proposition that God eternally knows *K*" as a fact that retains a certain truth value *at a given time*—namely, a time prior to the occurrence of the things known. While God's knowledge cannot be properly tensed to a specific time, it seems true at face value that a proposition about his knowledge can be so tensed because propositions themselves can be applied or considered at any given time, and thus if a proposition about God's knowledge of a future event has a definitive truth value (in this case, *K* is true), then it may seem that *K* has a definitive truth value in the past and cannot be any way other than it is. However, this cannot be the case when considering God's knowledge of *K*, for the truth of any proposition about God's knowledge depends not on what God knows *at some prior time* but rather on what God eternally knows—even as the future event itself occurs. Thus, a proposition tensed to some particular time about God's eternal knowledge does in fact have

16. Walls, "Fable," 69. Walls own solution is to distinguish what he differentiates as "foresight" and "foreknowledge," with the latter being what actually occurs and the former being what will occur absent intervening factors. "What God foresees, he can reveal to us, and indeed, his doing so maybe the very factor which prevents what he foresees from actually happening. However, it is part of the logic of foreknowledge that in many cases God cannot reveal to us what he foreknows. These are the cases in which we take appropriate steps to prevent what God has revealed from taking place." (Walls, "Fable," 70.) Walls's confusion here, however, is that God revealing his knowledge to humans is identical with his eternal act of knowledge and eternally simultaneous with what he knows; thus, if it were the case that revealing his knowledge would change the situation, then either it would not be in the power of God to reveal it, or God would reveal it differently such that the outcome matched the revelation.

a definite truth value *even at some point in the past*, but that truth value (even for God) never depends on the time in which the proposition is considered; rather, it depends on the time in which the subject of the proposition eventually occurs. Hence, in Plantinga's argument, God's eternal knowledge of *K* is true eighty years ago if and only if *K* eventually occurs, so a proposition about "God's eternal knowledge of *K* eighty years ago" has no truth value whatsoever if considered only in the context of what is past and what is now-necessary. Thus, no conclusions can be drawn about whether or not *K* itself is now-necessary (prior to its actual occurrence) and cannot be other than it is. In other words, even if a proposition about 1995 is considered in 1986, the truth value of the proposition does not depend on anything whatsoever that is specific to 1986—even God's knowledge of it; it only depends on what happens or exists in 1995, and since God exists immutably and eternally in both 1986 and 1995, his knowledge of 1995 offers no problem at all when considering the truth of some proposition in 1986.

In formulating his argument how he does, Plantinga confuses a successive/temporal perspective with a divine eternal perspective. The confusion of the two commits either an illicit category mistake or an apparent equivocation by holding one intellective framework (successive temporal knowledge) in place of another (eternal divine knowledge) and requiring that each impacts the other in ways that they simply do not. One cannot place eternal knowledge into a successive temporal framework without committing just such a fallacy. Thus, the truth of any proposition about God's "future" knowledge of *K* still depends entirely on whether *K* eventually occurs. As such, the proposition "God eternally knows *K*" does in fact have a truth value at every time (past, present, and future), but that very truth value is grounded on the eventual occurrence of *K* and nothing else. Therefore, even if *K* does occur and Plantinga's proposition is in fact true, the proposition is not true *per se* at any time prior to *K*, because the truth of the proposition depends not on anything that exists at some prior time but rather on what occurs at *K*. The only way Plantinga can proceed with his argument and remain consistent is to say that God's knowledge of *K* somehow exists *at some specific time* prior to *K*, but this is precisely Boethius's objection in the first place. Whether or not a proposition about God's knowledge of *K* is true or false always depends on *K* at every moment of time (past, present, and future).

Plantinga's confusion here is common among many contemporary philosophers who have made similar arguments. Often philosophers will refer to God as possessing some knowledge (or other divine attributes) "at time *t*" or some point in the past.[17] The confusion that enters with such terminology is that neither God nor the knowledge he possesses are essentially *at* any time at all. In fact, it is difficult to see what being *at* a particular time is meant to distinguish or describe of any item of knowledge; knowledge is knowledge, whether it is known in 1995 or in 2025. One may add an additional qualifier to some knowledge that is somehow dependent on the time in which it occurs such as "what time it is right now." Swinburne argues, "The proposition that 'it is now T1' (for example, October 2) can be known only by any person only at T1 (namely, on October 2)."[18] This would make the knowledge dependent on the time in question—generally that of the speaker, but some act of knowledge about the current time is only *about* that time, and there is no reason to think that some act of knowledge itself must also be *at* that time. Thus, knowledge *at* time *t* is better stated as knowledge *of* time *t*, which can be consistently held by an atemporal, eternal being.

Further, Plantinga's argument also appears to beg the question. What is at issue for Plantinga is whether or not Paul mows freely, given God's perfect eternal knowledge of Paul's eventual decision to mow or not to mow—it is the entire point of his argument to show that Paul does in fact mow and does so necessarily on account of God's knowledge of his future actions. However, Plantinga cannot come to any conclusion whatsoever about the freedom of Paul's decision until Paul actually makes his decision and either does or does not mow. If God's knowledge of Paul mowing or not is in fact always present with Paul's decision to mow (as Boethius argues), then nothing whatsoever can be said about whether or not Paul's act is free until Paul actually makes his choice and either mows

17. Richard Swinburne argues in just such a manner: "I shall consider what it means to say that 'there exists at a time *t* an omnipresent spirit, free, creator of the universe, omnipotent, omniscient, perfectly good, and a source of moral obligation.'" Swinburne, *Coherence of Theism*, 103. Also, Swinburne proceeds in like manner while defining what he calls "omniscience in the strong sense": "So I suggest that we say that the natural account of omniscience is that a person is omniscient at a time *T* if at *T* he knows *of* any proposition that is true, that it is true." Swinburne, *Coherence of Theism*, 177. In this way, Swinburne fully admits that his argument assumes God's temporality. "My argument so far has assumed that God is in time; he exists and knows propositions today, he existed yesterday and knew propositions yesterday, he will exist and know propositions tomorrow." Swinburne, *Coherence of Theism*, 194. This takes Swinburne far afield of the traditional view of God's timelessness and eternality.

18. Swinburne, *Coherence of Theism*, 175.

or not. As Kenny explains, God's knowledge does not possess any relation of past to future:

> Eternity, which has no parts, overlaps the whole of time; consequently, the things which happen at different times are all present together to God. An event is known *as future* only when there is a relation of future to past between the knowledge of the knower and the happening of the event. But there is no such relation between God's knowledge and any event in time is always one of simultaneity.[19]

In order to make his argument, Plantinga must *suppose* from the start exactly what is at issue—specifically the fact that Paul does in fact decide to mow. Hence, he begins his argument with "For suppose in fact Paul will mow his lawn in 1995." Once this is supposed, however, it should be no surprise at all that Plantinga eventually concludes that Paul has no choice but to mow and his act is not free—because it was already "supposed" by Plantinga toward this particular course of action that Paul, in Plantinga's argument, can no longer avoid. In other words, by beginning his argument with the simple fact that Paul does in fact mow, it is already necessary and inescapable that Paul does in fact mow—and this before God's knowledge of the event has even entered the argument. Thus, Paul's act of mowing is not *absolutely* necessary on account of God's knowledge; rather, it is only *suppositionally* necessary on account of Plantinga's premise, and here Plantinga is guilty of an equivocation by substituting what he has already assumed in place of what Paul can or cannot freely choose to do. As Boethius argues, God's knowledge of future contingent events does not "suppose" anything whatsoever at any time prior to what eventually occurs, and thus "propositions" about God's knowledge of future contingent events prior to the events themselves cannot be said to be true or false *at any time* prior to those events because God's knowledge is not tied to some time prior to those events.

In short, the proposition "God knows *K*" does in fact have a definitive truth value that transcends time, but the truth value of the proposition always depends on whether or not *K* actually occurs specifically at the time of *K*. Such a proposition about God's knowledge cannot be said to be true or false "before" *K* occurs without smuggling in a temporal component to God's knowledge. Once the proposition becomes temporally tensed, it has effectively exited the realm of God's eternal knowledge, even if the

19. Kenny, "Divine Foreknowledge," 407.

proposition is specifically *about* God's eternal knowledge. Propositions about God's eternal knowledge—while eternally true—cannot be true in any sense that is separated from their proper temporal contexts (i.e., "before" an event occurs) unless the proposition stops being about what is eternally known. In other words, even if it was true in 1915 that God eternally knew Paul will mow in 1995, God only eternally knows this because Paul, in fact, does freely mow in 1995, and thus the truth value of the proposition in 1915 depends on 1995, even if it is about God's eternal knowledge.

Further, one should not "suppose" *K* is true for the sake of argument if the entire point of the argument depends on whether or not *K* actually occurs: this presents the illusion (and confusion) that Paul's act is somehow determined from the start, which ends up concluding exactly what is assumed from the start—hence, begging the question. Once Paul's free act to mow is assumed, then it is suppositionally necessary that Paul mow and impossible for him to do otherwise. Given this, I believe Plantinga has failed to adequately resist the response provided by Boethius and Aquinas in defense of God's perfect knowledge of future events and substantial human freedom.

OBJECTION: TENSED TRUTHS

Another objection to the classically understood eternal omniscience of God is that of God's knowledge of tensed truths. Presented more explicitly as an argument against divine timelessness, this objection utilizes God's omniscience to suggest that a timeless being cannot know true propositions that are tensed to a particular time and place (since God himself cannot be so tensed). As J. P. Moreland and William Lane Craig explain,

> In order to know the truth of propositions expressed by tensed sentences like 'Christ is risen from the dead' God must exist temporally. For such knowledge locates the knower relative to the present. Hermetically sealed in timeless eternity, God could not know such tensed facts as whether Christ has died or has yet to be born. . . . Such ignorance is inconsistent with the standard account of omniscience, which requires that God know all truths, and is surely incompatible with God's maximal cognitive excellence.[20]

20. Moreland and Craig, *Philosophical Foundations*, 520.

Here, Moreland and Craig argue that a timeless God would have no way of knowing some "tensed truth," such as whether or not some event (like the resurrection of Christ) has already happened or is yet to come. Further, Moreland and Craig argue that this view depends on a "tensed" A-theory view of time, which holds that time itself is properly tensed to a "past, present, and future" in a real sense and that things actually come into and go out of existence as time unfolds.[21] Thus, according to the A-theory of time, only the present exists in a metaphysically real sense. While my own view of God's relation to time and how this does or does not impact divine omniscience is relative to the temporal nature of the knower,[22] I will avoid here an exhaustive discussion or defense of divine temporal philosophy and take Moreland and Craig's objection as given.

Given Moreland and Craig's view, it is not immediately clear why it would be impossible for a timeless, eternal, atemporal God to know tensed truths. If God's knowledge necessarily includes the events of all of time perfectly, as classical theologians have traditionally held (past, present, and future), there is no reason to think that God must himself temporally change in his own being or nature in order to know perfectly

21. Moreland and Craig themselves admit that their objections to divine timelessness collapse for anyone who holds to a B-theory of time.

22. My own view, which I will state here only weakly and entirely undefended, is that time itself manifests differently on the basis of the nature of the knowing agent who is perceiving and comprehending it. Thus, for humans who are limited to knowledge gained from an application of the senses to present reality, reality itself is therefore limited to the present—including all of the causal precursors and teleological successors associated with mutable things. This view of reality as temporally tensed to a real, existing present allows some things to undergo change and to go into and come out of existence as time unfolds. However, for any knowing agent whose knowledge is not subject to change or passive cognitive exposure to sense data (such as God, for example), time is only operative as a description of changing things and the causal operations of the world, and God's knowledge necessarily and always encapsulates all of existing reality through all times from an eternal vantage point. This does not mean that all of reality somehow exists simultaneously in some sort of massive cosmic contradiction, but it only means that God's knowledge comprises all of time at every tensed moment of time that humans perceive and experience. While God himself is not temporal, he certainly knows of anything that exists that it does in fact exist when it does in the chain of causal operations and cosmic change that define each punctiliar moment of time, and thus of any "tensed" truth claim that requires knowledge of a specific moment in time, God necessarily and eternally knows whether that claim is true or false, and his knowledge is eternally grounded in the time which that claim references or occurs. Thus, while humans correctly perceive time as one real present existence that contains within it all prior and successive causal operations of past and future, God knows and actualizes all past, present, and future reality as it temporally unfolds without requiring God himself to be temporally tensed or mutable.

when things happen any more than he must himself be extended in space in order to know where things are located. The change in the subject of God's knowledge (e.g., existing, created reality) as to what is "then" "now" and "will be" does not require or even suggest a change in God himself since his knowledge is eternally complete and unchanging. For example, if God knows perfectly that it is now 2:46 p.m., then there is no reason to think that any change in God's knowledge actually occurs when it becomes 5:31 p.m., because God's knowledge was always and is always eternal and complete in his divine nature—even his knowledge of the present reality perceived by a temporal agent (such as a human), whatever that may be. A change in the creation does not necessitate a change in the creator. Thus, God knows perfectly and eternally what time it is when existing reality is at 2:46 p.m. (including the world that presently exists), and he knows perfectly and eternally what time it is when existing reality is at 5:31PM. To claim otherwise is to assume real relations in the divine essence that depends on created things—as if the nature of God himself is somehow subordinate or dependent on that which he has created. Such an argument pits God (upon his creation of a temporal universe) as truly making a rock he could not lift, so to speak, which has always been understand as a metaphysical impossibility, even for God.

For now, it should be clear that God knows perfectly what is previous, present, and pending because those categorical truths are so tensed as an aspect of creation itself that depend only on a mutable creation (and not a change in God's knowledge) that God causes to be. In this sense, temporal change would only be actual in created reality as it unfolds along a temporal spectrum as a created aspect of existing reality, and there is no reason to think the divine essence would have to itself be essentially temporal in order for temporal reality to exist in this respect. In other words, God would cause reality to change from one moment of its existence to its next moment without ever experiencing time or change himself—since his knowledge is always eternal and complete, encompassing every moment of unfolding time. Such a God would certainly know "tensed truths," as Moreland and Craig suggest, as there are always things that were, things that are, and things that will be on account of the temporal existence of those things and their natures and the causal relationships involved—but those truths would not themselves be tensed to God and his own timeless nature but only to the things that undergo change. God would not have to be temporal to have such knowledge; he would only have to be the cause of temporal existence while he himself remained timeless and immutable.

Such a confusion as illustrated by Moreland and Craig betrays a subtle category mistake by assuming temporality as an aspect of the divine nature in order for God to possess the power to create a temporal reality. Asking God what time it is, for example, would be like asking God whether he is smaller or bigger than Venus and assuming that God's inability to answer such a question somehow betrays a limit to his omniscience. God is not smaller or bigger than anything because he is non-spatial and immaterial. Likewise, God himself is not temporally tensed—even if all of reality is so tensed. Thus, God can know perfectly what time it is for me when I ask or whether or not I am bigger or smaller than Venus without himself being temporal or spatial. How is it that an atemporal God can know what time it is? Because he knows perfectly the reality that he creates and sustains as it presently exists, and he can know this even if he himself is not extended in time or subject to temporal change. It is simply an anthropomorphic category mistake taking what is a reality for me—temporality—and applying it to God as if God himself must also be the same in order to comprehend what my finite intellect and perspective reveals to me. Remember that God does not know things by discovering them or observing them; he knows by causing them to be and act at every moment of their existence, and thus God can cause this perfectly and eternally, even if reality itself undergoes time and change. Much more could be said about this, including a discussion as to whether or not God stands in any sort of real relation to reality, for example, but this will suffice for now at least to demonstrate that this objection does not necessitate a denial of divine timeless omniscience.

4

God's Omnipotence

Also following from the understanding of God as *ipsum esse subsistens* (and of particular impact to the problem of evil) is God's omnipotence—traditionally defined as God having sufficient power to do anything possible. In consideration of the problem of evil, it would seem apparent that an omnipotent God would be capable of removing or pacifying the evil in the world at least in a more significant fashion than he does, and thus the persistence and prominence of evil in the world presents a challenge to his existence (or at least to his omnipotence). In consideration of such a challenge, one must first examine exactly what God's power entails. In this chapter, I will examine what it means to say that God is omnipotent and what such an attribute necessarily entails from a position of natural theology. I will also address a few objections to divine omnipotence and show how this approach to natural theology resolves those objections.

Considering God as *ipsum esse subsistens*, it can be reasonably said that God is necessarily without limit. The argument here considers God as divested of all potency (or "potential being," so to speak), since his essence is his existence and God is literally pure being itself. As pure substantial being, God is "pure act" or absolute actuality comprising no potency whatsoever, and a being devoid of potency who is his own existence must necessarily possess the power to actualize anything possible. Holloway explains just such a connection:

> That God's power is infinite, or without any limit whatsoever, is quite clear. For among creatures we see that the more perfect something possesses the form through which it acts, the greater

> is its power in acting. . . . Now, as we have seen in our discussion of creation, the form by which God acts is his own divine essence. But this essence, as identified with his act of existing, is not limited by any receiving principle. And so his active power is also infinite. As completely in act, God is infinitely powerful.[1]

Thus, as Holloway explains, God is omnipotent simply because his essence and existence are identical, which itself necessitates God's acts as always unlimited in scope because God's essence (as identical with his existence) is itself unlimited.

But perhaps a simpler way to approach God's omnipotence: any being that is capable of some act exhibiting any measure of power is necessarily limited by its own potency—or the range or measure of things such a being is naturally capable of doing on account of its own essence and act of being. A human may be capable of singing a song or memorizing a script, for example, but that same human cannot breathe water or lay an egg, since those acts lay outside the nature of a human. God's essence or nature, however, unlike humans, actually is his own act of being—given the identity of essence and being in God. As such, there can be no limit at all to what God can do, since his own act of being is determined only by his own existence—that is existence itself. Substantial existence itself, in other words, can actualize anything at all. Thus, literally anything that is possible to exist can be actualized by God, and by this we mean that God is in fact omnipotent. As Aquinas succinctly explains, God's power is essentially limitless: "Now His existence is infinite, inasmuch as it is not limited by anything that receives it . . . Wherefore, it is necessary that the active power in God should be infinite."[2]

It is important to note that God's omniscience only extends to what is actually possible—in other words, only that which does not entail a contradiction. Something that is impossible has no potency at all and thus cannot be actualized—even by God—because substantial existence can only actualize an essence or nature with at least some measure of potency (or possibility). It is therefore by definition that cannot do what is logically impossible. Classical theism has traditionally understood God's omnipotence in precisely this way—God can only do what is logically possible, and this constitutes no real limit on his power, since the power to actualize what cannot be actualized is no power at all. As George

1. Holloway, *Introduction to Natural Theology*, 381–82.
2. Aquinas, *Summa Theologiae*, I.25.2.

Mavrodes explains, "My failure to draw a circle on an exam may indicate my lack of geometrical skill, but my failure to draw a square circle does not indicate any such lack. Therefore, the fact that it is false (or perhaps meaningless) to say that God could draw one does no damage to the doctrine of His omnipotence."[3]

Though this understanding of divine omnipotence is widely accepted in the field of philosophical theology, it is not entirely unchallenged. William Rowe, for example, demonstrates what he argues is a weakness in Aquinas's view of omnipotence, which in fact bears a direct relation to Rowe's own evaluation of the problem of evil. First, Rowe defines omniscience: "For God's power, as Aquinas points out, extends only to whatever is possible. And there is nothing that is possible to be done that God's power is inadequate to accomplish."[4] However, Rowe offers a critique of this view and provides a qualifier to shore up the difficulty:

> But aren't there some things which, unlike making a round square, are not contradictory and yet such that God cannot do them? Committing suicide or some evil deed are not contradictory. . . . In view of this difficulty, it is perhaps necessary to amend Aquinas' explanation of what it means for God to be omnipotent. Instead of saying simply that what it means is for him to have the power to do anything that is an absolute possibility, we shall say that it means that God can do anything that is an absolute possibility *and not inconsistent with any of his basic attributes*. Since doing evil is inconsistent with being perfectly good, and since being perfectly good is a basic attribute of God, the fact that God cannot do evil will not conflict with the fact that he is omnipotent.[5]

Here, Rowe argues that classical theists often affirm a range of limitations to God's power that do not of themselves entail contradictions except when juxtaposed with further aspects of God's nature (such as doing evil or committing suicide), and he offers to amend Aquinas's definition to shore up this alleged weakness. However, it is not immediately clear how these alleged difficulties in fact pose a problem for the classical understanding of divine omnipotence. In fact, Aquinas himself resolves this very challenge without any such correction. As Aquinas explains, any objection to divine omnipotence that would relate to some defect in the

3. Mavrodes, "Some Puzzles Concerning Omnipotence," 221.

4. Rowe, *Philosophy of Religion*, 7.

5. Rowe, *Philosophy of Religion*, 7–8.

divine being or bodily motion (such as "God cannot scratch his nose") are already excluded by the classical understanding of omnipotence and require no such qualifier:

> Accordingly, as stated above, God's power, considered in itself, extends to all such objects as do not imply a contradiction. Nor does the objection stand that refers to things which imply a defect or bodily movement, since the very possibility of such things involves their impossibility to God. And as regards things that imply a contradiction, they are impossible to God as being impossible in themselves. Consequently God's power extends to things that are possible in themselves: and such are the things that do not involve a contradiction. Therefore it is evident that God is called almighty because he can do all things that are possible in themselves.[6]

For Aquinas, it does in fact entail a logical contradiction for God to do anything (or for anything whatsoever to occur under any circumstance) that would in itself contradict God's own essential nature. Such is precisely a logically impossible contradiction and needs no additional clarity.

Contrary to Rowe's objections, God's nature and attributes are not rules or limitations by which he acts; neither do they constitute an essential limiting factor that restricts the application and scope of God's other attributes by somehow limiting his power. Here, Rowe has committed a category mistake by assuming (without argument) that God consists of a complex construction of attributes (or properties) that define the scope of his being by providing limits and boundaries to just how "omnipotent" he could possibly be, so to speak. What Rowe misses is that God's attributes follow from the absolute essence of his being and are not limited in the way Rowe suggests.[7] As such, God's power is not limited by his goodness, but rather it is better to say that God lacks any imperfect powers. In this way, for example, God cannot damage or destroy himself, as Rowe suggests, because the capacity to destroy oneself assumes imperfections that God does not possess, such as existing as a contingent being or

6. Aquinas, *Quaestiones Disputatae de Potentia*, I.7.

7. In my view, it is precisely this misunderstanding of God's nature (as Rowe has here described) that gives rise to certain critical factors at play in an evaluation of the problem of evil. Rowe's position on these "limits" of God's power invite one to evaluate God's existence or nature based on how well he behaves in accordance with what other aspects of his nature demand (such as his perfect goodness), as if his own essence constituted a set of rules that God is obliged to obey. But if God is not bound by any such limits, then it makes little sense to evaluate his existence on such a basis.

possessing a mortal nature, for example. Thus, the power of self-destruction is not a power that God lacks but rather illustrates imperfections and limits in those beings that do possess such a power. In other words, the power to harm oneself is actually itself a limitation on one's own act of being (existing as a creature with a limited or finite life subject to annihilation). Such beings (humans, for example) are contingent beings that possess a mortal nature. Further, an act of self-destruction fails to achieve the good of its own being or ends, and thus God cannot do such a thing because he holds no imperfection in his will and cannot fail to always act toward the good he intends (more on this in the next chapter); thus the capacity to destroy or damage oneself is no real power at all but a limitation and imperfection in the things that possess such a power. God's "lack" of such a power, therefore, constitutes a perfection of God and no lack of power at all.[8]

A handful of other prominent objections have arisen in the philosophical literature since ancient times that are meant to challenge the classical understanding of divine omnipotence, some of which bear relevance to evaluations of the problem of evil and will here be further addressed. I will now briefly highlight two such objections to divine omnipotence: the paradox of the stone and the paradox of sin. Each presents a similar but distinct challenge to God's omnipotence and must be resolved in a manner that is sufficient to sustain the coherence of this classical attribute of God.

OBJECTION: PARADOX OF THE STONE

A common objection to the possibility of any being having a real sense of omnipotence (as defined above) is the paradox of the stone, which Mavrodes summarizes as follows:

8. One may continue along this same line of inquiry with a whole host of nonmoral examples of "limitations" sometimes attributed to God, or things that God in his essence cannot do such as sneezing, sleeping, discovering, or forgetting. But once again, as I have demonstrated here, God is not prevented from such acts because his divine essence is "limited" in some way by aspects of his nature, such as his immateriality or omniscience. It is not a limit on God that he cannot sleep or forget; rather, it is a limit on the creature that lacks the power to know at all times everything there is to know or to remain always conscious and immune to fatigue. Thus, it is logically impossible for God to be limited in these ways not because he lacks some power but because he is infinitely perfect and infinitely powerful. Such offers no threat to the classical definition of divine omnipotence.

> A more involved problem, however, is posed by this type of question: can God create a stone too heavy for Him to lift? This appears to be stronger than the first problem, for it poses a dilemma. If we say that God can create such a stone, then it seems that there might be such a stone. And if there might be a stone too heavy for Him to lift, then He is evidently not omnipotent. But if we deny that God can create such a stone, we seem to have given up His omnipotence already. Both answers lead us to the same conclusion.[9]

Thus, as Mavrodes explains, either God can create such a stone, which implies a limit on God (i.e., the power to lift stones of any weight), or he cannot create such a stone, which implies a limit on God (i.e., the power to create such a stone). Either way, so the argument goes, God's power is limited.

A number of solutions have been proposed, discussed, and defended by philosophers in response to this problem. One common and widely supported response is that creating such a stone itself entails a contradiction (in a similar way as drawing a square circle, for example). This, in fact, is Mavrodes's own solution: "The dilemma fails because it consists of asking whether God can do a self-contradictory thing. And the reply that He cannot does no damage to the doctrine of omnipotence."[10] Further, Mavrodes goes on to characterize the creation of such a stone as a "pseudo-task" with no real meaning in a realm of possibility: "Such pseudo-tasks, not falling within the realm of possibility, are not objects of power at all. Hence the fact that they cannot be performed implies no limit on the power of God, and hence no defect in the doctrine of omnipotence."[11] Some have disputed this solution as being inadequate, though I believe such a solution remains sufficient to unravel the paradox once the existence of just such a stone is properly considered as a "possible object," so to speak. Consider any being x and any stone y that holds the property "x cannot lift this." Stated in this sense, y seems in fact to be a possible object that could exist in relation to x. However, if x is meant to represent an omnipotent being able to lift stones of any possible weight, then it becomes immediately clear that y is no longer

9. Mavrodes, "Some Puzzles," 221. The dilemma presented by Mavrodes here is nothing new, with even ancient and medieval philosophers responding to forms of this objection dating back at least to Augustine, Averroes, and Aquinas, for example.

10. Mavrodes, "Some Puzzles," 221.

11. Mavrodes, "Some Puzzles," 223.

a possible or coherent object—in short, *y* cannot possibly exist for the simple reason that *x* is in fact omnipotent. As such, the stone *y* could only exist if it could simultaneously be both a stone that *x* cannot lift and a stone that *x* can lift, which is a contradiction. There results, therefore, no logical contradiction in the possibility of *x* being omnipotent if it is unable to perform tasks which are logically impossible. In order to sustain this objection to omnipotence, one would have to show how God's power is limited in either the creation or lifting of actual (or possibly actual) stones. As C. Wade Savage explains,

> God's inability to create a stone which He cannot lift is a limitation on His power only if (i) He is unable to create stones of any poundage, or (ii) He is unable to lift stones of any poundage—that is, only if He is limited in His power of stone-creating or His power of stone-lifting. But until it has been proved otherwise—and it is difficult to see how this could be done—we are free to suppose that God suffers neither of these limitations.[12]

Thus, per Savage, this paradox presents no challenge to the coherence of an omnipotent being, who remains able to both lift and create stones of any weight. As such, the paradox of the stone has not traditionally been seen as a genuine problem for the coherence of the divine attribute of omnipotence.

OBJECTION: PARADOX OF SIN

A related but distinct objection to divine omnipotence is what I will here refer to as the paradox of sin. This challenge refers to God's inability to do evil. Put succinctly, an omnipotent God would possess every possible power that does not imply a contradiction, and the capacity to sin necessarily implies no contradiction because creatures (e.g., humans) readily possess and utilize this power on a regular basis. However, as per classical theology, God in fact cannot sin—it is not a power God possesses, therefore either God cannot be omnipotent, or God can sin, and either way, classical theism is refuted. Just such an argument was mentioned briefly by Rowe as seen above, though Thomas Morris provides a more expansive explanation:

> A number of philosophers have suggested that necessary goodness is incompatible with omnipotence. The argument goes like

12. Savage, "Paradox of the Stone," 79.

> this: If God is supposed to be omnipotent, he is supposed to have every power it is logically possible to possess. Now, surely, it is logically possible to possess the power to sin. This is a power all too common among human beings. So it is a power which should be ascribed to an omnipotent being, in accordance with the definition or explication of omnipotence we are using. But one cannot have the power to perform a certain type of action A unless it is possible for one to perform actions of this type. Possibility is required for power. But we have just argued in the previous chapter that it is proper for the perfect being theologian to think of God as necessarily good, as being such that it is impossible for him to sin. On the perspective of perfect being theology, then, God must lack the power to sin. And so, on this way of thinking, he cannot be ascribed omnipotence after all.[13]

Here, Morris explains the objection as an inherent incompatibility between divine omnipotence and what he calls "necessary goodness." He argues that because the "power to sin" is well known among creatures (humans), then an omnipotent God must surely possess such a power as well. However, as with the error in claiming that God lacks the power to destroy himself, a similar response emerges when evaluating this objection.

The solution involves an understanding of exactly what the "power to sin" would rationally entail. Aquinas offers clarity that can be helpful here: "To sin is to fall short of a perfect action; hence to be able to sin is to be able to fall short in action, which is repugnant to omnipotence. Therefore it is that God cannot sin, because of His omnipotence."[14] As Aquinas explains, the "power to sin" represents a failure or imperfection in a creature and is more of a pseudo-power and thus no real power at all. Saying that God lacks this power, therefore, actually reinforces the argument for his omnipotence rather than serving as an argument against it. In short, if God were truly capable of sin, then he would not be omniscient or omnipotent. As such, it is not impossible for God to do evil because he is limited or prevented somehow by his goodness, as Rowe and Morris suggest. God does not avoid evil acts because he is "well behaved" according to some external moral code, for example. The "power to do evil," so to speak, is actually no real power at all but a failure in a thing to act correctly toward the good it intends. Thus, God cannot do evil because

13. Morris, *Our Idea of God*, 77.

14. Aquinas, *Summa Theologiae*, I.25.3.

the good is always perfectly known to him and his ends cannot fail. In this sense, the capacity to do evil is more of a limitation than a power. As such, the power to sin would not constitute a power that God lacks but rather a limit on his omnipotence. The power to sin would be more of a defeater to omnipotence rather than an aspect of it. Thus, it is better to say that a creature with the capacity to sin lacks a power God possesses. Sin is an impotence, thus to say that an omnipotent being cannot sin is a claim about the perfection of the being in question and the very definition of omnipotence.

The paradox of sin fails as a challenge to divine omnipotence, but the challenge of the problem of evil is not defeated on this basis. The question remains as to what God's relationship with good and evil truly is from the perspective of natural theology and also what it means that God is said to be perfectly good. In the next chapter, I will explore the nature of good and evil and the divine attribute of perfect goodness in greater detail.

5

God's Perfect Goodness

CENTRAL TO THE CONCEPT of God as revealed in classical theology, and of particular significance in regards to the problem of evil, is God's perfect goodness.[1] God is said to be *necessarily* good as an inevitable and undeniable attribute of his act of being. Thus, God's goodness is not generally intended as a description of or adjudication on God's accomplishments or achievements, but rather it is seen as a metaphysically necessary aspect of his divine nature. The question remains, however, as to how and on what basis God can be said to be "good" and how God's goodness informs our understanding of him. For example, most formulations of the problem of evil suggest that a perfectly good God should be expected to act and behave a certain way in relation to the state of any created world that contains evil, and if evidence in the world seems to contradict these expectations in some way, then the existence of God (as traditionally understood) can be reasonably doubted or denied. Therefore, once the nature of God's goodness is properly understood, the question follows as to how God relates to evil—specifically the nature of evil itself and whether

1. The concept of God's goodness has been described in various ways such as infinitely good, perfectly good, wholly good, omnibenevolent, omnigood, incorruptible, irreproachable, morally perfect, and others. While some of these terms bear subtle denotative distinctions, nonetheless the divine attribute referenced here—whatever it entails—is widely accepted as an integral aspect of the divine essence and a hallmark of classical theism. In this work, I will refer to God as "perfectly good" or God's "perfect goodness" in reference to this divine attribute. In my view, this phrase most closely aligns with what the classical attribute of divine goodness implies as an essential aspect of his nature. For the sake of my argument in this work, God's "perfect goodness" is meant to be interchangeable with other terms that are sometimes used to represent this divine attribute. As one will discover, however, I do believe that many other terms can be confusing and misleading.

evil (or more specifically gratuitous evil) can rightly be said to exist in the same world as a perfectly good God. Toward this end, I will consider how God (as *ipsum esse subsistens*) can be properly said to be "good" and what that goodness entails as an aspect of the divine *esse* from a position of natural theology. Of particular concern will be the question as to whether or not God's essential goodness entails a commitment to moral perfection, which is the aspect of God's goodness generally emphasized by the problem of evil.

ASCRIBING GOODNESS TO GOD

Exactly how one arrives at the conclusion that God is in fact perfectly good is a critical step in any discussion on the problem of evil. The question of God's goodness and precisely what such an idea entails, therefore, can be and has been approached in a variety of ways by philosophers and theologians. One possible approach is to argue from a position of natural theology, which I will do here, though a myriad of other options are often employed, such as arguing from a specific faith tradition, divine revelation, personal experience, and others. In fact, not all philosophers even agree that an argument for God's goodness is needed in the first place. Thomas Morris, for example, suggests that God's goodness is best characterized as an intuitive judgment rather than a philosophical argument:

> Why then have so many theists endorsed the belief that God is necessarily, or essentially, good? I believe that for a great many Christian philosophers and theologians, this conviction has not come as the result of an elaborate argument or proof at all, but that it is simply the result of an intuitive judgment that it would be better for God to be utterly invulnerable to evil than to be capable of wickedness. It is simply an Anselmian intuition that underlies most theists' endorsement of this belief. The highest form of perfection requires the impossibility of evil-doing on the part of the perfect being. Thus the necessity of God's goodness is a deliverance of perfect being theology, and does not stand in any obvious need of independent argument.[2]

Here, Morris attaches God's goodness to an Anselmian "perfect being theology" and suggests that one comes to a conclusion about God being good for no other reason that it is just simply better for him to be that

2. Morris, *Our Idea of God*, 50.

way; thus Morris offers no reason for such a conclusion aside from what he calls an "intuitive judgment." Despite the fact that Morris' conclusion about God's goodness in fact rests on prior arguments (such as those involving Anselm's own approach), just such an intuitive assumption is often common in the philosophical literature with God's goodness simply asserted as a universally accepted fact about God.

Nevertheless, whatever approach one takes toward assessing the reality and nature of God's perfect goodness, it has remained a staple of classical theology since ancient times. The resulting question follows as to what exactly God's goodness entails. Morris himself offers three models of divine goodness open to the theist in its interpretation and application, which I believe is helpful in narrowing the concept to a level of specificity that is necessary in evaluating the problem of evil: the *plentitude of being model*, the *duty model*, and the *benevolence model*:

> The *plenitude of being model* explicates that aspect of divine goodness which is distinctively metaphysical. According to this model, to say that God is good and to insist further that God is perfectly good is to hold that God is metaphysically, or ontologically, complete, without flaw, defect or lack with respect to his being. God, on this model, is the fullness of being in two respects. First, he himself exemplifies perfection in the Anselmian sense. And secondly, he is the metaphysical source of all being and thus of all other goodness.[3]

According to the *plentitude of being model*, Morris lays out a sense of metaphysical goodness attributable to God as exemplifying Anselmian perfection and the source of all created goodness. This is the closest analogy offered by Morris to the Thomistic position I will advocate for, in which God remains essentially and metaphysically good as a necessary aspect of his divine nature. More on this later.

A second option open to the theist is the *duty model*: "According to the *duty model*, God acts in perfect accord with all those principles which specify moral duties."[4] This model exemplifies something akin to what one may refer to as divine moral goodness, which suggests God's perfect adherence to all moral standards and duties as they apply to all rational beings. For example, under the duty model, God would be expected to adhere to moral directives that require one to intervene in the

3. Morris, *Our Idea of God*, 50; emphasis in original.

4. Morris, *Our Idea of God*, 50; emphasis in original.

face of evil and prevent or reduce evil in the world whenever it would be possible for him to do so. As Morris explains, "This model tells us that anything which *ought to be done* by a free moral agent in God's relevant circumstances is *perfectly done* by God without fail. God never acts in a way contrary to true moral principles."[5] Morris is clear that this model does not necessarily ascribe moral duties to God—as if God must obey a set of moral precepts that are somehow independent of his own existence and nature. Rather, Morris argues, God can be considered morally good because "his activity can be modeled on the conduct of an idealized moral agent who in the relevant circumstances does have duties and satisfies them perfectly."[6] Thus, God is not bound by moral duties the same way creatures are, but he nonetheless always perfectly acts in accord with those duties—hence the *duty model* serving as a means by which God can reasonably be called good.

The final option given by Morris is what he calls the *benevolence model*, which implies not only that God follows all moral requirements but also that he goes "above and beyond," so to speak, in generously doling out undeserved blessing beyond what would be expected or required.

> The *benevolence model* tells us that God does not do only that which would be morally required of a moral agent in his circumstances, but that he goes beyond the call of duty, graciously and benevolently doing good that need not have been done. He brings into existence good which is not merited, deserved, required, obligated or necessitated. Such is his gracious goodness.[7]

The benevolence model is an expansion on the duty model holding not only that God does in fact adhere perfectly to all moral duties and obligations, but he goes even further by always or often graciously providing more than what his essential goodness requires. This model holds that God is not only perfectly good in himself but demonstrates superfluous goodness above and beyond what is required of him by sowing good even where it is not due—like a consistently generous celestial benefactor for all of creation. These three models suggest a wide range of possible interpretations of God's goodness that would each lead to varied and distinct

5. Morris, *Our Idea of God*, 50–51; emphasis in original.

6. Morris, *Our Idea of God*, 60. The *duty model* of divine goodness seems to be the view that Morris himself endorses.

7. Morris, *Our Idea of God*, 51; emphasis in original.

conclusions regarding the problem of evil. Therefore, it is important to specify exactly what is entailed by the argument from natural theology I have presented here when one calls God "good."

God as Essentially Good

Upon consideration of God as *ipsum esse subsistens*, the first step toward establishing God as good begins with his essential perfection. As Holloway explains,

> We established, after the proofs for his existence, that the essence of God as known by us is most properly grasped under the aspect of subsistent Being. All the properties or attributes of the divine Being are what they are because of this fact. As subsistent Being, God must be pure act. Because God is completely in act, God is absolutely perfect.[8]

Thus, per Holloway, absolute perfection follows from God as essentially "pure act" or devoid of potency. Without any potential to be or become anything that is not already "in act" by God's very nature, God is therefore complete, perfect, and lacks nothing. As Aquinas explains, "Again, each thing is perfect according as it is in act, and imperfect according as it is in potency and lacking act. Hence, that which is in no way in potency, but is pure act, must be most perfect. Such, however, is God. God is, therefore, most perfect."[9] Brian Davies offers additional insight on Aquinas's view along these lines:

> As [Aquinas] sees it, an imperfect thing (e.g., a rotten egg) is something which is lacking what ought to be there (we object to rotten eggs because they are not what we expect eggs to be). In this sense, something imperfect fails because it is not what it could be, because, in Aquinas' language, it lacks a certain sort of actuality. And, since he takes God to be wholly actual, Aquinas therefore concludes that God can be thought of as perfect.[10]

Thus, per Davies, Aquinas argues that God's perfection follows from his being as "pure act," which in turn follows from God as subsistent being itself (*ipsum esse subsistens*). Aquinas also argues for God's essential perfection from his role as creator of all perfections:

8. Holloway, *Introduction to Natural Theology*, 245.
9. Aquinas, *Summa Contra Gentiles*, I.28.6.
10. Davies, *Thought of Thomas Aquinas*, 81.

> Since therefore God is subsisting being itself, nothing of the perfection of being can be wanting to Him. Now all created perfections are included in the perfection of being; for things are perfect, precisely so far as they have being after some fashion. It follows therefore that the perfection of no one thing is wanting to God.[11]

Thus, not only is God known as perfect by metaphysical necessity as a being of pure act: he is also known as perfect as the creator and sustainer of all finite perfections known by creatures and beings in the created world—and all on account of God as *ipsum esse subsistens*.

Turning to an idea of "goodness" as properly attributed to the divine essence, one must consider that being "good" is generally understood as a logically attributive adjective that bears some relationship with *what a thing is* that is being called good.[12] For example, a good shoe, a good pizza, and a good dog all say something specific and meaningful about the thing in question, but each refers to different aspects of those things. A good shoe, for example, has all of the defining characteristics one would expect to find in a shoe (durable materials, functional laces, unworn soles, and so on), while a good pizza would have completely different defining characteristics (pleasant aroma, delicious taste, certain nutritive properties, and so on). A pizza made out of leather and topped with laces would not be a "good pizza," so to speak. However, this does not suggest that the term "good" is entirely equivocal when applied to different things—rather it refers to how well a thing embodies the sort of thing that it is, or more precisely how completely or perfectly it may be *in act* (as opposed to a thing beset by certain privations—such as a shoe with a worn sole, for example). Thus, the goodness of a thing holds a direct relationship to its act of being in reference to the form of the thing that defines what sort of thing it is, or more precisely its perfection of being. Per Holloway, "A thing is said to be good insofar as it is perfect; for good is being as desirable, and hence according to its fullness or perfection of being."[13] Thus, for a thing to be considered "good," it not only possesses the perfection of being, but it also possesses an aspect of *desirability* as to how well it embodies the sort of thing it is.

11. Aquinas, *Summa Theologiae*, I.4.2.

12. For an excellent argument establishing that the term "good" is always logically attributive in this way (as opposed to predicative, for example), see Geach, "Good and Evil," 33–42.

13. Holloway, *Introduction to Natural Theology*, 247.

Here, the concept of desirability is introduced. In this respect, certain philosophers (such as those in the Aristotelian/Thomistic vein) often consider "the good" in large part to be synonymous with *being itself*, though, as Aquinas explains, with the added aspect of desirability:

> Goodness and being are really the same, and differ only in idea; which is clear from the following argument. The essence of goodness consists in this: that it is in some way desirable. . . . Now it is clear that a thing is desirable only in so far as it is perfect; for all desire their own perfection. But everything is perfect so far as it is actual. Therefore it is clear that a thing is perfect so far as it exists; for it is existence that makes all things actual, as is clear from the foregoing. Hence it is clear that goodness and being are the same really. But goodness presents the aspect of desirableness, which being does not present.[14]

Here, Aquinas describes goodness as an act of being with the aspect of desirability that speaks to its perfections.[15] As Davies further explains, "His meaning is that something is good insofar as it possesses what is desirable for it considered as what it is by nature. And with this thought in mind he concludes that being and goodness are seriously equivalent."[16] While all things actual possess at least some perfection (even if only the perfection of existence) and are therefore good, that which is *in act* and possesses more perfections is in a state of higher good. That thing which is *more perfect* is more desirable than a lesser thing that lacks some perfection or fails to thrive in some way, even in some small way, as the sort of thing it is. It is this ultimate actualization of inherent potency that speaks to a thing's goodness as it achieves its own perfections. Eleanor Stump offers additional clarification:

14. Aquinas, *Summa Theologiae*, I.5.1.

15. It is important to note here that "desirability" does not necessarily mean that someone or something must consciously "desire" the thing in some way (or at least exist as an object of admiration by a being capable of that sort of desire) in order to be good. Good soil, for example, may be that which provides a sufficient environment for a wild plant, even if no farmer is involved and the wild plant does not itself "desire" good soil in some cognizant way. However, when a thing achieves its own perfections as to the sort of thing it is (and as such achieves its proper ends, for example), then it is "desirable" in the sense that it is of a higher state of perfection than that which fails to achieve its own perfections (or does so not as well as that which is more perfect). Thus the "more perfect" implies an aspect of desirability as a more complete and fulfilled instance of the sort of thing it is.

16. Davies, *Thomas Aquinas on God and Evil*, 32.

> The ordinary sense of 'being' is being considered absolutely, that is, a thing's mere existence as the instantiation of a thing with a substantial form conferring a nature that includes a specifying potentiality. On the other hand the actualization of a thing's specifying potentiality is also the being of the thing, and the general sense of 'goodness' is being understood in this way . . . This is the state each thing naturally aims at, and it is in this state that the thing is said to have goodness.[17]

Thus, as Stump explains, the state of full actuality is what all things desire or move toward, and thus something is "good" whenever and to whatever extent it achieves these ends most fully. For something to be good, it has the aspect of desirability insofar as it succeeds in being in some way as the sort of thing that it is. Such a definition of goodness as presented here seems to embody most fully both the ordinary use of the word and the metaphysical import of the term when considering what goodness entails as applied to things in the world. In sum, something is good in the most basic sense on account of its own existence or actuality, and it is good in degree on account of how "perfect" it is according to the sort of thing it is.

Given this understanding of goodness, it becomes clear that God is not only rightly described as "good" in the proper sense (since it is his very nature to exist) but also that he is necessarily the highest and greatest good in existence (being entirely complete and perfect in his own nature or essence)—in fact, he just is the very embodiment of *goodness itself*. As Stump explains, "Since Aquinas takes God to be essentially and uniquely 'being itself' (*ipsum esse*), then on Aquinas's central meta-ethical thesis God alone is also essentially goodness itself."[18] As the concept of goodness is directly related to the concept of being, then God, whose essence includes his *esse* (as essentially "being itself"), is by necessity both the highest good and the source of all goodness in existence. Such a concept of God demonstrates that he is both perfect and complete—without flaw or limitation while possessing all perfections, and thus there can exist no privation or lack in the divine act of being.

It is important to note that this concept of goodness when referring to God, though analogically similar in significant ways, is pointedly

17. Stump, *Aquinas*, 67–68.

18. Stump, *Aquinas*, 90. Stump explains Aquinas's central meta-ethical thesis is essentially the identity of being and goodness, which differ only by the aspect of desirability as stated above. For a look at a more comprehensive presentation of the traditions associated with this view of goodness, see Scott MacDonald, *Being and Goodness*.

distinct from what humans often mean by the ordinary use of the term "good" as applied to certain creatures or objects. Goodness in created things is something that can be rightly attributed to a thing according to the degree of perfections embodied by the thing in question. It is an accidental characteristic that is applied by how complete or successful a thing may be according to its nature, for instance, when considered in certain relations or contexts. A good shoe may be well made, without physical flaws, and may adequately protect one's feet, though its goodness may diminish over time as the soles are worn, the stitching comes loose, the material is damaged, and so on. Eventually it is no longer a "good shoe," so to speak. The shoe is good because it is what it is meant to be—it fulfills the mandate of its nature to be what it is and do what it does most fully and completely. A good shoe does what it is meant to do according to its nature for a time and inevitably moves from good to bad when its functionality is reduced by wear or abuse. The goodness of the shoe is accidental to the shoe and dependent on its performance and behavior in a sense. But this sort of approach to understanding goodness leads to confusion when applied to the nature of God.

Unlike the shoe, God's goodness is essential to him. It is attributed to him by metaphysical necessity (as explained above)—not an accidental quality that depends on God's behavior or success, and thus (unlike human moral goodness, for example), it is not measured by the value, output, measure, or results of his actions, so to speak. For example, unlike the shoe, there is nothing God is "meant to do" or "meant to be" according to his nature that he must live up to. God's own act of being just is his very essence and nature, and thus God cannot be other than he is for all of eternity—entirely complete and perfect, lacking nothing. One cannot reasonably take God's perfect goodness and make an argument or case that in order to fulfill the requirements of his goodness or achieve some sense of moral perfection, he should behave in some way in order to accomplish what his perfect goodness demands or requires.

For example, Aquinas argues that God's goodness is not on account of his behavior but his eternal nature itself. He explains that the perfections of a thing are threefold: its own being, the accidents required for its operation, and the ends toward which it is ordered. For Aquinas,

> This triple perfection belongs to no creature by its own essence; it belongs to God only, in Whom alone essence is existence; in Whom there are no accidents; since whatever belongs to others accidentally belongs to Him essentially . . . and He is not

> directed to anything else as to an end, but is Himself the last end of all things. Hence it is manifest that God alone has every kind of perfection by His own essence; therefore He Himself alone is good essentially.[19]

As such, for Aquinas, God's goodness cannot be earned or achieved—it belongs to him by the definition of his very nature. Brian Davies further explains Aquinas's view:

> For Aquinas, however, God's goodness and God himself are not similarly distinguishable. Indeed, so he also wants to say, and as we have seen him saying, God's goodness and God's existence (*esse*) are not distinguishable either. We can, therefore, take it for granted that Aquinas takes "God is good" to mean something very different indeed from what we have in mind when picking out objects in the universe and calling them good.[20]

Here, Davies illustrates the uniqueness of God's goodness as an essential divine attribute identical with his own act of being. And while it is not on the basis of judging the success or failure of God's actions that his goodness is determined, one can rightly say that whatever is good anywhere in existence is good precisely because of the goodness of God. God, as described in classical theism, is the first efficient cause of all that exists, and since goodness and being are the same in referent, God is the cause of all that is good in the universe.

> Aquinas thinks of God's goodness (not to be thought of as an accident in God) as what accounts for the existence of all substances and accidents—whatever can be thought of as *having* (as opposed to *being*) *esse* (as actually existing without being the source of its being actual). Aquinas does not think that God's being good depends on him creating such things. He takes God to be essentially good.[21]

Thus, as Davies explains, it is the goodness of God that accounts for the existence of every being in the universe that has existence. In fact, this is precisely how God's goodness is known by creatures in the first place—as reasoning from effect to cause. Again, Davies:

> Created goodness comes in many different forms and is possessed by things that fall very short of (and are very different

19. Aquinas, *Summa Theologiae*, I.6.3.
20. Davies, *Thomas Aquinas on God and Evil*, 57.
21. Davies, *Thomas Aquinas on God and Evil*, 114.

> from) what God is by nature. But, as amounting to the possession of *esse*, all created goodness points to God as subsisting being itself (*ipsum esse subsistens*), whose goodness exists before that of creatures and is what makes them to be what creatures are insofar as they are good.[22]

Thus, God is not only perfectly good and goodness itself, he is also the cause of all that is good, which points back to him as the perfectly good creator.

What follows from this analysis of God's goodness is of particular import in consideration of the problem of evil. Arguments from evil tend to imply that God, on account of his perfect goodness, would be expected to behave in certain ways and create things that tend to thrive or succeed with as little suffering, failure, and death as possible. However, on account of the understanding of divine goodness as revealed from a being that is *ipsum esse subsistens*, it is difficult to establish exactly what obligations a perfectly good God would hold toward a universe he has created aside from providing and upholding the existence and degree of perfections things have as a matter of their created forms and natures.

God as Morally Good

Upon consideration of the metaphysically necessary goodness of God in the sense described above, the question follows as to exactly what such an analysis entails in regards to the obligations or responsibilities (if any) that God necessarily holds toward a creation plagued with cruelty, suffering, corruption, and all sorts of evil. The problem of evil suggests that God, on account of his essential goodness, does in fact hold an obligation or expectation to prevent or remediate evil wherever and whenever it is possible for him to do so, but is this truly evident from the above analysis of God as *ipsum esse subsistens*? Such a demand calls into consideration not only the *metaphysical* goodness of God but more specifically the *moral* goodness of God.

In William Rowe's original formulation of the evidential argument from evil, he presents his second premise as follows: "An omniscient, wholly good being would prevent the occurrence of any intense suffering it could, unless it could not do so without thereby losing some greater

22. Davies, *Thomas Aquinas on God and Evil*, 116.

good or permitting some evil equally bad or worse."[23] Rowe sees this argument as largely non-controversial and universally accepted among theists: "So stated, (2) seems to express a belief that accords with our basic moral principles, principles shared by both theists and non-theists. If we are to fault the argument for atheism, therefore, it seems we must find some fault with its first premise."[24] Thus, the bulk of Rowe's defense for his evidential argument from evil is devoted to his first premise, which is where he believes the theist must find fault. The alternative, as implied by Rowe, is that the theist must be prepared to redefine God in such a manner that makes his goodness either meaningless or radically different from what is ordinarily meant by the word. The critical factor tied up in Rowe's second premise, therefore, is God's *moral goodness*. Wykstra explains, "The heart of (2) is, I believe, a conceptual truth unpacking part of what it means to call any being—not just any omniscient being—morally good. . . . In this shorthand, the key idea of Rowe's second premise is that a morally good being would allow an instance of suffering only if the being believes that doing so serves some outweighing good."[25] Thus the question follows, in an evaluation of Rowe's second premise, as to what moral obligations apply to God and how God stands in relation to those obligations.

Richard Swinburne, largely in agreement with Rowe's second premise, offers one such analysis of what many philosophers hold to be God's moral obligations. Following an apparent Augustinian bent, Swinburne explains that God must always do only what is best:

> A theist normally holds that God is by nature morally perfectly good . . . When discussing the claim that God's actions are morally good, I suggest that what is usually meant by an action being 'morally good' is that overall, taking all reasons into consideration, it is better to do than not to do; the reasons for doing it override (are, as reasons, more cogent than) the reasons for not doing it.[26]

Here, Swinburne argues that God, in application of his divine omniscience, surveys all possible options and outcomes and consistently chooses the best course of action to take (if any) in any possible circumstance. Such

23. Rowe, "Problem of Evil," 336.
24. Rowe, "Problem of Evil," 337.
25. Wykstra, "Humean Obstacle," 140.
26. Swinburne, *Coherence of Theism*, 200.

an argument seems at first entirely plausible for the theist, upon reflection that a perfect being with the power and intellectual resources of God would certainly never fail to both intend the best possible outcome and always accomplish what he intends in every situation. "If God did not always do what on his evidence is probably the best where there was a best, or ever did a bad action, he would be less than perfect."[27] As such, Swinburne holds that God's moral goodness in this respect denotes a pivotal position for any theist. "I suggest that, in the sense of 'moral' that I am using, almost all theists hold that God is morally perfectly good, and that this is a central claim of theism."[28] Per Swinburne, therefore, it is both impossible and infeasible that God could create any living thing that fails to thrive in such a way that its own life is not "worth living" so to speak, because God is, on account of his divine nature, morally indebted to the well-being of everything or anything he creates. As Swinburne explains,

> . . . if God creates sentient creatures (including humans and the higher animals), he puts himself under an obligation to give them a total life that as a whole is on balance worth living; and so, if someone's life on earth is not on balance worth living, God is under an obligation to provide for that creature a further life after death such that his total life is worth living.[29]

Thus, for Swinburne, by creating living creatures in the first place, God has put himself under the moral obligation to provide a "better than not" existence for those creatures such that, given the whole picture, every creature experiences enough good to outweigh any possible amount of evil.

A further approach to affirming God's moral goodness speaks to God as the penultimate moral exemplar for created moral beings. In short, God is seen as both the source of human morality and the metaphysical standard that grounds it. Norman Geisler takes this approach:

> It is recognized that God is the ultimate standard for what is morally right: He is the ultimate Moral Lawgiver. The ultimate source of all moral perfection cannot be less than ultimately perfect; the ultimate measure of morality is by its very nature morally perfect. God can no less be perfect than a good yardstick can be less than three feet long.[30]

27. Swinburne, *Coherence of Theism*, 202.

28. Swinburne, *Coherence of Theism*, 204.

29. Swinburne, *Coherence of Theism*, 221.

30. Geisler, *Systematic Theology*, 347.

Here, Geisler combines the concept of God's metaphysical perfection with the idea of God as the metaphysical cause of the objective moral law to which all humans must adhere. Per Geisler, this entails that God must therefore possess a level of moral perfection himself that embodies his causal role as the origin of all moral laws. It is because of this, as Rowe explains, that the world as a whole can be rightly judged on its moral balance against any claim that it was created by a morally perfect being:

> But what is it to be perfectly good? Since God is unsurpassably good, he has all the features that unsurpassable goodness implies. Among these is absolute moral goodness. . . . For God's moral goodness has long been thought to be in some way the source or standard of what it is for human life to be moral. Furthermore, by virtue of his essential moral perfection, some judgments can be made about the world he has created. We may be certain, for example, that God would not create a morally bad world.[31]

Here, Rowe illustrates that given God's moral goodness (on account of God being the source of all moral goodness), God is obligated to create a world that is itself morally good. It is from this position that the argument from evil proceeds. If God is obliged to create a world that is on balance good and serve as moral exemplar to all moral creatures, then it seems reasonable to adjudicate the effects of God's interactions with the world according to basic moral principles (in the face of the experience of evil in the world, for example), and if one finds that God has acted (or failed to act) in any way incongruent with those principles, then it seems that his very existence as a morally perfect being can be rightly called into question.

Critique of God's Moral Goodness

However, a number of issues arise when considering God as a moral being in this respect. First, there is no *prima facie* reason to think that a creator instituting certain moral principles as an aspect of the created nature of created moral beings must himself adhere to those same moral principles when acting toward the well-being of those creatures. After all, God's own eternal, essential goodness is quite different from the goodness of created beings, who must strive toward "the good" by functioning

31. Rowe, *Philosophy of Religion*, 9–10.

and behaving according the sorts of beings they were created to be. Where creatures must strive toward goodness they do not yet possess by adhering to certain objective moral standards, for example, it makes little sense to argue that the source of all possible goodness (e.g., God) must also strive toward some standard by way of divine moral obligations if that standard is the ultimate metaphysical goodness that he already is as a necessary aspect of his divine essence. Thus, God's goodness does not imply or require him to behave in some way that comports directly with human moral precepts. Metaphysically, if God never obeyed any moral laws, he would still be perfectly good because he just is goodness.[32]

Second, attributing moral goodness to God seems to commit a category mistake by attributing the means of evaluating or determining creaturely goodness in a univocal way to how one evaluates or determines God's own goodness. As Davies explains, "According to this argument, standards for evaluating things other than God cannot be applied to God. In particular . . . we should not suppose that God is good or bad in accordance with the criteria we use to evaluate people morally."[33] The challenge for such a position is that if God is in fact a moral being in some analogical sense, then precisely where are humans meant to get the correct moral criteria for evaluating God's behavior? As such, humans tend to apply their own moral standards in such a comparison, often univocally. As Terence Penelhum explains, "In calling someone morally good, a speaker must have in mind some set of moral standards which the man he calls good follows in his conduct. . . . It is true that people's criteria of goodness differ. But in calling someone good I have to use *some* set of criteria. And these have, banally, to be my own."[34] Thus, the creature has no choice but to apply its own moral standards to God. "I

32. One may yet argue that God, by being the very goodness creatures strive for as their proper end in their moral pursuits, must himself possess the very moral perfection sought by creatures. However, even if it is so that God does in fact embody in an analogical sense, the proper object of creaturely desires and moral pursuits, this does not in turn require God to act toward the created world with a similar obligation as if the goodness of the created world were God's proper end. Even if God does hold some relationship to creaturely moral goodness in an analogical sense, it would be a perfect goodness that always maintains God himself as its proper object—never requiring him to act in some specific manner toward the goodness or perfection of created things. Thus, moral goodness, if it applies to God, is vastly different than the sorts of moral obligations held by creatures.

33. Davies, *Introduction to Philosophy of Religion*, 216.

34. Penelhum, "Divine Goodness and the Problem of Evil," 100–101; emphasis in original.

wish to conclude from this set of theses that in calling God good, a theist is committed to saying that God's reasons for permitting evils must be reasons that are acceptable according to the believer's own set of moral standards."[35] In the end, per Penelhum, the theist must be committed to the idea that the moral standards we hold ourselves to are the same that God must hold himself to, and if an act or command of God does not seem to fit with those standards, then the theist must call into question his own moral standards.

> We do not need to insist that God's moral authority depends on his decisions' coinciding with our moral intuitions; but we do need to insist that if we accept a purported moral decision as coming from God, our moral intuitions have to be put aside as misleading if they do not coincide with that decision. What is necessary is that the moral principles the theist holds to and the ones he ascribes to God are the same.[36]

Thus, as Penelhum explains, the moral standards between creatures and the creator must be identical if one is to make a moral judgment about the creator. As such, God must be placed in a moral community with creatures. As R. F. Holland elaborates, "When 'God' is conceived as a one among many he becomes subjectable to moral judgment; and within a moral community of course it would make perfectly good sense for the one by whom, or let us say the chief one by whom we are judged, to be submitted to our moral judgment."[37] Thus God must be reduced to "one among many" into a human moral community. However, it is difficult to place God into a moral community with any creature. Per Anthony Kenny,

> If it is difficult to attach clear sense to the evidence to be brought against the designer of the world, it is even more difficult to take seriously the idea of calling him before the bar of human morality. Morality presupposes a moral community: and a moral community must be of beings with a common language, roughly equal powers, and roughly similar needs, desires and interests. God can no more be part of a moral community with human beings than he can be part of a political community with them.[38]

35. Penelhum, "Divine Goodness and the Problem of Evil," 101.
36. Penelhum, "Divine Goodness and the Problem of Evil," 103.
37. Holland, *Against Empiricism*, 238.
38. Kenny, *What Is Faith?*, 87.

Kenny here demonstrates that God is a being of such distance and difference with human moral creatures that even if God were to hold to some moral community, there is no reason to think that it would be one that was in any way univocally commensurate with human moral intuitions. As such, D. Z. Phillips agrees that just such a challenge raises the question as to what God's perfect goodness could in fact be:

> To repeat for one last time in this chapter, my conclusions are meant to have force against those consequentialist philosophers of religion who see God as a member of a moral community he shares with us. What if we need to look in a radically different direction in order to understand what is meant by God's perfect goodness? That, as they say, is a totally different question.[39]

For Phillips, therefore, the correct understanding of God's goodness cannot be dependent on God's membership in a human moral community. Such an idea raises a number of problems and commits the fallacy of a category mistake—applying human moral obligations to God.

Third, God is by nature a metaphysically perfect being, and thus he lacks nothing that one could expect him to achieve by acting according to certain moral categories. Therefore, when one considers the proper definition of moral agency, one must also consider the distance between God and creatures and the wildly different goodness and perfections of each. As Davies explains,

> For how do we typically think of moral agents? Primarily, we think of them as people living in the world and capable of acting well or badly. . . . But they are all talking about people and what makes them to be (morally) good or bad (and what it therefore is for them to be moral agents). Yet God is not a human being. And if what I have said above has anything to recommend it, we have to think of God as radically different from anything created.[40]

39. Phillips, *Problem of Evil and the Problem of God*, 46. Phillips's own view of God is remarkably distinct from the argument from natural theology presented I have defended in this work. For example, Phillips is often characterized as a "religious nonrealist" that holds to a Wittgensteinian concept of God (what Phillips calls the "grammar of God") as a being whose existence depends in some way on the human conception of God. However, many of Phillips' insights surrounding the problem of evil, particularly surrounding the frequent over-anthropomorphizing of God in the literature surrounding the problem of evil and his critique of certain theodicies along this vein, are helpful on this point.

40. Davies, *Reality of God and the Problem of Evil*, 92.

In consideration of what God's goodness entails (as *ipsum esse subsistens*), God is already infinitely perfect and complete, lacking nothing. Therefore, according to the classical theist, God cannot be said to be in need of anything he does not already possess by way of his infinite essence in order to gain or improve upon the perfections that are part of his nature. Thus, as Davies explains, God has no dispositions and depends on nothing for his well-being.

> For most classical theists, however, God is simple and immutable, which means that he can have no dispositions since these belong only to things which are complex and changeable. And, so any classical theist would add, it is surely absurd to suppose that the God who creates everything from nothing depends for his well-being on anything, let alone dispositions which people need in order to thrive.[41]

Per Davies, God does not thrive because he possesses some disposition toward moral behavior, for example, or because he always does what is good or right. In fact, for God, there can be no meaningful moral context or standards to which God is obliged to act.

> One has duties or obligations as part of a definite, describable context. . . . In terms of classical theism, however, God has no context. He is the maker of all contexts and is the cause of there being situations in which people have duties and obligations. If classical theists are right, God has no role or job with standards to which he must conform.[42]

Thus, it makes little sense to speak of God as having moral obligations that he is beholden to or that his goodness somehow depends on his behavior in this sense. As such, God cannot be morally good or bad. Per Herbert McCabe:

> It is blasphemous nonsense to say that God is wicked, but it is equally inappropriate to say that he is morally good. We can say this only in the sense that he is the cause of moral goodness in creatures. Moral good and evil, we saw, belong to rational beings that achieve or fail to achieve perfection. And we saw that this perfection of rational beings could be nothing other than the possession of God, the *bonum universale* (universal good). It follows that there can be no sense in which God can be said to

41. Davies, *Introduction to the Philosophy of Religion*, 229.

42. Davies, *Introduction to the Philosophy of Religion*, 229.

> achieve or fail to achieve this perfection, and hence no sense in which he can be said to be morally good or bad.[43]

Here, McCabe illustrates that God's goodness speaks rightly to his causal role as the source of all creaturely goodness (including creaturely moral goodness), but that is as far as the comparison should go. The moral goodness of creatures is the strive to achieve a perfection as their proper end, which is found in the infinite goodness of God. Given this understanding, what is it that we can say God strives for in a similar moral sense that he does not already possess? Ascribing moral duties to God, therefore, engages in a degree of anthropomorphism that fails to recognize God's essential perfection as the object of his own will.

This rejection of the classification of God as a moral agent in this respect is not a new concept but is nevertheless consistent with many aspects of classical theology. Thomas Aquinas, for example, specifies active human virtues as indicative of that which cannot be ascribed to God: "Now, since human virtues are those by which human life is directed, and human life is twofold, contemplative and active, the virtues belonging to the active life, so far as they perfect this life, cannot befit God."[44] Thus, those active virtues that compel a creature to act toward some good end that is lacking to the creature (such as making good habits, resisting temptation, nourishing the body, directing the passions, and so on) cannot be attributed to God, who at all times lacks no such perfections that would oblige him to act in some manner. Morality, in its basest sense, involves the achievement of some good that is lacking in a creature by way of an action that one is compelled or expected to perform, and thus only mutable, imperfect beings are those who possess such obligations. Davies explains,

> For Aquinas, our moral life is that of changeable beings ever seeking goods that they lack at various times. Yet God, he thinks, is the simple, unchangeable source of all the perfections of creatures. So it never occurs to Aquinas to consider whether

43. McCabe, *God and Evil*, 106.

44. Aquinas, *Summa Contra Gentiles*, I.92.6. Note that Aquinas holds the contemplative virtues (such as wisdom, knowledge, and intellect) to be really present in God as the exemplar of the human contemplative virtues. These, however, are not virtues to which God is obliged to act in some way (as is necessary for the premises of the problem of evil), but rather these are virtues that apply as perfections to an immaterial nature. For more on Aquinas's view of the contemplative virtues as applied to God, see Aquinas, *Summa Contra Gentiles*, I.94.

> God is morally good as having the virtues that make for our moral goodness.[45]

The result of such an analysis, according to Davies, is a distinct anthropomorphizing of God under categories that should and do apply only to creatures. "The notion of God as subject to duties or obligations (and as acting in accordance with them) would, I think, have been thought of by [Aquinas] as an unfortunate lapse into anthropomorphism, as reducing God to the level of a human creature."[46] Thus, if one is to resist the urge to make God a creature under the same or similar obligations under which creatures are driven (or directed) to act, then one must be willing to admit that God holds no moral obligations to act in some manner or situation in the same way creatures do. Furthermore, just such a position, as described above, has no bearing at all on God's metaphysical goodness; God's perfect goodness does not depend on his behavior, and God is not compelled to act toward adherence to some moral directive to which he is obliged.

ASCRIBING MORAL GOODNESS TO GOD

Given this understanding of God's goodness as the sort that is metaphysically necessary, though not the result of some good behavior or adherence to moral precepts, there remains a sense in which God's goodness and creaturely morality may nevertheless intersect. This speaks to certain moral virtues or categories that can be rightly attributed to both creatures and (at least analogically) to God. Thus, it is not entirely impotent to say of God that he is always loving or just or that he always does what he says he will do, for example. Such acts as love, justice, and trustworthiness on the part of creatures speak to their own achievement of certain moral virtues on account of right behavior, and yet God is often said to act in ways that similarly reflect divine love, justice, and trustworthiness as well—though not in an obligatory sense in the same way that creatures do. As such, there seems to be a sense in which one may refer to God as possessing or exhibiting what would be seen in humans as morally good behavior.

45. Davies, *Thomas Aquinas on God and Evil*, 60.

46. Davies, *Thomas Aquinas on God and Evil*, 62.

God's Goodness as Moral Exemplar

One such way in which God can be said to exhibit a sense of moral goodness, as consistent with the classical view of God as *ipsum esse subsistens*, acknowledges him as the prime exemplar of human moral virtues and the creator of all human morality. As Brian Shanley argues, "Now since creaturely moral goodness is surely a spiritual perfection, it must have its exemplar source in God, even though God's moral goodness is not a state to be achieved through virtuous actions but rather identical with his very being."[47] Thus, for Shanley, God necessarily possesses the exemplar source for all creaturely moral goodness. Likewise, from Aquinas:

> Following what has been said, it remains to show how virtues may be posited in God. For just as God's being is universally perfect, containing in itself the perfections of all beings, so His goodness must in a manner contain the goodness in each and every thing. Now, virtue is a certain goodness in the virtuous, for according to it is one called good, and his work good. Therefore, the divine goodness must contain in its way all the virtues.[48]

Here, Aquinas illustrates the sense in which classical theologians refer to God's goodness as the source of all creaturely virtues, which Aquinas argues must preexist in him. Precisely how these virtues exist in God, however, as Aquinas explains, is not as one who must achieve said virtue through habit or behavior or in the submission of the appetites, for example, but rather simply as an exemplar to said human virtue.

> Consequently the exemplar of human virtue must needs pre-exist in God, just as in Him pre-exist the types of all things. Accordingly virtue may be considered as existing originally in God, and thus we speak of "exemplar" virtues: so that in God the Divine Mind itself may be called prudence; while temperance is the turning of God's gaze on Himself, even as in us it is that which conforms the appetite to reason. God's fortitude is His unchangeableness; His justice is the observance of the Eternal Law in His works.[49]

Hence, for Aquinas, God does in a way possess all human virtues, but the way such virtues are attributed to God is not by God's behavior in

47. Shanley, *Thomist Tradition*, 116.
48. Aquinas, *Summa Contra Gentiles*, I.92.
49. Aquinas, *Summa Theologiae*, I-II.61.5.

some circumstance and thus is far different from how those virtues apply to humans. Temperance in creatures, for example, involves a binding of the passions in sight of a higher or greater good, while temperance in God, who is devoid of passions, just is his eternal, unbroken gaze toward his own perfect goodness—entirely and eternally unaffected by anything apart from the highest good of his own divine being.[50] Thus, God is not temperate in his character because he knows how to repeatedly and effectively keep down unwelcome evil desires but rather because he has no such desires at all in the first place. Temperance, therefore, has its proper source in God's nature, but God is not morally obliged toward temperance such that he must make an effort toward it and work to achieve it, so to speak, or that his own divine temperance is somehow determined or proven by how God behaves or acts in some situation. As Davies explains,

> If Aquinas takes moral virtue to exist in God, it is only because he thinks that nothing God produces can fail to have some grounding in God's nature. It is not because he takes God to be morally virtuous in any sense that we can fathom and adjudicate on (or in any sense that we ought to try to fathom and adjudicate on).[51]

Thus, God has virtues only in this limited sense, insofar as what he creates exists in him, and he serves as an exemplar cause of all creaturely morality devoid of any sense of evil, passion, or imperfection.

God's Goodness as Moral Justice

A second sense in which God can be said to have or possess moral goodness speaks to God's divine justice.[52] As Shanley argues,

50. For Aquinas's own definition of temperance in this respect, see *Summa Theologiae*, II-II.141.

51. Davies, *Reality of God*, 99.

52. Here I do not mean to limit discussions of justice to the remuneration of wrongs but rather in the broader sense as always giving to things their due. Criminal acts, for example, in fact do call for remuneration, and justice demands that they be punished, though justice in the divine sense encompasses much more than this, such as always giving to humans (on account of the created human nature ordained by God) what is properly due to the human, such as a rational intellect, a physical body, a desire to seek the good, and so on. The correct sense of what divine justice entails is important in consideration of the problem of evil. The evidential problem of evil, for example, holds that all evils that arise in the world must by justified by some greater good in order for God to allow them to come about unhindered. Any evil with no corresponding

> When discussing God's justice, the most important moral virtue in this context, Aquinas says that while any moral virtue connected with the passions can only be metaphorically attributed to God, the moral virtues connected with the will and its acts can be attributed to God non-metaphorically or analogously . . . So Aquinas does consider the moral virtues to be attributable to God, especially when it comes to the will and its pre-eminent virtue of justice.[53]

Justice, in its basest sense, entails always giving to things their due, and precisely what is due to things is determined by their created nature and the world in which they exist. Per Aquinas, "Furthermore, it was shown above that because God wills something He also wills those things that are necessary to it. But that which is necessary to the perfection of each thing is due to it. Therefore, there is justice in God, to which it belongs to give to each one what belongs to him."[54] As the creator of every creaturely nature, God decides what is rightfully due to anything he creates and always provides this for every created thing. It is in the nature of a maple tree to have leaves and produce sap, for example, and thus God, on account of his divine justice, cannot cause a maple tree (at least one that is unhindered by outside factors or privations) to have no leaves or sap by its nature, which would entail a contradiction. An important distinction follows: the maple tree is not *owed* things like leaves and sap until God himself declares that it is so, and only then, in a suppositional sense, can one say that God is suppositionally obliged to provide what the nature of the tree requires when he creates such a tree. God does not dole out justice (or anything else for that matter) because he is somehow indebted to things like the maple tree, but rather God first decides what is due and then always follows through by providing precisely that. Davies explains,

> One can, of course, say that God is truly (and not metaphorically) just. But God's justice cannot amount to him paying what he owes to anything, for God is the debtor of nothing created. Rather, it amounts to him giving creatures what is owed to them

---

justifying good associated with it is considered gratuitous or even "unjust evil," so to speak. The relevant point of consideration here will be whether or not the nature of a creature includes a life without evil and whether God's divine justice requires him to provide for every creature such a life.

53. Shanley, *Thomist Tradition*, 115.

54. Aquinas, *Summa Contra Gentiles*, I.93.6.

> given the natures that they have as his creatures (natures of his making and design).[55]

Thus, in this sense, God's justice is necessarily directed toward certain things according to their due, and what is due to a thing is determined by its nature, which in turn is created by God. Thus, it all reduces to God's own will (as opposed to some moral obligation toward justice) as to what is due and what is not. "In ascribing justice to God, however, all Aquinas retains of this notion is that of bringing about what is owed, and he does so on the assumption that what is and what is not owed always derives from God's will."[56] Such introduces a sense of suppositional necessity that is relevant to this understanding. If God has decided that mature humans are rational beings by nature, then all mature humans (absent interfering privations) will be rational beings. God always gives to the human what is due in this respect. Likewise, if acts of moral evil on the part of a human necessitate judgment and punishment according to the created nature of the human, then God (whether directly by divine action or indirectly by means of his natural created order) will always mete out those consequences as required by the suppositional nature of the human according to God's perfect justice. As for moral obligation, however, divine justice does not necessitate that God owes something more than what a creature's nature essentially requires to any created being. If it is within the created nature of the human creature, for example, to be a moral being beholden to certain moral directives and obligations, then it is because God has created humans to be in that way—not because God himself holds to similar moral obligations. Though this comes from God (and is in a sense directed toward God as the highest good), the morality of the human begins and ends with humanity and is binding only on human creatures.

In relation to the existence of evil in the world, there is yet another sense in which divine justice is sometimes said to require God to act in some way. Here, one may argue that God must either bring good from evil, allow evil only in sight of a greater good, or risk the charge of being unjust (by allowing gratuitous evil). Even Aquinas himself seems to make this argument: "For it would not please God that someone should suffer from adversity unless he wished some good to come to him from it. . . . The name of the Lord is truly blessed by men inasmuch as they have

55. Davies, *Thomas Aquinas on God and Evil*, 117.

56. Davies, *Thomas Aquinas on God and Evil*, 64.

knowledge of his goodness, namely that he distributes all things well and does nothing unjustly."[57] Here, Aquinas argues that God's justice seems to require that adversity (or evil) suffered by a creature would be unjust without some concomitant good. Again, Aquinas:

> Although every created thing is from God and is good according to its nature, yet, if something harms us or brings us pain, we believe that such comes from God, not as a fault in Him, but because God permits no evil that is not for good. Affliction purifies from sin, brings low the guilty, and urges on the good to a love of God.[58]

Thus, for Aquinas, all evil permitted by God must be for the good of the creature on account of God's justice, which is precisely the position of the problem of evil. However, it is important to note that Aquinas is not here implying or arguing that God holds some obligation to a creature who experiences evil *as the debtor of the sufferer*. He is simply making a statement as to how the universe is properly ordered by its creator and how the function of the universe does in fact (at least sometimes, or often) bring about evil that is itself ordered toward some good—not because it *must* (on account of God's divine justice or goodness, for example), but because it simply *does* (on account of God's grace, for example). As Aquinas argues, the ordering of the universe in this way necessitates the good of the whole, though not always for the good of the sufferer:

> To realize this we should consider that whatever happens in the world, even if it be evil, accrues to the good of the universe . . . However, the evil does not always accrue to the good of that in which it is. Thus, the death of one animal accrues to the good of the universe, inasmuch as by the destruction of one thing something else begins to be, although it does not accrue to the good of that which ceases to be; because the good of the universe is willed by God according to itself and to this good all the parts of the universe are ordained. The same seems to apply to the relationship of the noblest parts to the other parts, because the evil affecting the other parts is ordained to the good of the noblest parts. But whatever happens to the noblest parts is ordained only to their good, because his care for them is for their sake, whereas his care for the others is for the sake of the noblest.[59]

57. Aquinas, *Expositio Super Iob as Litteram*, I.4.
58. Aquinas, *Expositio in Symbolum Apostolorum*, article 1.
59. Aquinas, *Super ad Romanos*, 8.6.

Thus, God orders the universe such that evil suffered is often ordered toward the good of the whole rather than for the good of each individual created being. Here, Aquinas makes clear what he intends in reference to divine justice bringing forth good from evil—not from of a sense of moral obligation on account of the divine goodness but rather on account of the ordering of the universe in such a fashion that evil befitting to one thing often accrues toward the good of something else, and this in turn ordered toward the "noblest parts" of creation.[60] As such, it is unclear how such a view of divine justice bringing about the goods of the universe (according to the ordering of its nature as created by God) could be used to argue for a sense of divine moral obligation toward the mitigation of evil in that very same creation. The critical factor of such an argument, for Aquinas, is rather the simple fact that good does come from evil, which he posits more as an encouragement for the saints rather than a justification of God's divine goodness.[61]

God's Goodness as Moral Consistency

A third sense in which God is said to be held to a sense of moral obligation is the argument that God, while not *obliged* to act in a moral manner, nevertheless *chooses* to do so in every circumstance and thus is properly open to adjudication of his acts in the same sense as if he did hold those obligations. Such an argument is advocated by Thomas Morris, who distinguishes between God behaving in *obedience* to some rule and God always behaving *consistently* with the same rule.

> Behavior which results from obeying a rule can be distinguished logically from behavior which accords with the rule but does

60. For Aquinas, the "noblest parts" refer to the saints of God, who are directed by nature toward the ultimate and highest possible good for all of creation in the beatific vision. As Aquinas explains, "But the most excellent parts of the universe are God's saints . . . Therefore, whatever happens to them or to other things, it all accrues to the benefit of the former. . . . because even the evil of sinners accrues to the good of the just." Aquinas, *Super ad Romano*, 8.6.

61. The fact that good comes from evil is of importance to Aquinas in the understanding of the evils in the universe but not in terms of justifying God's permission of them in the sense implied by the problem of evil. What is noteworthy here is Aquinas's view of the proper end of human happiness—finding its ultimate fulfillment in the beatific vision of God himself. For Aquinas, all saints enjoy this fulfillment of their good, and the evils faced by the saints are ordered toward this good. Such evil, therefore, is not a necessary condition nor product of the ultimate good of humans. It is, nonetheless, a good that follows the evils of privation for the intellectual creature.

> not result from an attempt to obey it, even though the two forms of conduct may be empirically indistinguishable to an observer. Something similar to this distinction can help us to understand the relation between God and moral duties, and thus the legitimate application of the duty model to God. We can hold that moral principles which function as prescriptive or proscriptive for human conduct stand in some other relation to divine conduct. We can even go so far as to claim that they are merely descriptive of the shape of divine activity.[62]

Here, Morris argues that someone ascribing moral goodness to God need not defend the position that God stands in some obligatory relation to a set of moral precepts to which he is beholden. Rather, one may argue that God acts consistently with the moral duties ascribed to creatures, though he himself does not do so because he is compelled but rather does so freely. For humans, Morris argues, our flawed natures stand under an obligation to moral precepts outside of ourselves, while God does not.

> But the important difference is as follows: We human beings, imperfect and weak as we are, exist in a state of being bound by moral duty. In this state, we act under obligation, either satisfying or contravening our duties. Because of his distinctive nature, God does not share our ontological status. Specifically, he does not share our relation to moral principles—that of being bound by some of these principles as duties.[63]

Thus, for Morris, God's relation to moral duties is not of obligation but the divine will.

> Nevertheless, God acts perfectly in accordance with those principles which would express duties for a moral agent in his relevant circumstances. And he does so necessarily. So although God does not literally have any duties on this construal of the duty model, we can still have well-grounded expectations concerning divine conduct by knowing those principles which would govern the conduct of a perfect, duty-bound moral agent who acted as in fact God does. We understand and anticipate God's activity by analogy with the behavior of a completely good moral agent.[64]

62. Morris, *Our Idea of God*, 60.
63. Morris, *Our Idea of God*, 60.
64. Morris, *Our Idea of God*, 60–61.

Therefore, according to Morris, one can rightly expect God to behave in a moral manner in an analogous way similar to how creatures are expected to behave, though not because he stands under a moral obligation but rather because he necessarily chooses to act in such a manner.

> Part of God's goodness does consist in his acting in perfect accord with those principles which would provide duties for a lesser being. This use of the model would then be an explication, not of God's moral goodness, but of his volitional and thus, more generally, axiological goodness. When religious people claim that God is morally good, meaning that he acts in accord with moral principles, they are merely using that axiological conception with which they are most familiar, moral goodness, to describe or model an aspect of divinity functionality isomorphic with, though ontologically different from, human goodness.[65]

Thus, for Morris, one can speak of God's moral goodness in an analogical sense and also rightly adjudicate on God's behavior from a moral perspective even if God does not stand under moral obligation in the same way that creatures do.

However, how can one rightly come to the conclusion that God always necessarily acts in accord with human moral principles? The bar for such a belief seems inordinately high, especially since there is no guarantee or requirement that God behave in some specific way in some specific circumstance. One cannot merely assume (even in a suppositional sense) that God always acts in accord with moral precepts (even though he is not obliged to do so) and then proceed to use perceived divine moral failures as an argument against his existence in a way consistent with the problem of evil. Any perceived evidence of divine moral failure in this sense would serve not as an argument against his existence but only as a counterexample to the original assumption that God always acts consistently with moral obligations. As such, one would have to argue that God's nature somehow requires him (out of necessity) to always act in accord with certain moral directives, which would just make him beholden to moral obligations, which is exactly what Morris tries to avoid. As explained above, it is not clear how such a concept would follow from a position of natural theology (*ipsum esse subsistens*), and without an argument on that (or similar) basis, Morris's consistency argument fails. Furthermore, arguing for the necessity of God's actions in this sense seems to contradict the

65. Morris, *Our Idea of God*, 62–63.

very point of exception that Morris seeks to achieve and returns God to a status of moral obligation, even if applied through a means of semantic analogy. As such, this model falls short of ascribing moral duties to God in a sense that can be adjudicated on by moral creatures, even if God always or often does act consistently with creaturely moral precepts.

God's Goodness as Moral Revelation

The fourth and final sense in which God (as *ipsum esse subsistens*) can be considered "moral" in an analogical sense depends on what (if anything) God has communicated via divine revelation about what he will and will not do. Such an argument is distinct from the approach in this work that depends on natural theology to draw conclusions about God and his nature, though it is worth considering as a possible means of advancing the idea that God is in fact a moral being subject to creaturely moral evaluation and correction. As Anthony Kenny explains, "Remember that we have been speaking throughout within the bounds of natural theology. If an alleged revelation claims that God has entered into moral relationships with human beings, then we enter into a different realm of discourse."[66] Though God is not committed *per se* to univocal moral obligations in the same way that humans or other creatures are, God can in fact promise to act or behave a certain way in certain situations—including a spoken divine commitment to abide by human moral precepts, for example—and this would suppositionally create a type of obligation akin to what humans experience as morality. For sake of space and scope, I will here refrain from investigating or examining any purported divine revelation that purports to place God into a suppositional moral community with creatures, because it is only the possibility of this that is worth addressing here. Even if God does in fact promise to behave in a moral manner, this would not somehow alter God's essential goodness to now depend on his behavior as the problem of evil requires, nor would it create an actual moral obligation for God in the same way that creatures identify or experience moral obligations. In such a case, God would not be placing himself into a moral community, and he would not be doing so because his nature somehow requires it—he would instead be willfully and freely choosing to do so, which is nothing like the sort of moral obligations ascribed to creatures. Even if God were to promise (via divine revelation,

66. Kenny, *What Is Faith?*, 87.

for example) to behave in some specific moral way, any counterexample to this would only serve to cast doubt on the revelation itself and not the existence or nature of God.

God as a Moral Being

In summary, God (as *ipsum esse subsistens*) can rightly be said to be metaphysically good, both in reference to not only his acts but also his very nature or act of being. Taken in the classical sense, God is goodness itself. The perfect goodness of God is a metaphysically necessary aspect of his divine nature as understood by God as subsistent being itself. Thus, God's goodness does not depend on his behavior or performance in some way but is rather an eternal, essential attribute. Further, God's goodness is seen and known from effect to cause as the metaphysically necessary source for all created goodness in the world—every act of being that exists and depends on God for its existence.

With this nature of goodness and the divine essence properly considered, it is difficult to see how one could argue that God is a "moral being" subject to moral obligations and duties in the same way that creatures are—who must adhere to some moral standard as a necessary aspect of his nature. God as subsistent being itself does not rely on anything external (such as adherence to a moral code, for example) to be properly considered good, and holding God to some human moral standard on account of his perfect goodness is an anthropomorphism that commits an illicit category mistake. As such, God cannot be rightly considered a "moral being" in the sense that arguments from evil often imply.

Further, given this analysis, other arguments for considering God a moral being in an analogical or suppositional sense fail to place God under a sense of moral obligation that can be adjudicated on by rational moral creatures. Though God is in fact the exemplar of all human moral duties and obligations, this does not imply that God himself must adhere to those same duties and obligations because his own nature is his proper end, while human moral creatures are ordered to him. Though God is rightly said to be and have divine justice, this does not obligate him to act or behave in some manner toward his creation beyond providing what the natures of created things require for their existence. Also, God acting consistently with moral obligations does not necessitate that he must do so and does not provide the creature with cause to evaluate his behavior in the sense required by the problem of evil. And finally, even if God himself may promise to act or behave in a moral manner in some circumstance, this does not place him under a moral obligation. As such, given these considerations, there does not seem to be any sense in which God can be said to exist under a moral obligation toward the well-being of creatures or the mitigation of evil. In the following chapter, I will explore precisely what evil itself implies or entails and how evil can be said to exist in a created universe without violating the goodness or nature of God.

6

The Nature of Evil

WITH THE METAPHYSICALLY NECESSARY goodness of God in mind, it follows to examine the nature of evil itself and what relationship a perfectly good God may hold to evil. What is evil *per se*? And what is suffering? What sort of existence or nature do things like evil and suffering have in the present world? What are the causes of evil? How does evil relate to God as an aspect of the created world? Did God create evil? These are the sorts of questions that follow when considering whether evil serves as *prima facie* evidence against the existence of God, and the proper answers to these questions carry much weight in the problem of evil.

A critical premise of the problem of evil argues that God, on account of his perfect goodness, must necessarily minimize or mitigate any evil in the universe as much as it is possible for him to do so. As such, if one discovers some instance of evil that God could have done something about and yet failed to do so, as the argument goes, then it follows on these premises that an omnipotent, omniscient, perfectly good God does not exist. One could argue, for example, that even the God of natural theology that I have proposed (given the sense of metaphysical perfection I have thus far defined and defended) does in fact suggest such an expectation of God as beholden to at least some essential perfections for the world he created and all it contains. Once God has become a creator, for example, one may argue that his creation becomes necessarily beholden to him for its own good, which may seem to preclude the possibility of any genuinely gratuitous evil in such a world. In other words, it may seem that God enters into an obligation of sorts to any world he creates, and on account of these creative acts, he is obliged to such a world to provide for its good—or some measure of good that is at least on balance better than whatever evil or suffering such a world may also include. As such, given the rampant lacks, deficiencies, and failures of the things (and creatures) he has allegedly created in the actual world, one may argue on this account that God must not exist. If this argument succeeds, the evidential problem of evil would yet have grounds to proceed, and the theist would be left once again to explain away proposed instances of gratuitous evil in the world.

However, a careful examination of the nature of evil and how it relates to and inhabits the world helps to mitigate the possibility of success for this line of argument. In fact, upon reflection, I believe there is no good reason at all why the God of classical theism could not exist simultaneously with a world containing evil—even perhaps *gratuitous* evil that is not causally associated with some greater good. The difference lies with a precise definition of what is meant by the term "evil" and what this term entails. As a rejoinder, it is of note that some philosophers argue that this sort of examination of the nature of evil represents either a distraction or hindrance to discussions surrounding the problem of evil. Michael Peterson, for example, makes this argument:

> Recognizing the problem of evil as a serious challenge to Christian theism, it might seem advisable to begin our investigation with a precise definition of evil. However, the attempt to offer such a specific definition at this point frequently ladens the meaning of evil with preconceived ideas and thus hinders objective discussion. . . . Therefore, it is advisable for present purposes to leave open the question of definition and proceed with a broad, commonsense notion of evil evoked by the things we typically call 'evil.'[1]

Here, Peterson argues that an approach to specificity as to the definition and nature of evil ends up reducing the discussion to a system of "preconceived ideas" that often distract one from any discussion of the problem of evil itself, or conflating matters to a point of confusion. In order to escape the pitfalls of such an approach, Peterson argues that one should simply begin with what everyone naturally agrees about the definition of evil and go from there.

> The set of commonly recognized evils includes, at the very least, such things as extreme pain and suffering, physical deformities,

1. Peterson, *God and Evil*, 10.

> psychological abnormalities, the prosperity of bad people, the demise of good people, disrupted social relations, unfulfilled potential, a host of character defects, and natural catastrophes. This list specifies the sorts of things that are commonly considered evil without prejudicing later discussions.[2]

Thus, for Peterson, the term "evil" is widely understood along the lines of the laundry list of examples he provides and generally needs no further analysis. The advantage for Peterson would be to bypass the distraction (and possible confusion) of a nuanced philosophical analysis of evil and lean on what he considers a more or less universally recognized denotation of the term.

However, even if one could agree on specific instances of evil in the world that conform with a more-or-less instinctive, universal human perspective (as Peterson suggests), it is difficult to proceed directly from mere mutual agreement on *specific instances of evil* to any meaningful metaphysical conclusions related to God and his relation to that evil. The alleged conflict between the existence of God and the existence of evil involves the nature of each, and omitting any discussion of the nature of evil altogether would lead to conclusions regarding the impact of evil on the existence of God that would be at best proportionately unclear—or at worst entirely unfounded. For instance, taking "physical deformities" as one of Peterson's examples, all may agree that this is in fact an instance of evil, but taking it as an evidential basis for a philosophical objection to God's existence requires further argument—specifically one must also explain what it is about physical deformities *per se* that makes this evil incompatible with the existence of God. Is it that a physical deformity really exists in some way with its own form or nature in such a fashion that it must have been instantiated by a creator? Is it that God holds a moral obligation to prevent or alleviate physical deformities in created things? Perhaps one may suggest that God should be expected to create only beings with natures that preclude even the possibility of physical deformities. Whatever the argument, simply stating that something is evil does not rise to a metaphysical challenge without additional justification, which must include at least some consideration as to what makes some evil (like physical deformities) an instance of evil in the first place. Thus, without a careful understanding of the natures of God and evil, the outcome of any argument from evil would struggle to rise above idle

2. Peterson, *God and Evil*, 11.

speculation based largely on instinctive human definitions and perceptions without rigorous philosophical support.[3] As such, one must offer at least some analysis of the nature of evil in order to demonstrate that some particular evil is incompatible with God's nature and existence.

In this chapter, I will offer just such an analysis of what is meant by the term "evil" and consider what the nature of evil would be as a thing in itself—and what sort of form or nature evil can be said to possess when instances and examples (such as physical deformities) occur in the context of the natural world. I will argue that evil itself has no nature at all that is separate or distinct from the things in which it inhabits or affects; it is not a force in the universe or a thing in itself that must be (or can be) actualized by a creator as an "existing thing" so to speak. Rather, I will argue that evil is and can only be a privation of the good in real existing things with no actual existence of its own. As such, evil cannot be said to be caused directly by God (considering both moral and natural evil), though it can be caused indirectly by the natural products and acts of created things. I will then conclude with a direct comparison of the nature of God and the nature of evil given the Thomistic approach to natural theology presented above, as well as the nature of evil addressed in this chapter. I will conclude that the existence of God is fully compatible with the existence of evil in a universe created by him—even evil that may be genuinely gratuitous.

EVIL AS PRIVATION

A common approach to the evidential problem of evil is to identify some tragic event (or deficient state of being) that evokes more or less a universal agreement and acceptance that it is in fact evil and then proceed to an argument or syllogism from there. William Rowe, for example, makes just such a claim: "In developing the argument for atheism based on the existence of evil, it will be useful to focus on some particular evil that our world contains in considerable abundance. Intense human and

3. As I will argue in the chapter eight, there remains an argument from evil that embraces the concept of evil specifically from a human perspective and leads to a new approach to the problem of evil speaking not to the existence of God per se but to the personal confidence one places in God and his goodness in the face of evil. Thus, while a careful understanding of the nature of evil is helpful in dissolving the *philosophical* problem of evil (as I will argue), its application is arguably limited in some way to that context and leaves certain questions concerning the nature and existence of evil unresolved—what I will later refer to as the "why" question of evil.

animal suffering, for example, occurs daily and in great plentitude in our world. Such intense suffering is a clear case of evil."[4] Likewise, John Hick defines suffering as a mental state distinct from physical pain, thus requiring a certain level of advanced cognition or mental acuity: "Pain is . . . a specific physical sensation. Suffering, however, is a mental state which may be as complex as human life itself. The endurance of pain is sometimes, but not always or even usually, an ingredient of suffering."[5] Further, Eleanor Stump points to suffering itself as a failure to thrive or to achieve one's desires: "A human being suffers when he is kept from being what he ought to be, or when he is kept from having the desires of his heart, or both."[6] Such aspects as these are typical of the literature surrounding the evidential problem of evil—taking an example of evil (usually some instance of suffering, pain, failure, or cruelty—the more egregious the better) and focusing on making the case as to why such an evil should or should not be mitigated by an omnipotent, omniscient, perfectly good being. The question remains, however, as to what the nature or existence of evil (such as in these examples) truly entails and how it is that evil actually occurs. One may ask what it is that makes something like suffering an example of evil in the first place, for example, and how one answers such a query may have a wide-reaching impact on the soundness and validity of the evidential argument. Without addressing the specific nature of evil *per se*, one can fall prey to answering or justifying some specific instance and miss the whole picture that the problem of evil entails. Thus, instead of focusing on a particular instance or example of evil, I intend to present a more expansive definition of evil (specifically from an Augustinian/Thomistic perspective) that is meant to encompass every possible instance of evil (both real or imagined) in order to put such a definition against the existence and nature of God.

When properly considered, evil always seems to entail some failure or lack in a thing that keeps it from being "all that it can be," so to speak, according to the sort of thing that it is. This concept of evil as a *privation of the good* is commonly attributed to Augustine, who explains the concept of evil in his work *City of God*—"For evil has no positive nature; but the loss of good has received the name 'evil.'"[7] In this way, it can be said that every instance of evil occurs when something that is otherwise

4. Rowe, "Problem of Evil and Some Varieties of Atheism," 127.

5. John Hick, "Soul-making and Suffering," 173.

6. Stump, "Problem of Suffering," 14.

7. Augustine, *City of God*, 318.

good (as a thing that has *being*, for example) somehow fails to thrive as fully as it could according to its nature. It is not simply the "absence of some good" that is evil *per se*, else anything that does not exist would be evil; rather, evil is a privation of what already exists and is by definition good. From Aquinas:

> Absence of good, taken negatively, is not evil; otherwise, it would follow that what does not exist is evil, and also that everything would be evil, though not having the good belonging to something else; for instance, a man would be evil who had not the swiftness of the roe, or the strength of a lion. But the absence of good, taken in a privative sense, is an evil; as, for instance, the privation of sight is called blindness.[8]

Here, Aquinas lays out the concept of evil as something that always occurs as a privation of the good of some existing thing, which entails a lack or defect in something that properly belongs to a thing as an aspect of its nature. Further, while a thing itself experiencing some privation can be considered "evil" as a subject or entity, evil *per se* cannot. Again, Aquinas: "And we can similarly understand evil in one way as the subject that is evil, and this subject is an entity. In the second way, we can understand evil itself, and evil so understood is the very privation of a particular good, not an entity."[9] Thus, per Aquinas, only the subject that experiences evil in some way can be considered an entity or something with *esse* or being, while evil *per se* has no existence or being of itself. Blindness, for example, has no existence apart from a creature that itself possesses a sighted nature and is yet deprived of sight due to some absence or defect in its ocular operations.

In this way, evil is generally defined by its relation to that which is otherwise good. Good, as a reminder, is a term synonymous with being but with the added qualifier of desirability that indicates how well a thing actualizes its own potential according to its nature. Thus, the goodness of a thing depends on the sort of thing that it is, and it is not a term applied in the same way to everything of which it is predicated. A good shoe, for example, is different than a good dog or a good pizza. While the term "good" is identical in each case and retains the same meaning,

8. Aquinas, *Summa Theologiae*, I.48.3.

9. Aquinas, *De Malo*, I.1. Aquinas does argue that the subject experiencing privation is itself considered evil as an entity, though he does not mean that evil as a nature has been actualized in some way in the subject in question—rather, the subject is "evil" as a thing in privation, not as evil *per se*.

it is applied differently to different things. Something is "good," therefore, when it achieves some end toward which it is ordered or thrives in whatever way its nature defines. When applied to creatures with a moral nature, it also speaks to its moral acts and choices, such as that of a "good citizen" who follows the law, pays their taxes, and contributes to society.

With this in mind, every instance of evil or "badness" is therefore a term applied to things that are otherwise good and limited or lacking in some way, or it is prevented somehow from realizing the fullest extent of its nature. As Brian Davies explains, "As we generally use the word 'bad' a bad *X* is one that somehow fails to function well considered as what it is."[10] Thus, per Davies, badness applies to an absence of being in some respect to an already existing thing. "For how do we defend our claim that something or other is bad? We do so, as we *always* do so, by noting how it is lacking in some respect. We are lamenting an absence of being, the fact that what could and should be there is not there."[11] In this way, evil does not and cannot exist in any way on its own or as a thing in itself. Once more, Aquinas: "No being can be spoken of as evil, formally as being, but only so far as it lacks being. Thus a man is said to be evil, because he lacks some virtue; and an eye is said to be evil, because it lacks the power to see well."[12] As such, it may be bad for a car to have a flat tire or for a citizen to skip out on his taxes, but the car is still a car and the citizen is still a citizen, and both retain a sense of "goodness" in that respect, even though they fail in some way to be everything they could or should be. As Davies argues, "So my argument is that badness exists in so far as things are good to a certain extent but lacking in one or more respects."[13] This definition of the nature of evil as privative is apparent in each of the instances of evil above in some fashion as well. Suffering, for example, represents the failure of some creature (particularly a sentient creature) to live up to its greatest potential in the experience of some external or internal condition or physical malfunction causing it pain. Physical deformities are failures of a creature to embody the sort of physical function that it is meant to possess by its nature. Evil can also describe things like pain, agony, sorrow, despair, cruelty, indifference, laziness, hatred, selfishness, and so on. These are all examples of ways in which a creature may fail to thrive or live up to all it can or should be on account of the nature it

10. Davies, *Reality of God*, 175.

11. Davies, *Reality of God*, 177.

12. Aquinas, *Summa Theologiae*, I.5.3.

13. Davies, *Reality of God*, 180.

possesses. Each are losses of goods or perfections that such a creature might expect to have or be somehow deficient without.

Not all philosophers embrace this understanding of evil—particularly in the context of the problem of evil. H. J. McCloskey, for example, offers at least three main objections to the use of evil as a privation in the analysis of the problem of evil. First, McCloskey argues, "In the first place, the view rests on the technical and morally irrelevant use of the word 'good' as equivalent with 'being.'"[14] Though McCloskey does not elaborate in detail on what he means by this particular objection, he seems to be saying that goodness cannot be identical with being because such a concept does not comport with what is normally meant by the word "good" (in a sense of moral relevance, for example) and excludes entire categories of goodness, such as moral goodness. However, referring to goodness and being as really the same thing in referent fits perfectly with every sense in which the term "goodness" is in fact ordinarily used, including in the moral sense (more on that below). Anything that exists is at least good insofar as it exists, and anything that thrives or functions as it should is good on that basis as well. However well something embodies the very nature it possesses determines how good a thing is or truly can be. An amputee who is without his right arm is still good as an existing human and may also have a good intellect, a good left arm, good respiration, good ambulation, and so on. The whole human does not become "bad" because of a missing limb, though the amputee is certainly lacking something belonging to its nature and is in a state of deficiency in this respect. In short, the amputee still has *being* and may yet thrive in many ways despite the privation of the missing arm, and this fits well with the way the term "good" is ordinarily used when applied in this sense.

Second, McCloskey also argues that there are instances and examples of evil that do not fit well with this description. For example, he argues that pain is just such an exception:

> Secondly, while it is true that if we consider evils such as loss or lack of organs, the talk about privation has some plausibility, this is not so if we consider pain. Pain is not an illusion, nor is it simply the absence of a good, e.g., pleasure. Pain is positive. It has a real nature, and its evilness flows from that nature, not from its being the absence of something else. It is pointless to tell the child whose body is bruised and broken by the landslide, and who is wracked by pain, that he is experiencing simply a

14. McCloskey, "Problem of Evil," 189.

> privation of the proper good of the body. His suffering may be associated with a privation of the proper good of the body, but it is much more and other than this. And its existence needs to be justified.[15]

Here, McCloskey argues that pain has a nature of its own and produces an effect because of that nature—namely suffering. As such, per McCloskey, pain is an evil which has existence and requires an explanation. However, it is not clear what sort of nature pain could be said to possess as a thing that exists if that is what McCloskey here implies. First, pain simply cannot occur in any sense without a subject to experience it—which does not imply some "existence" that it has in and of itself and (contra McCloskey) rather perfectly embodies the definition of evil as privation. Second, pain is not necessarily "evil," even when it occurs and is often actually a "good" resulting from the proper functioning of a creature's body. Feeling pain when touching a hot stove, for example, alerts a human to remove her hand in order to avoid the further suffering and privation of being burned. While undoubtedly unpleasant, it is not necessarily "evil" when it occurs but rather a simple description of a human body functioning exactly as it should in some dangerous or harmful circumstance. In fact, the human biological disorder Congenital Insensitivity to Pain (CIP) that prevents a human from feeling pain altogether is itself an evil privation that leaves the human with a very dangerous and difficult condition. Nevertheless, it is certainly true that pain can occur at times when it seems more than is necessary, or even when its causes may be entirely unknown and irremediable. My wife, for example, is the victim of hip bursitis, which at times causes her significant, ongoing pain with no immediate or obvious means of mitigation. Such instances doubtless result in undue suffering without any obvious or commensurate benefit, and when this occurs, it is in a distinctly privative sense that denotes a lack of thriving or functioning according to the sort of nature that a thing may possess. The argument that pain (like hip bursitis) is a privation that can only exist as an aspect of something good (like my wife, who in fact is *very* good) does not imply that pain is itself good or that it is illusory or cannot itself produce other effects as a privative absence of being.

Third, McCloskey argues that moral evil itself serves as an exception to the concept of evil as a privation of the good.

15. McCloskey, "Problem of Evil," 189.

> Moral evil lends itself even less than physical evil to interpretation as privation of good. And the only truth in the privation account of moral evil seems to be that if evil is present, good is absent. Wherever there is evil, there is necessarily absence of right order. But this does not mean that evil is simply absence of right order. It is the presence of evil order. Of course, it is possible to set up a linguistic system such that good actions are defined as those in which evil order is absent, or one in which evil acts are explained as those in which right order is lacking; but if we simply consider particular evil acts and particular good acts, we see that each sort of act has a real positive nature of its own. For example, the act of the cold-blooded, sadistic murderer who kills not for gain but from hatred has a positively evil nature, and just as positive a nature as the act of the benevolent man who helps all those who seek his help because he knows it to be right so to act.[16]

Here, McCloskey argues that "evil order" is a sort of thing in itself that is more than a mere absence of a good moral order. Per McCloskey, one could define goodness as the absence of "evil order" for example, though this way of thinking seems to draw back once again to the identity of goodness and being. The absence of moral dysfunction in a creature (as per McCloskey's argument) does not denote the absence of anything at all in a creature but rather the *presence* of a fully functional and successful moral nature. As such, when moral dysfunction is absent in moral beings, moral goodness necessarily remains. However, it is difficult to see how the absence of moral goodness suggests a new "evil nature" bent toward immorality as McCloskey here implies. The moral nature of any creature is always directed toward that which is its highest good, and creatures that fail to achieve this do not in fact have a deficient or evil *nature*—rather, they have a good moral nature inflicted with the privation of moral failure (or perhaps a willful ignorance or rejection of what one knows to be morally good). If McCloskey's interpretation were upheld, then there would be no meaningful difference in moral good or moral evil, for the creature would be always acting according to whatever nature it has—whether good or evil. In such a case, a wife who murders her husband out of hatred or rage would be no different than a praying mantis that devours its mate after copulating with it—both are simply acting according to their natural proclivities and impulses (the murderous wife exhibiting an "evil nature," according to McCloskey). In fact,

16. McCloskey, "Problem of Evil," 190.

McCloskey's theory here suggests that a person with an evil moral nature who performs an act of kindness would actually be a moral failure for doing so—in violation of their "evil nature," so to speak. It is not that the moral reprobate is *morally different* than other humans or adheres to different moral principles (as far as the nature they possess)—rather the reprobate fails to live up to the *good moral nature* they necessarily possess as a positive aspect of their own humanity. Also, it does no good to suppose that an "evil nature" is simply a description of evil moral behavior (and not a nature *per se*), because if this were the case, then McCloskey has lost his objection to privation. Moral evil is, therefore, quite simply a privation of moral goodness that occurs exclusively in moral beings. It is not and cannot possibly be an aspect of a wicked creature's "evil nature," as McCloskey here suggests.

EVIL AND ITS CAUSES

Considering evil as a privation of the good does not in itself resolve the problem of evil. As McCloskey observes, "And even if [evil were a privation of being or of right order], the problem of explaining it would remain, for sin and pain do not become justified and do not cease to be a problem merely by being described as a privation rather than as an intrinsic nature."[17] Per McCloskey, the question remains as to what the causes of evil would be and whether God can be said to cause evil directly (as an end in itself), or act with evil intent (toward a lesser good), or serve as an indirect cause of evil (such as causing a good thing to exist that itself causes or suffers from a privation). Evil, even as privation, must be caused in some respect because the possibility of privation (at a minimum) exists in the natural potency of created things, which in turn is definitive of the nature of those things as created by God. Further, privation is inherently accidental to a thing—it is never something that is natural or essential to that which it inhabits. Thus, evil is always something that is caused. It may be caused by things that happen to the subject from the external world (such as natural evil), and it may be caused by the thing itself failing to achieve its own perfections (such as moral evil). In either case, evil is something that happens to an otherwise-good thing, and it is always caused to be.

17. McCloskey, "Problem of Evil," 190.

If evil is always caused, then what exactly are the causes of evil? It is first evident that evil must have a cause, for something that limits or reduces the natural function and being of an existing thing must itself be an entity acting on that thing, else it would be in the nature of a thing to be in privation, which is a contradiction. As Aquinas explains,

> It must be said that every evil in some way has a cause. For evil is the absence of the good, which is natural and due to a thing. But that anything fail from its natural and due disposition can come only from some cause drawing it out of its proper disposition. For a heavy thing is not moved upwards except by some impelling force; nor does an agent fail in its action except from some impediment. But only good can be a cause; because nothing can be a cause except inasmuch as it is a being, and every being, as such, is good.[18]

Here, Aquinas illustrates that only that which is good can serve as a cause of evil, which may seem at first to be a puzzling admission. If evil, by definition, is the privation of the good, how can something good (functioning properly as it intends, for example) cause evil in itself—or something else? As Aquinas argues, evil as privation cannot be the cause of anything at all (since it is not something that exists); therefore, only that which is good can be the cause of evil. "Again, what does not exist is not the cause of anything. So, every cause must be a definite thing. But evil is not a definite being, as has been proved. Therefore, evil cannot be the cause of anything. If, then, evil be caused by anything, this cause must be the good."[19]

Further, in order for something to be corrupted or fail in some respect to be what it is by nature, it must be acted on or prevented by some external agent-cause, which is itself either defective in its own action or teleologically ordered toward some good that accidentally results in evil or suffering for something else. For example, a thriving zebra may find its life cut short by a hungry lion, and the death of the zebra—while itself an "evil" for the zebra—results in a "good" for the lion in the nourishment it receives and provides for its pride. Thus, something good operating exactly as its nature requires may have the natural effect of causing evil in something else. This is always necessarily the case for privative evil. If some creature existed and thrived with no interference at all and yet still failed to be what it is or should be, then such a thing would actually be

18. Aquinas, *Summe Theologiae*, I.49.1.

19. Aquinas, *Summa Contra Gentiles*, III.10.3.

deficient *according to its own nature*, which entails a contradiction. In other words, such a "naturally deficient thing" would be, by nature, deficient of its nature, which presents a self-contradictory paradox. Thus, all evil (as privation) comes from some cause or being acting on the victim that somehow prevents it from thriving as the sort of thing it is. Further, evil can never be caused directly (as an end in itself) but always *accidentally* as the byproduct of some good agent-action that itself is teleologically ordered toward the good.

> Besides, whatever is properly and of itself the cause of something tends toward a proper effect. So, if evil were of itself the cause of anything, it would tend toward an effect proper to it; namely, evil. But this is false, for it has been shown that every agent tends toward the good. Therefore, evil is not the cause of anything through evil itself, but only accidentally.[20]

Thus, as Aquinas here explains, since evil must be caused by some agent, and any agent-action tends toward the good (in a teleological sense), then evil can only be caused accidentally on account of some good.

The obvious question that follows is what those causes might be and whether or not God himself is or could be the cause of some or all of the evil in the world. In fact, affirming God as the direct cause of any sort of evil is an unpalatable idea that has potential theological consequences for theists. Aquinas, for example, argues as follows: "No one in his right mind entertains any doubt as to whether God does anything from an evil intention. For there cannot be anything evil in the highest good."[21] But if evil nevertheless occurs as an aspect of the created world—even the evil of privation—then how is it that the very creator and sustainer of the world either causes, allows, or tolerates the evil that such a world and its creatures produce? Therefore, it is important to proceed to an evaluation of the causes of evil *per se*, whether or not God can be said to be the cause of evil, and whether or not this raises any challenges or problems for the existence of a being such as the God of classical theism. After all, if God serves as an agent-cause of every good thing that exists (as *ipsum esse subsistens* suggests), and all evil comes from an agent-cause, is it not therefore plausible that God himself can cause evil?

There are two senses to consider that must be causally operative as the causes of evil—evil caused by some failure or defect in an agent-cause

20. Aquinas, *Summa Contra Gentiles*, III.10.4.

21. Aquinas, *Expositio Super Iob*, 10.1.

and evil caused by a failure or defect in the privative subject itself (on account of a nature given to the possibility of corruption, for example). Given the understanding of God from a position of natural theology I have proposed, it is clear that God cannot cause evil directly on account of some failure or defect in himself. God is necessarily perfectly good lacking nothing, and thus any evil that exists cannot be caused by some failure or lack in God. Per Aquinas, "As appears from what was said, the evil which consists in the defect of action is always caused by the defect of the agent. But in God there is no defect, but the highest perfection, as was shown above. Hence, the evil which consists in defect of action, or which is caused by defect of the agent, is not reduced to God as to its cause."[22] One may argue that God is in fact said to cause evil directly in some theistic traditions—such as inflicting a plague as an act of judgment, for example—though this would only serve as a counterexample if God did so by mistake or on account of some confusion or deficiency in himself that prevented him from correctly acting on the good he intended. To be clear, this does not mean that God must be morally justified in order to inflict a plague or otherwise affect a created being in some privative manner. Rather, this means that whatever God does and however he acts, he necessarily does so without any flaw in himself, and thus he cannot be an agent-cause of evil due to a failure or defect in his own knowledge, will, or perspective.

Considering the second possible sense of the causes of evil, there is no reason to think that God cannot or should not be able to create a being with a nature given to corruption or privation—particularly one that exists in a created natural world where some things thrive at the expense of others. In this way, the existence of beings that experience privation can (and must) be caused to be by God, and thus God is the cause of evil in this sense. Once again, Aquinas:

> But the evil which consists in the corruption of some things is reduced to God as the cause. And this appears as regards both natural things and voluntary things. For it was said that some agent inasmuch as it produces by its power a form to which follows corruption and defect, causes by its power that corruption and defect. But it is manifest that the form which God chiefly intends in things created is the good of the order of the universe. Now, the order of the universe requires, as was said above, that there should be some things that can, and do sometimes, fail.

22. Aquinas, *Summa Theologiae*, I.49.2.

> And thus God, by causing in things the good of the order of the universe, consequently and as it were by accident, causes the corruptions of things.[23]

Here, Aquinas illustrates that God, as creator of the universe, causes the existence of creatures according to their created natures, as well as the good of the creation order itself that governs the operations of the world and the creatures it inhabits. By extension, it is apparent that many created things suffer in privation on account of the natural operation of the world that functions properly as decreed by God. This does not mean that God has caused the evils of the universe directly as an end in themselves but rather that God has caused a universe to exist in a natural state that functions by the operation of existing things causing privation in varied senses among other existing things. Thus, in the machinations of the natural world, God can be said to be the author of the good of that world (including a nature that allows for the possibility of corruption), while created agent-causes in turn directly cause the evil that results.

One may naturally inquire as to how a world where good existing things thrive on account of evil acts (such as a lion receiving nourishment by killing a zebra) could be one created by a perfectly good God—after all, God, in this sense, is responsible for at least some evil in this respect. This introduces what Brian Davies calls "evil suffered" as a way to distinguish this aspect of evil that has God as its cause (as opposed to evil resulting in a flaw in the agent-cause itself, such as moral evil). As Davies argues, this presents no contradiction:

> Aquinas finds no absurdity in the suggestion that God might have made a world in which nothing at all is bad. But he does hold that, on the supposition that God has made a world of interacting thing with certain definite natures, then certain goods willed by him shall necessarily derive from, or be bound up with, certain evils. Here we come to his notion of evil suffered.[24]

23. Aquinas, *Summa Theologiae*, I.49.2.

24. Davies, *Thomas Aquinas on God and Evil*, 68. Davies distinguishes two categories of evil by which to evaluate its causes—*evil suffered* and *evil done*. Evil done, per Davies, is the evil of moral failure in an agent-cause that fails to act toward the highest good because of a fault in its own being. This sort of evil, per Davies, cannot be attributed to God in the same way that God cannot have or possess a lack or flaw in this sense and is not compelled to act toward any sort of moral obligation. Evil suffered, however, is different for Davies, as it is the sort of evil experienced by the natural operation of the world as described above. See Davies, *Reality of God*, 173–92.

As Davies here explains, there is no reason to think that God should have or would be required to make a world in any particular way whatsoever, simply on account of his perfect goodness or divine nature. So long as what God creates is good, at least in the sense that is has being and operates correctly according to the natural operations God has put in place (and it is difficult to imagine what sort of non-being it would be possible to create in any literal sense), God can create any world whatsoever—even one where the evils of natural privation can and do occur. The important point for Davies here is that evil suffered is not a thing that exists and is not caused to be (or have *esse*) in some sense by God. "In a similar way, evil suffered has no independent existence. It 'is there' only in the sense that something is missing. But what is *not there* cannot be thought of as made to be by the source of the being of things. It cannot be thought to be made to be by God."[25] As such, God's creative activity in relation to evil suffered is only as the first efficient cause of that which is good itself—the being subjected to the evil in question. "My claim is that when it comes to evil suffered all we have is the creative activity of God bringing about what is good—that God brings about everything that is good and does not directly bring about anything we might think of as evil suffered."[26] In this way, God is the cause of evil only *indirectly*, because God causes the universe as well as its agent-causes to exist, and these things in turn produce evil on account of the natural order or the failure in the agent-cause to act toward the highest good. This results in both natural and moral evil (or "evil suffered" and "evil done," to use Davies's terminology).

One may argue, of course, that such a claim is only "moving the goalposts," so to speak, and really contributes little to the argument upon consideration of the problem of evil. If God does not create or actualize evil *per se*, does he not at least create or actualize a deficient being (such as the agent-cause in the case of moral evil)? Is God not responsible for the existence of a natural order in a universe that makes evil and its consequences not only possible but necessary for its operation (such as that of natural evil)? Even more broadly, does God not actualize the circumstances that enable beings to become deficient and suffer evil in the first place, such as the corruption and deficiency that exist upon creation in the potency of moral creatures and the natural world? In this sense, however, one must proceed with an additional premise that God cannot or

25. Davies, *Reality of God*, 178.

26. Davies, *Reality of God*, 178.

should not create such a world or a creature with the capacity to produce or experience evil. Without this additional step, one cannot conclude on the basis of what has here been said about the causes of evil that the existence of evil in the universe provides *prima facie* evidence against the existence of God. Once again, Davies: "To say that God is guilty by neglect is to say that there is something he ought to have done but has not—it is to hold him morally accountable. But it is a mistake to think of God as morally accountable."[27] If the argument that God is under no moral obligation to create a world with no evil (or as little as possible) without some justification for doing so is sound, as I believe that it is, then there is no reason whatsoever that God could not or should not create just such a world as that which presently exists—where flawed moral agents act immorally and where the operation of the natural order at times results in privative effects on the varied constituents of that universe. In the end, the important aspect to consider is that God cannot and does not cause evil as an end in itself, and no evidence of evil in the universe of which I am aware indicates that he does so.[28] Per Davies,

> My argument is that for God to ensure results is simply for God to create (to make to be what can be singled out as a genuine substance or positive property). And, I am saying, privations are not creatable things. So God does not make them to be even if he makes a world in which they can be noted as being the privations they are. If he is the 'author' of privations, he is so only as making to be that which is not a privation, and not as willing (creating) evil as an end in itself.[29]

Here, Davies illustrates the impossibility that God can be said to be the cause of evil. However, one may seize on Davies's claim that God in fact does not will evil "as an end in itself" and seek to present evidence or argument that God does exactly this. If one could present such evidence of

27. Davies, *Reality of God*, 190.

28. In order to sustain the argument that God acts toward evil as an end in itself, one would have to present evidence of some instance evil that either has its own act of being, was effected by a divine lack in some respect, or was caused as an end in itself in juxtaposition with the natural order of the universe (such as unnatural suffering apart from any agent-cause or the regular operation of the natural order). Such an example would serve as a strong evidential case for God's non-existence. However, I do not believe that any such evidence of evil has ever been discovered or even suggested in this context, and I have encountered no such example myself in the philosophical literature. More on this in the following section.

29. Davies, *Reality of God*, 190.

God acting in such a manner, one would have a good *prima facie* reason for thinking that God does not exist. However, as I intend to show, this has never been achieved and is no simple task.

EVIL AS AN END IN ITSELF

Considering the concept of evil here presented as a privation of the good and the classical concept of God as *ipsum esse subsistens*, there remains a sense of evil that is *by definition* impossible for God to cause—that is, evil as an "end in itself" so to speak. God being perfectly good and causing the existence of only what is good cannot be said to cause evil for its own sake. Such would present a contradiction to the divine essence as understood above. If one could identify some instance where God has caused evil for its own sake—or some evidence of evil that occurs in the world that is not associated with the privation of the good (having some existence or act of being on its own, so to speak, which could only come from God as the cause of all that exists)—then it seems that one would appear to have a *prima facie* reason to reject the existence of an omniscient, omnipotent, perfectly good God on that basis. Hence, the evidential problem of evil could be restated in these terms and, in my view, would remain an unresolved problem for theists. However, the prospect of identifying some instance of evil of this sort is remarkably difficult and highly implausible given what is known of the present universe. To my knowledge, such an example has never been discovered or observed.

Aquinas offers some insight into why God cannot be said to cause evil as an end in itself, and though God can cause some goods that may naturally or by extension cause some evil to occur, his ends are always good.

> Now the evil that accompanies one good, is the privation of another good. Never therefore would evil be sought after, not even accidentally, unless the good that accompanies the evil were more desired than the good of which the evil is the privation. Now God wills no good more than He wills His own goodness; yet He wills one good more than another. Hence He in no way wills the evil of sin, which is the privation of right order towards the divine good. The evil of natural defect, or of punishment, He does will, by willing the good to which such evils are attached. Thus in willing justice He wills punishment; and in willing the preservation of the natural order, He wills some things to be naturally corrupted.[30]

30. Aquinas, *Summa Theologiae*, I.19.9.

Here, Aquinas illustrates the problem of God (or any intellectual creature with the power of will, for that matter) being said to cause evil as an end. As Aquinas explains, the will is by nature (and by definition) always directed toward the good, and thus the will never causes evil directly or even accidentally apart from some good that is willed that may itself result in evil. A glutton, for example, certainly wills the evil of gluttony when he eats in excess of his physical needs, though the evil of gluttony in itself is not the object or desire of his will—rather, it is the good of physical delight and pleasure in the act of eating that is willed directly, and gluttony is what results in pursuit of that good (however defective or depraved such a means may be toward achieving the ends sought by the glutton). Thus, it is not the evil act itself that is willed as an end in itself, though evil may yet be the result. God, however, always wills the highest good (literally the good of his own being and essence), and as such, even the good he wills may result in the privation of other goods. In this way only can God be said to be the cause of evil. God may will the good of justice, for example, and thus sinners may experience the evil of suffering as recipients of divine judgment. God wills the good of the natural order, and thus some things experience corruption and privation according to their natures for the good of other created things (as the death of a zebra nourishes a lion or the burning of a fawn nourishes a fire). Such instances of evil are not and cannot be in contradiction with God's nature or his perfect goodness. However, if one could identify such a case where God has in fact caused evil for its own sake or any evidence of evil that occurs in the world that is not the sort of evil associated with the privation of the good or the regular operation of the natural world, then it seems that one would have a *prima facie* reason to reject the existence of God on that basis.

What sort of evidence of evil could one properly identify as evil caused by God as an end in itself (whether evil suffered or evil done)? Here I will propose a few possible means that an argument from evil may pursue toward this end with at least some prospect of success if such was achieved. The task at hand, in order to sustain the problem of evil in the face of the natural theology I have here proposed, would be to posit some sense of what I will call *inexplicable evil* such that this instance of evil is unexplainable as the natural result of a good natural order or the result of a deficient moral agent-cause acting toward some otherwise-good intent. I will propose here three possible examples of inexplicable evil that the non-theist may seek to identify in pursuit of their argument.

First, one could seek to discover or identify some instance of inexplicable evil or suffering in the world that arises without cause or any referent or dependence on what is otherwise good—such as more suffering than is called for (something unnaturally excessive beyond the regular operations of the world or the nature of the suffering creature). Such an instance of evil would have to be entirely beyond the web of causes and dependencies that exist in the natural order, and it would have to be set apart from the activities of any agent-cause within that created order acting toward the good in some way (however corrupt or confused such acts may be).[31] An innocent fawn burning in a distant forest fire (to use Rowe's example) is not an example of undue or excessive suffering so long as the suffering it endures is consistent with the operation of the natural world and the nature of the fire and the fawn itself (with a natural capacity for pain) in which the fawn and the fire both exist. Per Davies, "But the actual suffering of an actual fawn is only more suffering than there need be (and is therefore, as Rowe likes to say, 'pointless') if it lacks natural causes, if it is scientifically inexplicable. Assuming that it is scientifically explicable, however, then it arises because something other than the fawn is flourishing at some level."[32] Fawns burn and suffer in forest fires, to use Rowe's example, because fawns by nature are flammable and their pain receptors are activated in the presence of fire or extreme heat. This is good evidence that the natural world is functioning exactly as its nature requires, and thus it is not evidence against the existence of God. One may argue, "But isn't God the cause of this natural world in which fawns are able to burn and pain receptors unleash agony when they do?" The answer, of course, is that God is in fact the cause of the existence of the natural world (including the natures of fawns and fires), but the existence and natural operation of a world that functions according to its design is hardly good evidence against the existence of a designer. A better example of excessive or undue suffering would be something like an entirely healthy, thriving fawn suddenly and inexplicably wracked with intense pain in such a way that all reasonable natural explanations have been excluded, and no external agent-cause was acting on the fawn

31. Such an example would also have to be *inexplicable* as the result of any possible agent-cause or natural operation—however far removed or difficult to observe or verify (such as the acts of spiritual beings like angels, for example). Though excluding such agent-causes as possibilities in the face of some inexplicable evil as described here would be appropriate, in my view, in absence of any additional evidence one might have that such beings actually exist and act by their natural powers toward those ends.

32. Davies, *Reality of God*, 182.

to cause this pain (toward some perceived good end, for example). An inexplicable, unnatural bout of suffering would be a better argument in support of the evidential problem of evil than the case of a fawn naturally burning to death in a forest fire. Another example may be a creature with an inconsistent or undefined nature, such as the existence of a human with the nature of a dog.[33] In such a bizarre scenario, it is difficult to imagine how such a creature could be found or identified, but this, it seems, would serve as another sufficient example of an instance of evil (a nature deprived of its nature) from the failure of the natural order to operate as directed without any natural cause or agent interference.

> According to Aquinas, however, in the case of evil suffered, there can never be more evil than there need be. He thinks that any evil suffered that is *more than there need be* would be *lacking a natural cause*. It would be scientifically inexplicable. He therefore suggests that the evil suffered in the world is neither *more* or *less* than what we can expect in a material world in which scientific explanations can be given for what happens.[34]

Here, Davies illustrates the problem for the non-theist who attempts to find evidential examples of evil sufficient to countermand the existence of God. One must demonstrate that suffering is either more than is called for in the world in which it occurs or is entirely without natural explanations. To my knowledge, no such evidence has ever been presented or discovered.

Second, one could posit the existence of inexplicable evil as an entity in and of itself—with its own act of being that is not itself privative in any sense on what is otherwise good. An example of this may be a

33. It is important to note here that sometimes creatures do erupt in what may seem like inexplicable pain, such as an infant with colic who may scream through the night in inconsolable suffering. Likewise, there may be some humans who truly think they are dogs and may truly believe that they have a canine nature. However, such instances cannot be counterexamples to the nature and existence of God, so long as they are explicable as part of the natural order (such as an unknown physical or medical explanation of the colicky infant) or a defect in the mental operations of the agent (such as the human who thinks he is a dog). One would have to have a reason to believe that the infant's suffering had literally no natural cause—as if its own suffering were simply a part of its nature and not a privation, and one would also have to conclude that the dog-human did not merely "think" he was a canine (as per some intellectual defect or privation of the mind) but rather that the human truly *was* a canine with a human body. It is difficult to see how this could be done given what is known of the function of the natural world, though either example would seem to fulfill the demands of the evidential problem of evil and require an explanation.

34. Davies, *On Evil*, 22; emphasis in original.

physical pocket of "non-existence" in the existing world that inhabits some aspect of the universe. Something like empty space or a black hole would not be enough, however, for these are things that exists on account of the natural laws of physics functioning properly in the regular operation of the cosmos. Further, the absence of existence is not the same thing as "substantial non-existence," which would seem to indicate something that could not be caused by God. Such a discovery would not only offer *prima facie* evidence of the non-existence of God, but it would shake the very foundations of reality itself and what it means for something to exist or not. Admittedly, I have no idea what this sort of thing might be (or *not be*?) or how someone would go about demonstrating this through observation or philosophical argument, but nevertheless it seems this would be a possible significant example of an existing contradiction that God could not possibly have actualized. If a non-theist could identify such an example, they would have a good argument against the existence of God.

Third, one may posit the existence of some nature or form in a thing that is itself naturally (or by design) directed toward evil as an end in itself. This would be some existing thing, such as an agent or being, that always necessarily acts toward evil as an end in itself and is naturally incapable from knowing or acting toward the good it desires or perceives. Once again, it is difficult to imagine what such a being would even be or how it could be said to act at all. One may propose something like the existence of fallen angels or demons (such as from biblical Christianity), but this would not serve as such an example if such beings were created as essentially good and became corrupted by their own acts of will as intended toward the good of their own pride, for example (such as how Satan and his fellow demons are typically described in classical Christianity). Likewise, even a horribly wicked human who, through some measure of extreme madness or depravity, always does the most evil and vile thing he can think of in every situation (which unfortunately is not entirely beyond the scope of imagination) would not suffice as a sufficient example by itself because the nature of humans are always driven to the good, and even the most morally corrupt individual still acts toward some idea of the good that they intend—even if wildly confused about what the true highest good actually is. Such a being that would serve as a sufficient example for evidence of such a naturally evil agent-cause would have to be one that has the nature of evil itself as its end and always, by nature, acts toward that evil end with no good in mind whatsoever. To my knowledge, no such being (angel, human, or animal) has ever been discovered in the world.

One may respond to these suggestions by claiming that I have set the bar too high and that these sorts of things simply do not and cannot exist in a world acting under a regular natural order and populated with moral beings. To this I can only say that the absence of these sorts of things is exactly what one would expect in a theistic universe, which has been my point all along. If God in fact created the world, as theists believe, then none of these things will in fact exist. The inability to discover such things in the world does not mean that I have set the bar too high—it simply means that there is no evidential reason to deny God's existence in the observable, natural world. That is precisely what makes these sufficient counterexamples or counterevidence to theism. The point I am making is that we should not be surprised to find that nothing of these sorts actually transpire if in fact the universe we inhabit is a theistic one. Given these clarifications, it is difficult to see how a non-theist could possibly proceed with an evidential argument from evil on the basis of God's perfect goodness from any natural example of evil occurring in privation to that which is otherwise good in the created universe. However, if any such example were proffered that met these conditions as I have here laid out, my own position on theism would be in need of revision.

EVIL AND THE NATURE OF GOD

After examining in detail the nature of God and evil as described above, it is now possible to consider more carefully the compatibility of both—specifically whether the existence of evil in principle (particularly gratuitous evil) constitutes *prima facie* evidence against the existence of God. It is important to note that the concept of evil as privative is not itself sufficient to resolve the problem of evil. In fact, some think that evil as privation is entirely beside the point altogether. H. J. McCloskey, for example, emphasizes what he sees at the shortfalls of such an approach for the theist.

> The point I was concerned to make is this. If all evil is to be explained as privation of some sort, and the world is in all other respects good, then, I suggest, the theist who holds that God to be perfectly good does not have to create the best of all possible worlds, does not need to explain the existence of evil further. If the privation theory were true, there would, for such a theist, be

> no evil of the kinds which give rise to the problem of evil to explain and justify. I suggest that the pressure felt by those theists who seek to explain the nature of evil in terms of privations to offer solutions to the problem of evil, comes from a vague awareness that the privation account is not adequate; that at best, it can only be part of the story, for the evilness of the occurrence of the privations needs to be explained—its nature (its evilness is not to be explained in terms of some sort of privation), and the reason a benevolent, omnipotent being allows it to exist.[35]

Here, McCloskey argues that the general sense of the theist in consideration of the privation theory of evil seems to be instinctually insufficient to resolve the problem and only "moves the goalposts," so to speak—leaving open the question of why a world rife with privations or imperfections in created things should be one that is caused by a benevolent, omnipotent God. For McCloskey, an important question remains regarding the "evilness" that results from a privative world and why God should allow such a world to persist as it does (or even cause it to be in the first place). Even if evil is not a thing in itself that God creates and sustains as an entity with existence in the created world, then why does God create a world filled with beings that thrive on the corruption of other beings, beings with the potential for suffering and cruelty, and beings that are in every practical sense imperfect instances of their own natures? Here I will seek to evaluate the nature of God in light of the existence of evil *per se* and what (if any) impact or contradiction follows between the existence of each given the understanding of God from natural theology that I have defended.

The first question to consider in measuring the nature of God against the concept of evil is whether the existence of a perfectly good God makes the existence of any evil whatsoever impossible or unlikely. Given the understanding of evil as privation in the sense described above, one may hastily conclude that God cannot create evil, simply because evil is no thing at all. Per Davies, "God, therefore, is not causally responsible for the existence of evil or badness, for, *in the sense I have tried to explain*, evil or badness does not exist."[36] However, as we have seen, even evil considered as privation exists in some fashion in the created world—even if only as an aspect or accidental property of created things themselves. Per Aquinas: "Now it is in this that evil consists, namely, in the fact that a thing fails in goodness. Hence it is clear that evil is found in things, as

35. McCloskey, "Evil and the Problem of Evil," 14.

36. Davies, *Reality of God*, 180.

corruption also is found; for corruption is itself an evil."[37] Thus, there is evil in the things God has created, and by extension, God is its cause (whether directly or indirectly) because he has made these things to be. Once again, Aquinas:

> But the evil which consists in the corruption of some things is reduced to God as the cause. And this appears as regards both natural things and voluntary things. . . . Now, the order of the universe requires, as was said above, that there should be some things that can, and do sometimes, fail. And thus God, by causing in things the good of the order of the universe, consequently and as it were by accident, causes the corruptions of things.[38]

Thus, for Aquinas, God can be said to cause the evil of corruption, which happens naturally on account of the good of the order of the universe God has created. The universe that exists is one in which some things are destroyed or consumed for the good of other things by natural processes, and the evil that results from such a design is the natural consequent of the universe God has created. Furthermore, it seems that God could have created a world vastly different than the present one, such that the natural order of such a world would not result in the occasional corruption or destruction of its inhabitants. The key question follows as to whether there is anything in the nature of God that implies or guarantees that he should create such a world with as little evil and corruption as possible.

In answer to this question, Herbert McCabe offers a helpful summation of what the nature of God entails in light of what one may expect him to be and do, which is consistent with the argument in this work as to God's responsibilities toward creation from a perspective of natural theology. Per McCabe, there is nothing God should be expected to do in regards to the sort of world he might create.

> For creatures such as us, what we do not will and what we do not do can be as morally significant as what we do will and do. To fail to do what one ought to do is as wicked as to do what one ought not to do. But this is precisely because we exist in a moral context in which we ought to do this rather than that. We are born with a nature that determines what it shall be good for us to do and what evil. But, as I have tried to show throughout this essay, there is no such context for God. God is not any kind of thing. There is nothing that it is natural for God to do, and

37. Aquinas, *Summa Theologiae*, I.48.2.

38. Aquinas, *Summa Theologiae*, I.49.2.

> nothing unnatural. He cannot have duties or a way of life. He has no function and no place in any order. All creatures are *his* and hence are ordered towards him. And he is not *his*. Before he does anything there is no reason for doing it rather than not doing it. There is not even a 'before.' He does not have good reasons for what he does. Rather, he *is* the reason for what he does.[39]

Here, McCabe argues that God is under no obligation or natural inclination to behave in some specific manner, and he is not ordered toward some end apart from himself as creatures are. So long as the good of the world is directed toward the highest and best good of God himself as its proper end and evil does not exist in the world objectively as an end in itself (either in created beings or in God himself), then any logically possible world at all is one God can create, including a world inhabited by beings that experience corruption, suffering, and evil. There is nothing in the existence of such a world that implies the non-existence of God, and God is free to create just such a world if he so chooses. Whatever inherent contradiction the non-theist may intend to demonstrate by positing evil *per se* against God's nature and being is not immediately obvious or apparent.

A subsequent consideration is precisely what sort of world one might imagine that is not the one that presently exists—and what conclusions (if any) one can hope to draw from such theoretical worlds. Per Aquinas, according to Davies, one must always start from the world that presently exists and reason from there. Just such a world is one of a type of suppositional necessity that cannot be ignored or set aside in evaluating God and evil.

> If it is logically possible for something to be, then, thinks Aquinas, God can make it to be. But, Aquinas also thinks, we have no means of determining what logically possible things God will make to be. For Aquinas, we must start by noting what God has, in fact, made to be. Reflections on the topic of God and evil must, so he thinks, start from that, and not from assumptions we might have dreamed up (on what basis?) concerning what God is or is not likely to create.[40]

As Davies here explains, God can create any world at all so long as it is logically possible for him to do so (such that it contains no contradictions). Thus, any effort to reason to an evaluation of why God created the

39. McCabe, *God and Evil*, 127; emphasis in original.

40. Davies, *Reality of God*, 24.

present world as he did must begin with the world one presently inhabits. Unless the present world is in fact rife with logical contradictions and impossibilities (which would in fact be good evidence against an omnipotent, omniscient, perfectly good creator), then it can be one created by God. In order to sustain the argument that God could not have created the present world on account of the evil that obtains among its creatures, one would have to demonstrate how the existence of evil presents a logical or probable impossibility such that it could not or should not occur in any possible world *at all* (since it is only a logically impossible world that God is unable to create). Of course, if one were to identify such an evil in the present world, then its very identification would preclude the argument because in order to identify something in the present world, it would have to exist in at least some way. As such, I am not sure how such an approach could have any possibility of success.

One may follow such a response by arguing that the present world does not include any logically contradictory or impossible quantity of evil, yet there is nonetheless *too much* evil in it. But what exactly constitutes "too much" in this context? It is here that the concept of gratuitous evil, as often employed by the evidential argument from evil, takes center stage. Gratuitous evil is some evil that has no related good associated with it that justifies its existence in an overall-good universe, and it can be argued to be "too much" evil in either a qualitative or quantitative sense. One may argue, for example, that there is too much evil *qualitatively* such that some instances of evil are so incredibly horrific or severe that no good could possibly justify their existence in the actual world—such as a natural disaster or terrorist attack that results in the deaths of thousands (or millions) of people. One may also argue that there is too much evil *quantitatively*, such as the sheer number of children in the world (and throughout history) who have experienced horrific suffering from conditions such as hunger, disease, cruelty, or abuse. While the possibility of gratuitous evil in a world created by God will be addressed more extensively in the following chapter, here it is only the question as to what precisely constitutes "too much evil' and whether such a concept *by definition* excludes the possibility of an omnipotent, omniscient, perfectly good creator.

First, the problem of excessive evil reduces logically to an argument about the existence of any evil at all. As Bruce Little explains, "If a horrific evil is horrific because of how it compares to another evil, then logically this will mean that all evil should be prevented."[41] As Little argues, comparing one to another and ruling out only the most egregious examples would reduce to the absurdity of denying the very possibility of all evil altogether, which I have already argued is unnecessary in defense of theism. Thus, as long as it is possible for any evil at all to exist, then it is possible for God to exist, regardless of how prevalent or prolific the evils in the universe may be. Further, the limit of the evil that comes about in the world can be, should be, and is properly defined by the natural operation of the world it inhabits (and any moral creatures such a world may contain). Thus, the most important thing to consider in the concept of too much evil is the nature of the world we find ourselves in and whether the evils we discover follow naturally from its regular operation. In this vein, Davies (interpreting Aquinas) offers an important clarification as to what would constitute too much evil in such a world:

> According to Aquinas, however, in the case of evil suffered, there can never be more evil than there need be. He thinks that any evil suffered that is more than there need be would be lacking a natural cause. It would be scientifically inexplicable. He therefore suggests that the evil suffered in the world is neither more or less than what we can expect in a material world in which scientific explanations can be given for what happens."[42]

Here, Davies explains that the only evil that could pose a problem for the existence of God would be an evil that happens outside the bounds of the natural operation of the world it inhabits. If every instance of evil identified in the world is simply a natural byproduct of creation, then evil is sufficiently explained and able to exist in a world created by God—regardless of how severe it is or how much of it there might be. As such, there is no *prima facie* contradiction between the existence of God and the existence of evil. Whether or not God could have created a world in some other fashion to avoid these evils is entirely beside the point. If God can create a world containing evil, and this is logically possible and consistent with his own nature and act of being, then there is nothing preventing God from doing so—even if some other possible world has less evil (or even none at all). What is at issue here is that the present world does not entail a contradiction by including evils that follow naturally from its regular operation or by the actions of agent-causes that may

41. Little, *Creation-Order Theodicy*, 164.

42. Davies, *On Evil*, 22.

cause evil as the result of some moral privation. However, even if it is *possible* for God to create a world containing evil (even perhaps genuinely gratuitous evil, as I have argued), and this is not inconsistent with his divine nature and act of being, there remains the question of whether it is *probable* that God would create such a world, given the range of options available to him that may have included much less evil or even perhaps no evil at all. Why might God want to create such a world as this in the first place, and what good reasons might he have for making the world as it is? This brings us to the crux of the evidential problem of evil, which I will address in the following chapter.

7

God and Gratuitous Evil

THUS FAR I HAVE argued that the existence of God does not preclude the possibility of evil, but this alone does not explain why there should be any evil at all. Even if God's existence is not contradicted by evil, and even if God is under no moral obligation (on account of his perfect goodness) to prevent or mitigate evil whenever it is possible for him to do so, it follows to consider even still why evil should exist. If God could have created the world without evil, why would he not do so—even if he did not *have* to? Is there any good reason why there is the severity and abundance of evil to the degree it exists in the present world? It is not enough, one may argue, that evil presents no contradiction to God's existence and that God is under no moral obligations concerning evil; surely God must also have at least *some good reason* for allowing evil as a possibility (or likelihood) in a world created by him. Thus, we return once more to Epicurus's ancient query: "Whence cometh evil?"

Granting what I have argued thus far, one may argue that it remains possible that God could have made things differently than he has, and if a few relatively simple changes or differences would have made the world a better place or reduced the suffering and cruelty in the world even by a little, would God not have done so if he could? It is here that evidential arguments from evil thrive, and the question arises as to whether God could have done better than he did in creating the world in some different way. Humans live in a world where evil runs rampant, and at least some evil that does occur (even as a privation of the good) seems to have no explanation or reason to justify its existence in a world created by God. God, it seems, could have created a perfect world with no privations at all, or perhaps even no *potential* for privation, and yet he chose not to do so and has made instead a world where suffering, loss, pain, and death occur *en masse*. Barring any apparent reason why God would do this, many of the evils humans know and experience on a daily basis seem to be truly gratuitous—without any associated greater good that explains why a good God would allow those evils to occur. Does gratuitous evil, therefore, serve as *prima facie* evidence against the existence of God as the evidential argument demands—even if God's perfect goodness is understood in a non-moral sense?

Further, it is often argued that the nature of God requires him (on account of his divine perfection) to always do the best he could do, and as creator of the universe, it is suggested that God must necessarily create the very best and highest goods and the least and fewest evils possible in any world he may choose to create. If so, then it seems upon reflection that God could have done better by reducing the suffering in the world by at least a small margin at minimum without greatly impacting the balance of his creation. Such an idea invites a return to the problem of evil in the demand for an explanation from the theist as to why there should be any evil at all that God could have prevented—even if he did not *have* to do so on account of his infinite, perfect goodness. After all, just because someone does not *have* to do something, it may yet be true that perhaps they *should* do it. For example, a human does not *have* to give time or money to charity in order to feed the hungry or care for the sick, but humans of the highest moral good with the means to do so certainly *should* when able. What more can be said of God, who is necessarily a being of the highest possible good and has the most possible means at his disposal? Such an argument could be framed in a non-moral sense to evade the arguments offered above—speaking not to God's moral obligation to mitigate evil in his creation but rather God's own *love* and *compassion* toward creatures who are victims of intense and horrific suffering. Most theistic traditions, after all, describe God as just a sort of "omnibenevolent" being who wants the best for what he has made. If this is true, then an argument from evil may yet persist.

In this chapter, I will revisit what it means for God to be committed to creating only the "best of all possible worlds" and whether such a concept (whatever it entails) is a legitimate expectation of God and follows from the approach to natural theology I have thus far defended. I will then briefly examine a slate of theodicies and defenses that are often posited in response to the question of gratuitous evil and consider what sort of merit these arguments hold in an analysis of the problem of evil. I will conclude that God is under no obligation to create the best of all possible worlds, God needs no good reason to prevent or mitigate gratuitous evil in the world, and there yet remains no contradiction between the natures of God and evil sufficient to require a denial of the existence of either.

THE BEST OF ALL POSSIBLE WORLDS

A central point of focus in many discussions on the problem of evil tends to circulate around the concept that God is constrained by his nature and infinite wisdom to always and only create the *best of all possible worlds*, and since the present world is the one that exists as created by God, then it must necessarily be the best possible world. One influential early advocate of this idea is Gottfried Wilhelm Leibniz, who argues in his seminal work *Essais de Théodicée*[1] that God's nature being infinitely good simply requires his absolute best. "It is true that God is infinitely powerful; but his power is indeterminate, goodness and wisdom combined determine him to produce the best."[2] Further, Leibniz argues that if God has done other than the very best, then God himself would be guilty of a greater evil than the sum of all the evils of the universe, and his goodness and wisdom would be rightly called into question. "If God chose what would not be the best absolutely and in all, that would be a greater evil than all the individual evils which he could prevent by this means. This wrong choice would destroy his wisdom and his goodness."[3] Likewise, Alvin Plantinga (characterizing Leibniz) further explains that the present world by necessity must be the best of all possible worlds:

> Before God created anything at all, he was confronted with an enormous range of choices; he could have created or actualized any of the myriads of different possible worlds. Being perfectly good, he must have chosen to create the best world he could; being omnipotent he was able to create just any possible world he pleased. He must, therefore, have chosen the best of all possible

1. The original title of Leibniz's work is *Essais de Théodicée sur la bonté de Dieu, la liberté de l'homme et l'origine du mal* (Essays of Theodicy on the Goodness of God, the Freedom of Man and the Origin of Evil).

2. Leibniz, 72.

3. Leibniz, 72.

> worlds; and hence *this* world, the one he did create, must be (despite appearances) the best possible.[4]

Here, Plantinga illustrates the logical zenith of Leibniz's argument that the theist must be absolutely committed to the precept that no possible world could be better and contain fewer evils or more goods than the actual world. If this is in fact the case, then it is up to the theist to justify the present world as the best possible one and make arguments as to why some other imagined world with fewer or less severe evils than the present one would be a world that was not within the power of God to create.[5]

Other theists often agree that God is constrained by his nature to always do the best that it is possible for him to do. Geisler and Corduan, for example, argue that any resolution to the problem of evil requires the theist to show that "there could be no better world or non-world."[6] They go on to argue that anything else would simply preclude the existence of God.

> The theistic God cannot be expected to do better than what is possible, for this is impossible and he cannot do what is actually impossible. On the other hand, it seems eminently fair to show God did the best that it is possible for him to do. Anything less than the most nearly perfect possible would be incompatible with an all-perfect Being.[7]

For Geisler and Corduan, the burden of proof rests on the theist in any response to the problem of evil to conclude that the present world is the best world God could possibly have made. As they explain, anything less would be an act of evil for God. "God must do his best or else it is an evil for him. . . . Hence, the theist must show that what God produces in this world of free but evil beings is the best possible world that could

4. Plantinga, *Nature of Necessity*, 168.

5. It is precisely this position that leads many theists to defend against the problem of evil by proposing various theodicies as a means of resolving the question as to how every instance of evil that arises in the world is necessary in some fashion and results in some greater good or prevents some greater evil. For if any gratuitous evil existed without some justifying good associated with it, then one could reasonably conclude that a better possible world exists, and God's omnipotence, omniscience, or perfect goodness would be rightly called into question. It is on the basis of this very argument, for example, that Plantinga himself builds his "free will defense" as an attempt to uphold the possibility that the present world is the very best that God could possibly have achieved.

6. Geisler and Corduan, *Philosophy of Religion*, 310.

7. Geisler and Corduan, *Philosophy of Religion*, 310

be produced."[8] Likewise, Bruce Little makes an argument that seems to echo back to arguments from evil that question God's classical attributes:

> If this world is not the best of all possible worlds, then one of the following must be true: (1) God chose not to do His best, which seems to question His goodness; (2) God did not know which world would be best, which questions His omniscience; (3) God knew which world would be the best and wanted to actualize it but lacked the power to do so. This, of course, would question His power. All three possibilities seem unacceptable, leaving the only one possibility—this is the best of all possible worlds.[9]

Here, Little illustrates what he takes to be a necessary conclusion drawn from foundational theistic concepts implying that God must have and has done his very best and the world we inhabit is just that—the best of all possible worlds. However, is this a reasonable conclusion given the proper understanding of God as *ipsum esse subsistens*? Is God required to only and always create the "best possible world," as others have argued?

Given what is known of God by natural theology, I hold that any concept in which God is constrained to create only a "best possible world" necessarily confuses *God's* best with *the* best, in a matter of speaking. Returning to Aquinas for a moment, the question he considers is whether God could have made anything better than he has, which Aquinas affirms in at least one sense:

> The goodness of anything is twofold; one, which is of the essence of it—thus, for instance, to be rational pertains to the essence of man. As regards this good, God cannot make a thing better than it is itself; although He can make another thing better than it; even as He cannot make the number four greater than it is; because if it were greater it would no longer be four, but another number. For the addition of a substantial difference in definitions is after the manner of the addition of unity of numbers. Another kind of goodness is that which is over and above the essence; thus, the good of a man is to be virtuous or wise. As regards this kind of goodness, God can make better the things He has made. Absolutely speaking, however, God can make something else better than each thing made by Him.[10]

8. Geisler and Corduan, *Philosophy of Religion*, 312.
9. Little, *Creation-Order Theodicy*, 153.
10. Aquinas, *Summa Theologiae*, I.25.6.

Here, Aquinas demonstrates that God cannot make something that he has already made better than it is because, suppositionally speaking, it has already been made as good as it can be (on account of the sort of thing it is by its present nature as determined by God). As such, God cannot grant a human the power of flight, for example, without giving that human a volant nature (i.e., causing the creature to essentially cease being human and become something else). However, as Aquinas argues, God could have created something else better than what he has made—including an entire world with more goods and less evils than the present one. This means that what God has chosen to create is always the best it could ever be *on account of what it is* but that God could surely have made something better if he had wanted to. Etienne Gilson explains further:

> What is true is that the present world is perfect in itself. It is the best possible world which it was possible to make with the kind of beings God chose to create. But he could have created another one, made up of better beings and which was a better universe. . . . For an infinite creator, there is no such things as a best possible finite universe. The same question could have been asked about any created world. Just as God was free to create or not create a universe, He might have created it better or worse without His will being subject to any kind of necessity.[11]

Thus, per Gilson, God could create *any* possible world whatsoever—even one that has fewer goods and more evils than some other possible world, so long as that which he does create is the best it could be, according to the sort of thing God means to make and the natures he creates that define the things in that world. As such, God cannot improve *even one single thing* in the world he has already made that operates according to the order and nature of that world as he has already made it. Once more, Aquinas:

> The universe, the present creation being supposed, cannot be better, on account of the most beautiful order given to things by God; in which the good of the universe consists. For if any one thing were bettered, the proportion of order would be destroyed; as if one string were stretched more than it ought to be, the melody of the harp would be destroyed. Yet God could make other things, or add something to the present creation; and then there would be another and a better universe.[12]

11. Gilson, *Christian Philosophy*, 128.

12. Aquinas, *Summa Theologiae*, I.25.6.

Here, Aquinas illustrates that given the way the world has been made, it cannot be improved upon by changing something into something else—only by adding something new. Also, taking highly theoretical "possible worlds" that do not exist to compare to the actual one in a sort of cosmic value-judgment is extraordinarily difficult because God has not in fact made those worlds, and such theoretical worlds are not evident or observable in any way beyond limited imagination. God's "best" is therefore a measure of achieving what he intends by what he does choose to make—not a comparison with other non-existent worlds that he did not choose to make.

Further, God is not beholden to some standard of good as an external property or object that he seeks to achieve in whatever he does or does not do. From a Thomistic perspective considering God and his nature, the good of the created universe is not the object of the divine will as something God intends to accomplish or gain by his creative acts. An infinitely perfect God has nothing to gain or achieve by creating anything at all. God is infinitely good and perfect whether or not he creates, and he would lose nothing if no universe existed and would gain nothing if one did. Thus, "goodness" in any world (either qualitatively or quantitatively) is patently irrelevant when considered in context with the infinite perfection of its creator. As Gilson observes, the confusion is one of the divine relation to creation.

> In every case, since all that is good insofar as it is, any universe created by God would have been good. Every difficulty that could arise on this point springs from the same confusion. It supposes that creation establishes a relation between God and creature as with an object. Hence one is led naturally to search out the cause determining the divine will in the creature. But in reality, creation does not introduce into God a relation with the creature. Any relation here is unilateral and is established only between the creature and the Creator as between a being and its cause.[13]

Thus, as Gilson explains, God does not enter into a real relation with creatures upon their creation, but rather, the relation between creature and creator is an entirely unilateral one from the first cause (God) to his effects (all of creation). In this sense, every possible world that it was possible for God to create—whether it contained more or less goods or evils than any other world (including the present one)—would have been

13. Gilson, *Christian Philosophy*, 128.

inherently and equally "good" to God as exhibiting exactly the perfections it required according to its nature. If this is so, then every possible world God could create is always the best it could possibly be. In other words, no world can be reasonably said to be "better" than any other possible world.

Further, it is difficult to see how God would be under any sort of obligation to create only a world with the most *possible good* imaginable (either qualitatively or quantitatively). If every world—regardless of the goods it inhabits—is just as "good" as any other world, then it would seem that God would be free to create any such world he wanted to. As such, the only way God could create a world "better" than the present world is if the present world were somehow defective or imperfect in some way *in its nature*. In other words, things would have to exist in such a world that failed to be what they are; such things would have to both be and not be at the same time, for example, and such would amount to a world that could not possibly exist as one created by God. On this account, therefore, the presence of evil *per se* in any created world—so long as that evil exists as a privation of the proper function of the natural world or within the potency of moral agents—would be an insufficient example of something that would make one world "less good" than another. Rather, the sorts of defects necessary to require divine revision of some created world, as I have argued, would yield an overall world mired in contradiction and chaos. It is admittedly difficult to imagine such an inferior world that could not have possibly been created by a perfect being, and it would certainly look nothing like the present world that now exists. Therefore, it is hard to see how one could argue that God could "do better" than what he has already done.

Additionally, it would seem to be prohibitively difficult (or perhaps entirely impossible) for a finite human mind to conceive of any possible world whatsoever apart from the actual world to a sufficient degree of nuance to make any meaningful judgment between the two. As Anthony Kenny explains, "A material world of precarious competition is the only world of which we have experience, and our imaginations are too feeble for us to be sure whether other forms of world are genuinely conceivable."[14] One may argue, for example, that one can easily imagine a world identical to this one but where tsunamis never occur; after all, such a world seems to be within the scope of possibility and would

14. Kenny, *What is Faith?*, 82.

seem to be a "better" world than the present one (at least by some accounts). A world without tsunamis would be one without massive coastal disasters in which thousands of lives are inevitably lost—not to mention devastating property damage that results on a massive scale. Once such an imagined world is posited, however, it is clear upon reflection that the world being described would necessarily be vastly and wildly different in a myriad of other ways that it is difficult to imagine in any coherent manner. Exactly what a tsunami-free world would entail is either enormously difficult or simply impossible to know—having different natural laws, wildly different weather patterns, varied effects of this new weather-system on the world and its overall operation, and likely further cascading implications throughout the rest of the world that are difficult for a finite mind to predict or comprehend. No world could possibly be "exactly like this one but without tsunamis," simply because tsunamis are part of the natural operation of the present world, and eliminating tsunamis from the design of the world could carry with it a heap of other intolerable consequences—perhaps even worse than tsunamis. Likewise, Peter van Inwagen describes in detail just such an undertaking, illustrating well the futility in attempting to describe another possible world (much less use such a concept in a philosophical argument):

> One should start by describing in some detail the laws of nature that govern the world. (Physicists' actual formulations of quantum field theories and the general theory of relativity provide the standard of required 'detail.') One should then go on to describe the boundary conditions under which those laws operate: the topology of the world's space-time, its relativistic mass, the number of particle families, and so on. Then one should tell in convincing detail the story of cosmic evolution in that world: the story of the development of large objects like galaxies and stars and of small objects like carbon atoms. Finally, one should tell the story of the evolution of life. These stories, of course, must be coherent, given one's specification of laws and boundary conditions. Unless one proceeds in this manner, one's statements about what is intrinsically or metaphysically possible—and thus one's statements about an omnipotent being's 'options' in creating a world—will be entirely subjective, and therefore without value.[15]

Without the painstakingly impossible path that van Inwagen has set out, the practicality of comparisons with this world to other possible worlds

15. Van Inwagen, "Ontological Arguments," 375–95.

seems grossly unfeasible as a means to construct a coherent philosophical argument. In short, "Our own universe provides the only model we have for the formidable task of designing a world."[16] Therefore, if one begins with the world that exists, then it is unclear what one could hope to compare it to in order to determine whether or not it is the best it could be.

Therefore, if God in fact has created the present world, as the theist claims, then it is entirely within the scope of the present world in which one must make a case regarding the problem of evil (not some comparison to a non-existent possible world, for example), and the evil of the present world is not difficult to explain. Fawns exposed to fire burn because their flesh is combustible. Abused children suffer because of the immoral and heinous acts of their abusers. God actualizes the world, and the evils of the world proceed from its natural operation or the acts of its inhabitants. In order to make a case against the existence of God, therefore, one would need to demonstrate some instance of evil that occurs beyond the scope of created reality and its natural operation, which I surmise to be an even more formidable task than imagining some other possible world.

Finally, on theism, any possible world that may exist can do so only by the creative decrees of an eternally existent being of the highest and most complete goodness and perfection. Thus, infinite goodness necessarily exists in every possible world. Such a fact makes any attempt at value-judgments between possible worlds utterly insignificant at best or entirely incoherent at worst. As such, every possible world includes God's infinite goodness and majesty, and thus every possible world is equally good in that respect. The only way a theist could conclude that some possible world is better than another is if the goodness of the world itself somehow added to or complimented God's goodness is some beneficial way so as to make that world better than another. But God's own act of being is eternally complete and perfect—no possible world including any imaginable quantity (or lack) of goodness can add even the slightest bit of improvement to what God already is on account of his own divine nature. Therefore, there is no reason to think God should be constrained to create any one world over another as no possible world contributes anything to God's own infinite goodness. Thus, the philosophical concept of a "best possible world" in relation to that which God must create seems to be either meaningless or incoherent.

16. Van Inwagen, "Problem of Evil, Air and Silence," 159–60.

Despite the foregoing analysis on the inherent issues with "best possible world" semantics, the evidential problem of evil is not entirely resolved on this basis alone. The next point of consideration in evaluating the problem of evil is the concept of "gratuitous evil," or evil without some greater good to justify it such that God should be expected to prevent or refuse to allow it on account of his perfect character and nature. For proponents of the evidential argument from evil, the existence of God simply precludes the existence of gratuitous evil, and thus if one can identify evil in the world that is likely to be gratuitous, then one has sufficient cause to consider the existence of God as equally unlikely. Before addressing the possibility of gratuitous evil specifically in light of a Thomistic natural theology, however, I will first address some ways in which other philosophers have sought to resolve the question of gratuitous evil—including theodicies, defenses, and theistic skepticism.

A FAREWELL TO THEODICY

The most common method among theists of counteracting evidential arguments and its use of gratuitous evil is the practice of *theodicy*. Coined by Leibniz in the eighteenth century, the term "theodicy" refers to any attempt to justify God's permission of evil—effectively attacking Rowe's first premise: "There exist instances of intense suffering which an omnipotent, omniscient being could have prevented without thereby losing some greater good or permitting some evil equally bad or worse."[17] Addressing Hume's own logical problem of evil, Alvin Plantinga describes the method of theodicy most often employed: "Now one reply would be to specify God's reason for permitting evil or creating a world that contained evil. (Perhaps evil is necessary, in some way, to the existence of good.) Such an answer to Hume's question is sometimes called a *theodicy* . . . an answer to the question why God permits evil."[18] Thus, the theodicist is occupied with the task of justifying an omnipotent, omniscient, perfectly good God's permission of evil in the universe. Bruce Little offers a more expansive explanation of what the theodicist means to achieve:

> The task of the theist is to demonstrate how God can be morally justified in permitting evil in this world. This would undercut the atheist's argument. The responsible theist creates a theodicy

17. Rowe, "Problem of Evil and Some Varieties," 12.

18. Plantinga, *God, Freedom, and Evil*, 10.

> that is philosophically sound, theologically consistent, and existentially satisfying for the sufferer and sufficient to answer the objections from the argument from evil.[19]

As Little explains, the task for the theodicist involves an explication of God's moral justification for allowing the quantity and severity of evil to exist as it does in abundance in the present world, and the theodicist must do so while upholding sound philosophical reasoning, theological understanding, and personal satisfaction. As Little also explains, given the lackluster results of theodicists to the present day, the prospect is difficult and the outlook is grim. "Theists currently involved in the work of theodicy generally agree that the argument from evil has yet to receive a sufficient answer, and understandably so as it is a most difficult task."[20] In fact, as D. Z. Phillips explains, the most common result of attempts at theodicy is woeful inadequacy and dissatisfaction. "The embarrassing result is that what seems like a sensitive account of suffering to the theodicist will strike others as almost a paradigm of insensitivity. This comes as an understandable shock to the theodicist. Theodicy, which is supposed to explain evil, is said, at its worst, to contribute to it."[21] For Phillips, it is the entire practice of theodicy that is flawed, and instead of offering solace to the sufferer, the theodicist more often assaults them further by denying the reality of their pain. In the realm of biblical Christianity, for example, the story of Job illustrates how efforts to explain or justify God in the face of suffering (as undertaken throughout the book by Job's three friends) not only fall flat but also add to Job's own suffering. In fact, God himself brings condemnation to Job's friends—all of whom are occupied with offering their own "theodicy" of sorts for Job's suffering, namely their argument that God is justified in punishing Job because of some unknown sin in Job's life. God asks, "Would you really challenge my justice? Would you declare me guilty to justify yourself?"[22]

19. Little, *Creation-Order Theodicy*, 134.

20. Little, *God, Why This Evil?*, 11.

21. Phillips, "Theism Without Theodicy," 148.

22. Throughout the book of Job, Job's three friends explain Job's suffering as being the result of Job's own sin, and Job's response to his friends is that he himself is just and does not deserve what God has done to him. Job calls out for an explanation, all the while extolling his own virtue as the basis for his questioning of God. God here questions Job—pointing out that by extolling his own righteousness (as a lack of justification for his own suffering), Job is implying that God himself is not righteous in his own acts involving Job. God's response here points out the disparity between him and Job, and Job's lack of standing to cast doubt on what he knows is true of God's own character

(Job 40:8). As such, even in the realm of biblical Christianity, one can argue that the task of the theodicist is not theologically supported. However, is this characterization of theodicy justified? I will here offer a brief critical evaluation of a few attempts at theodicy and consider what merit they may hold in terms of this discussion.

Swinburne's Greater Good Theodicy

The most common means of justifying God's permission or tolerance of evil in the world is to identify some greater good associated with the evil in question such that the good itself would be unattainable without at least the possibility of evil. As Michael Peterson explains,

> For many who think about the problem, it seems to be a deeply held intuition that for an evil to be justified—and for God to be justified in permitting it—the evil must be necessary to a greater good. If it were not strictly 'necessary,' then a God who is all-powerful, all-knowing, and all-good could achieve the specified good through other means.[23]

As such, most direct attempts at theodicy purport to provide exactly this—the possibility of some good associated with some evil such that the good itself cannot be actualized without it—even by God, and the good itself must outweigh the evil to such a degree that it is righteous and just for a supremely good, all-powerful being to allow both the good and the evil to occur.[24]

One such approach is that of Richard Swinburne, who describes his own approach as an attempt to identify the greater goods that God may invoke as a justification for evil:

> This paper is a contribution to theodicy. I accept that an omnipotent being can prevent any evil he chooses, but I deny that a perfectly good being will always try to do so. If a perfectly

and nature. For helpful commentaries on the book of Job that relate to the context of the problem of evil, see Aquinas, *Expositio Super Iob ad Litteram*; Stump, "Aquinas on the Sufferings of Job"; and Brown, *Job*, 370–74.

23. Peterson, *God and Evil*, 103.

24. In a way, every theodicy is exactly this—an attempt to counter Rowe's first premise by describing goods that God could not achieve without at least the possibility of evil. This sort of approach to resolving the problem of evil is often called a "greater good theodicy," or what Brian Davies calls the "means-end approach." See Davies, *Reality of God*, 19–24.

> good being is to allow evil to occur, he must have the right to do so, and there must be some good that is brought about by allowing the evil to occur and could not be brought about by him in any better way, and so great that it is worth allowing the evil to occur.[25]

Here, Swinburne lays out the terms of his theodicy: he must show that (1) God has a right to allow evil, (2) there is some good that results from or causes the evil to occur that could not exist without it, and (3) the good is of sufficient value to outweigh the evils associated with it. If Swinburne can in fact achieve these goals, it seems that his solution would serve as a successful counterexample to Rowe's first premise, and the evidential problem of evil would be resolved. However, I do not believe that Swinburne meets his own criteria.

Swinburne suggests that many theodicies are caught up in the goods of pleasure and the evils of pain and miss a wide range of other goods in the universe that also serve as justifying principles when set against the evils associated with them. He suggests several, such as free will, desire, love, and doing good deeds as goods that, in their highest forms, tend to result in at least the possibility of evil in the world. Additionally, says Swinburne, some goods cannot arise at all unless evil exists—goods such as compassion, sympathy, charity, and courage, for example. Here I will address one such argument from Swinburne, which he employs as a theodicy for natural evil—the good of the freedom of choice.

The problem of natural evil is always a quick rejoinder for the nontheist when the theist presents arguments related to free will as the explanation of evil in the world. Swinburne argues that the existence of natural evil in the world is also related to creaturely free will as a necessary component for God to provide a world where creatures are able to observe and learn how to do both good and evil to others such that this knowledge makes the freedom of choice possible.

> For example, I believe that the occurrence of natural evils is required for humans to have the power to choose between doing significant good or evil to their fellows, for the reason that the observation of the processes which produce natural evil is required for humans to have the knowledge of how to do significant evil to their fellows. Without that knowledge, the choice between good and evil will not be available.[26]

25. Swinburne, "Some Major Strands," 30–31.
26. Swinburne, "Some Major Strands," 31–32.

Here, Swinburne argues that humans must be able to observe a world filled with natural evils such that they are able to choose between the very real possibilities of doing good or doing harm to others. Without such a world where natural evils are possible and abundant, says Swinburne, humans would have no knowledge of good and evil and would be frustrated in any attempt to reject good in favor of evil (as genuine free will must allow). As such, Swinburne holds that God has created a world where creatures are able to harm others in order to give to them the greater good of a freedom of choice, and this implies that the world must be filled with natural evils such that God cannot intervene to prevent them without sacrificing this greater good.

Swinburne is correct that many philosophers writing on the problem of evil become transfixed with pleasure and pain as a focus of the problem of evil and miss a world filled with myriad other goods that likewise exist in tandem with the evils in the world. However, Swinburne does not explain how an omnipotent God could not have found some other means of instilling knowledge in creatures about the possibility of good and evil without placing them into a world filled with actual evil. Birds, for example, are simply born with the natural knowledge and inclination to perform all sorts of tasks that they are not required to observe in the natural world, such as flying, foraging for food, gathering materials, and building nests. None of these behaviors seem to be learned from the bird's observation of the world, and yet the bird possesses sufficient knowledge to do all of these things. Could God not have instilled in humans a similar "natural knowledge" so to speak without having to immerse them into a world of natural evils? It seems that God could have done this—even without violating the free will of creatures—by instilling a natural knowledge of things like pain and suffering that requires no observation or direct experience of those things. Thus, Swinburne's (2) has not been adequately established because the good of the knowledge of doing evil does not require natural evils to actually occur.

Further, it is difficult to see how the freedom to do harm (and thus the freedom to choose between good and evil) is a greater good than an entire world plagued with natural evils. If one creature gains the knowledge and freedom of choice from its observation of a world of natural evils, how does this justify the evils that occur to so many other creatures (such as nonhuman animals) in the same world that do not have genuine free will? There seems, at least at a glance, to be a colossal disparity between a small amount gained and a massive amount lost. As such, it seems that Swinburne's (3) is not satisfied either as the good of freedom of choice arguably does not sufficiently counterbalance the evils of a world full of suffering non-sentient creatures.

Perhaps the most problematic element of Swinburne's theodicy, however, is not whether he meets his own bar. Rather, Swinburne seems to have illicitly identified a deity that is nothing like the God of classical theism that most theists seek to defend in the first place. As John Hick points out, Swinburne's God is an anthropomorphized "human writ large," so to speak, rather than the omnipotent, omniscient, perfectly good creator of the universe. As Hick explains,

> It is indeed Swinburne's concept of God which lies at the heart of the misgivings which some of us are bound to feel. He speaks about God as another person existing within a common moral community with ourselves, so that he has rights and duties in relation to us, as we have in relation to him.[27]

If we are to consider God as *ipsum esse subsistens*, for example, then God does not share a moral community with his creatures and holds no moral obligations toward his creation akin to similar human obligations. As such, Hick explains, Swinburne's concept of God is far afield of the sort of God the non-theist means to disprove in the first place by the problem of evil.

> The picture of the deity that we receive is that of the human person magnified to infinity in some of his attributes (such as omnipotence and omniscience), but on the same level as us in that there are things which he is not permitted to do, others that it is his duty to do, and also in his having humanlike anxieties and desires.[28]

As Hick explains, in order to assume that God can and cannot do certain things in relation to creatures and holds certain duties and obligations toward others (in the same sense that humans hold duties and obligations to each other), one has anthropomorphized the deity into a being not unlike a human himself, though with his powers and knowledge multiplied. However, if God holds no true moral obligations toward creatures, as I have argued above, then Swinburne's own approach to theodicy is misguided and ultimately ineffective.

27. Hick, "Richard Swinburne," 60.

28. Hick, "Richard Swinburne," 61.

Hick's "Soul-Making" Theodicy

Proceeding to John Hick's own attempt at theodicy, which has become a landmark example of theodicies in discussions on the problem of evil, Hick argues that evil in the world is justified because it plays a significant role in the process of what he calls "soul-making."[29] In a similar vein to Swinburne, Hick seeks to justify God's permission of evil in the world by identifying a greater good—that of the possibility of a range of moral virtues that could not obtain without the presence of at least some evil in the world. As Hick explains, it is a higher good for a creature to achieve moral virtue through struggle and effort (and the possibility of failure) than one created in a state of moral perfection from the start. "The value-judgment that is implicitly being invoked here is that one who has attained to goodness by meeting and eventually mastering temptations, and thus by rightly making responsible choices in concrete situations, is good in a richer and more valuable sense than would be one created *ab initio* in a state either of innocence or of virtue."[30] For Hick, the divine design of the world is for the purpose of harboring and guiding creatures to their highest and best good, much like a human parent sets up an environment suited for the growth, maturation, and well-being of a child.

> If, then, there is any true analogy between God's purpose for his human creatures, and the purpose of loving and wise parents for their children, we have to recognize that the presence of pleasure and absence of pain cannot be the supreme and overriding end for which the world exists. Rather, this world must be a place of soul-making. And its value is to be judged, not primarily by the quantity of pleasure and pain occurring in it at any particular moment, but by its fitness for its primary purpose, the purpose of soul-making.[31]

29. Other philosophers have taken up the mantle of Hick's argument and argued in a similar vein. Geisler and Corduan, for example, offer a similar soul-making type of theodicy. They argue that the present world is justified because it is a means to the best possible world. "In summation, it is impossible for God to create directly a world with achieved moral values of the highest nature. He must first allow evil as a precondition of the greatest good. Hence, this world with freedom and evil is the best way to produce the morally best possible world." Geisler and Corduan, 353. In short, per Geisler and Corduan, the present world (including evil) is the best way for God to achieve a morally perfect world in which creatures are able to achieve moral virtue.

30. Hick, "Soul-making and Suffering," 168–69.

31. Hick, "Soul-making and Suffering," 171.

Thus, for Hick, the value of the world and its regular operation (including evils) is to be measured in its ability to achieve the good intent of "soul-making" where the human creature is placed in an environment in which he is able to achieve the highest good of moral excellence.

Central to Hick's idea here is that a world created without the possibility of pain and suffering, such as a world in which God always intervenes to mitigate or prevent suffering, would be a world in which real moral choices and decisions lack any meaningful consequence or real value. "We can at least begin to imagine a world custom-made for the avoidance of all suffering. But the daunting fact that emerges is that in such a world moral qualities would no longer have any point or value. . . . If to act wrongly means, basically, to harm someone, there would no longer be any such thing as morally wrong action."[32] As such, in order to facilitate moral good and evil, Hick argues that God must instantiate a world where harm (and therefore pain and suffering) remains a real possibility.

Hick goes on to describe how a world without pain would be a world without any meaningful moral choices and without certain moral virtues that represent the highest and best good that a human can experience and achieve, such as compassion, charity, and love. He further explains natural evils in the world (such as hurricanes, tsunamis, earthquakes, etc.) in a similar vein—as that which inspires and empowers humans to acts of mercy, charity, and compassion.[33] Thus, as Hick concludes, the sort of world one would expect as a home for creatures who strive to achieve the highest goods of moral and spiritual excellence is one in which evil abounds. "It seems, then, that in a world that is to be the scene of compassionate love and self-giving for others, suffering must fall upon mankind with something of the haphazardness and inequity that we now experience. It must be apparently unmerited, pointless, and incapable of

32. Hick, "Soul-making and Suffering," 179.

33. The consideration of natural evil in Hick's theodicy may seem at first to be an issue, since nothing in the existence of natural evil intersects with free will or human moral achievement in the sense Hick implies. However, Hick and others have addressed this challenge in an attempt to shore up these difficulties. For example, in support of Hick's basic approach, philosopher Diogenes Allen has expanded on Hick's ideas with an eye on natural evils specifically as an opportunity for creatures to understand more about their own nature, show kindness and compassion to one another, and even to participate in the sufferings of Christ. For more on the intersection of the soul-making theodicy with natural evils, see Allen, "Natural Evil and the Love of God," 439–56; and Allen, *Traces of God*.

being morally rationalized."[34] As such, for Hick, the "greater good" in operation that justifies God's permission of evil in the world is the greater good of human moral virtue.

While Hick is correct that some moral virtues do result specifically from the experience of evil in the world (such as charity and compassion, for example, which can only arise in response to the suffering of others), what is not clear is that God would be somehow morally justified in permitting evil on that basis. As such, a glaring difficulty with Hick's soul-making theodicy is that it not only fails to offer an explanation that would justify the vast amounts of evil in the world, but it also seems to make God even more of a moral monster than first thought by suggesting that evil for God is a means to an end (on account of its necessity in the task of soul-making). As Bruce Little explains,

> One difficulty of [greater good] theodicies when carried to their logical conclusion is that the very God who is to help in times of need is also the God who wills the suffering in the first place. . . . Stated rather crassly, if it serves God's purposes to allow some terrible evil in your life, you should rejoice because His purposes are being served at your expense.[35]

In other words, following Hick's theodicy to its logical zenith, one comes to the bizarre and confusing conclusion that evil—upon serving its purpose to facilitate a greater good—should not be something derided or resisted at all but rather celebrated. If evil makes it possible for humans to gain moral virtues that would be entirely unrealized in a world without evil, then evil only *appears* to be bad or wrong while it is in reality just another good—a means to an end.

Further, the idea that God wills a world with evil (or even directly wills evil itself) in order to bring about soul-making for creatures does the exact opposite of justifying God as a supremely perfect moral being. "Regardless of the benefits to others when it comes to opportunities to do good and so on, what are we to make of an agent who *arranges* for people to contract cancer? I should have thought that most moralists would regard such a person as simply vicious."[36] As Davies here explains, the practice of instantiating a world filled with evil falls short of providing a moral justification for God. "It is, of course, true that we cannot choose to help people

34. Hick, "Soul-making and Suffering," 186–87.

35. Little, *God, Why This Evil?*, 103.

36. Davies, *Reality of God*, 130.

unless they are in need. It seems odd, however, to suggest that one is morally justified to put people in need so that others can help them."[37]

In point of fact, borrowing an example from human history, Nazi physician Sigmund Rascher engaged in extensive biological and medical research in Germany during World War II. A problem for the German Army at the time was how to treat and prevent hypothermia, which had become a pressing concern given the harsh winter conditions German troops faced along the Eastern front, as well as a particular difficulty for German pilots flying at high altitudes or finding themselves shot down in the frigid waters of the North Sea. In pursuit of a remedy for this issue, Rascher experimented on unwitting prisoners of the Dachau concentration camp by exposing them to prolonged ice baths and forcing them to stand naked in freezing temperatures for prolonged periods until hypothermia was induced. Rascher would then oversee efforts to re-warm the subjects of his experiments through various methods—including having some thrown into boiling water. As a result, somewhere between eighty and ninety victims died agonizing deaths throughout Rascher's experiments. Despite the cruelty of his methods, these experiments did arguably offer at least some new insight to German researchers at the time regarding the impact and effects of severe hypothermia.[38] The question follows: Was Rascher morally justified in his experiments on his victims because of the proposed benefits of his research that could aide vast numbers of German soldiers—not to mention the potential benefits to medical science as a whole? One cannot fathom any moralist considering any sum of knowledge gained or humans helped through such horrific acts as morally sufficient to justify Rascher in his actions. Regardless of the alleged benefits of his efforts, doubtless anyone today would argue that he was anything other than a moral monster. However, this seems to be exactly what theodicies of the soul-making variety attempt to establish. For Hick, God is morally justified in inflicting horrendous suffering on unwitting subjects so that others (or even at times the subjects themselves) can benefit in ways that advance their own moral character.[39] Such a suggestion seems disgusting and inexcusable.

37. Davies, *Reality of God*, 131.

38. See Berger, "Nazi Science," 1435–40. The actual value of Rascher's experiments in the medical field at the time is widely debated—especially considering that most of his efforts failed to yield practical results.

39. Richard Swinburne himself argues along this vein in a similar manner as a throwback to his own theodicy—that the evils of the Holocaust, for example, can and

Another problem with Hick's theodicy (and theodicies of the "greater good" variety in general, for that matter) is that such an explanation seems to make evil itself a good—seemingly denying that what we think is evil is *really evil at all* as opposed to some beneficial means used by God to enact or accomplish a noble end. For example, given Hick's view, what is to be said of people who mean to intervene in the face of evil to hinder or prevent it? If the existence of some evil is necessary for this greater good, are we not somehow hindering that greater good if we intervene? In a lengthy argument that is worth quoting in full, William Rowe makes just such an argument:

> Suppose a certain level of actual, otherwise gratuitous, natural evil must occur in order to provide rational motivation for humans to develop certain good qualities and dispositions in themselves. If so, God will then permit this level of otherwise gratuitous, natural evil in order to provide us with the requisite rational motivation to develop in these ways. But now consider some agent who is in a position to prevent some serious animal suffering that is about to be occasioned by natural forces. We will suppose our agent is in a position to rescue the fawn from the fire (occasioned by lightning) before it is severely burned. Our agent can reason that if she prevents this otherwise gratuitous, natural evil, God will have to permit the occurrence of some other equally severe, otherwise gratuitous, natural evil in order to maintain the level necessary to provide humans with rational motivation to develop in virtuous ways. Knowing this, our agent may well be deprived of rational grounds for her motivation to prevent this otherwise gratuitous, natural evil.[40]

Here, Rowe illustrates the challenge for any greater-good theodicy that claims the existence of horrific evils is a necessary condition for some greater good intended by God: if all evil brings about some greater good or prevents some greater evil, then God is justified in using evil as a means to an end that is good, which does not sit well with one's natural moral inclinations. Likewise, "If all evil is allowed by God for from it He will bring about a great good, then the evil should not be stopped, for

did serve to benefit the sufferers if at least in their own individual character. As Swinburne argues, "But I am saying that God, who has rights over us that we do not have over others, is not less than perfectly good if he allowed the Jews for a short period to be subjected to these terrible evils through the evil free choice of others—in virtue of the hard heroic value of their lives of suffering." See Swinburne, "Some Major Strands," 45.

40. Rowe, "Ruminations About Evil," 83.

in doing so, the good would be stopped."[41] Thus, as Little here argues, any effort by humans to prevent, eliminate, or even minimize evil in the world must, it seems, be guilty of sacrificing a wealth of greater goods (whether known or unknown) that God could have achieved if the evils had been allowed to flourish unhindered. "If all evil allowed by God necessarily becomes an evil that brings about a greater good, then the only evil present in the world would be God-allowed evil. Should the believer be successful in preventing this evil, he would also defeat the good that would have come from that evil."[42] If one is to view the presence and prevalence of evil in the world as a necessary condition for some greater good that God aims to accomplish, it stands to reason that one should do whatever one can to "stay out of evil's way," so to speak, and allow it to continue whenever possible—or even perhaps to perpetrate evil (the more horrendous the better) in order to facilitate God's good purposes for it. As such, it seems that Hick's theodicy falls short of satisfying the challenge of gratuitous evil.[43]

Eschatological Theodicies

Another approach of a greater good theodicy is what I will refer to as an "eschatological theodicy," meaning any explanation of evil in the present world that appeals to a separate or subsequent world (such as an eternal paradise, for example) as the proper factor that outweighs or overwrites the evil in question and justifies God's permission of it.[44] For the escha-

41. Little, *God, Why This Evil?*, 112.

42. Little, *Creation-Order Theodicy*, 168–69.

43. A number of other criticisms of Hick's argument are possible, though for the sake of space, they will not be addressed here in detail. For example, a common rejoinder is that Hick's argument does not seem to come close to justifying all instances of evil and suffering—such as those that happen in isolation away from any human participation or involvement (such as Rowe's fawn, for example). Further, it would seem that if God's intent for allowing evil and suffering were the well-being of "soul-making" in his creatures, then it is puzzling that encountering evils in the world often has the opposite effect—driving sufferers and those around them to states of despair, destruction, and devastation, ending up bitter, angry, hateful, vengeful, or utterly broken by their experiences. If God means for suffering to actualize virtue in creatures, then it seems an inconsistent means at best. Rather it is surprising that God's method of using evil for soul-making seems to fail in its aim as often as it does.

44. Some, such as Marilyn McCord Adams, argue that this approach is not strictly a theodicy because it involves "defeating" or "overcoming" the evils faced in the present world, as opposed to a typical theodicy, which argues that the evils themselves must have justifying goods associated with them. However, since the moral justification of

tological theodicist, the horrific evils experienced in this life simply pale in comparison to the endless joy of heaven to such a degree that one would consider their own suffering to have been worth it in the end (or utterly insignificant) once paradise is attained. As such, so the argument goes, once God has created sentient creatures, he becomes indebted to those creatures to provide them a life that is on balance an overall positive—with more good than bad—such that the joys of life were worth its toils. Per Swinburne,

> . . . if God creates sentient creatures (including humans and the higher animals), he puts himself under an obligation to give them a total life that as a whole is on balance worth living; and so, if someone's life on earth is not on balance worth living, God is under an obligation to provide for that creature a further life after death such that his total life is worth living.[45]

As Swinburne argues, if the evils of this life do at times outweigh its good, then God becomes the debtor of the sufferer and owes the creature an afterlife of sufficient joy to overwrite or overcome the gratuitous evil she has experienced. Thus, the joys of the afterlife become the "greater good" that justifies the evils experienced in the present life.[46]

One advocate of this approach to theodicy is Marilyn McCord Adams, who argues that God's own goodness depends on whether or not creatures become beset with gratuitous evil in the course of their lives. She argues, "For God cannot be said to be good or loving to any created persons the positive meaning of whose lives He allows to be engulfed in and/or defeated by evils—that is, individuals within whose lives horrendous evils remain undefeated."[47] Thus, for Adams, if a creature ex-

---

God on account of the evils in this world is what is sought by the eschatological approach in identifying good that follows from (or after) the evil of the present world, I will here classify this as a "theodicy."

45. Swinburne, *Coherence of Theism*, 221.

46. It is notable that Swinburne himself holds some unorthodox views of heaven and hell that make his own approach somewhat unique, though the variances in question are not relevant to my argument here and will not be further addressed. However, for more on Swinburne's view of heaven and hell in the context of arguments from evil, see Swinburne, "Theodicy of Heaven and Hell."

47. Adams, "Horrendous Evils," 214. Adams specifically defines her version of gratuitous evil (what she calls "horrendous evil") as "evils the participation in (the doing or suffering of) which gives one reason *prima facie* to doubt whether one's life could (given their inclusion in it) be a great good to one on the whole." (Adams, "Horrendous Evils," 211.) Thus, given Adams own definition of horrendous evil, its gratuity depends subjectively on the experience of the creature, and the good that results must be a good also

periences a life of devastation, suffering, and heartache (for example), then a perfectly good God must "defeat" those evils either in this life or the life to come. "It is enough to show *how* God can be good enough to created persons despite their participation in horrors—by defeating them within the context of the individual's life and by giving that individual a life that is a great good to him/her on the whole."[48] As Adams argues, therefore, every creature that experiences any sort of evil in this world must be duly compensated in some fashion that effectively "defeats" the evil in question in order for God's goodness to remain consistent. For Adams, just such a defeater of evil begins in divine relationship and has its ultimate fulfillment in the beatific vision of God. "Retrospectively, I believe, from the vantage point of heavenly beatitude, human victims of horrors will recognize those experiences as points of identification with the crucified God, and not wish them away from their life histories."[49] Thus for Adams, the beatific vision (as often described in Christian theology) reveals to the beholder how each moment of suffering has in some way enhanced one's identification with the sufferings of Christ and thus one's relationship with God, such that the evils experienced are properly justified for God.

Another approach to an eschatological theodicy is offered by Thomistic philosopher Edward Feser, who argues in a similar vein that the finite sufferings of this world pale in comparison to the infinite joy of an eternity with God in heaven—in the presence of the beatific vision. "For even the worst evils we suffer are finite. Therefore there is every reason to think that God can and will bring out of the sufferings of this life a good that so overshadows them that this life will be seen in retrospect to have been worth it."[50] As Feser argues, God brings from the evils of the

dependent on the perception of and experienced by the creature that suffers. Hence, God owes the creature its own good to its own satisfaction (as opposed to any other related good associated with evil, such as the good of the natural order or even the good of God's own being or essence). Thus, Adams's own theodicy is by definition opposed to many other greater-good theodicies, and it is incompatible with the idea that goodness is an aspect of reality that exists beyond the experience of the creatures in the world.

48. Adams, "Horrendous Evils," 217; emphasis in original.

49. Adams, *Horrendous Evils*, 167.

50. Feser, *Last Superstition*, 162. Feser does not here explain how his view would address the Christian concept of the eternal torment of hell for unbelievers and how the evils in this world and the evils of hell are somehow justified on account of the beatific vision in the manner he suggests. While such an argument as Feser offers here may be of some value to those who do experience the joys of heaven in the beatific vision of God, it would seem of little comfort to those condemned to eternal damnation as

present world a second world in which humans experience the joys of the beatific vision and consider the evils faced in the present world as worth the price of admission, so to speak.

Eschatological theodicies of this sort are right to shift the focus of the problem of evil from its implied preoccupation with immediate, observable goods as associated with some evil and turn towards the significance of the divine being and essence as the highest possible good that all created beings necessarily strive toward (as realized ultimately in the beatific vision). After all, it is the goodness of God that drives the motion of the universe in its natural operations, including the various causes of evil that operate in the created world. However, a number of concerns arise that do not seem to cohere with the view of God I have thus far espoused—at least as a means of justifying God's permission of evil in the world. First, the eschatological theodicy commits the same error as other theodicies by attempting to resolve the problem of evil with a moral justification of God for his permission of evil. Simply put, God does not owe to creatures an overall balance of life to include the resplendent joys of heaven in order to justify the suffering they may experience in their interactions with the natural world and other moral agents. Second, it appears that the proposed solution in the eschatological theodicy is wholly unrelated to the problem posed in the first place. In short, it provides no explanation for the suffering in the present world that could not have been achieved without it. The claim that God in some future experience will actualize the sort of world that one might expect an omnipotent, perfectly good being to have created in the first place (such as a perfect, sinless, painless paradise) does nothing whatsoever to explain why he made the world as he did rife with evil and suffering, or why the present world persists as it does if a better world were presently possible. For that matter, it is not clear how the sufferings of the present world are somehow necessary for the joys of heaven to be realized; it seems that God could have granted the beatific vision to any creatures at any time without first subjecting them to a world of pain and suffering. As such, it is difficult to see how God could not have just started with the beatific paradise in the first place and just skipped the present world, with all of its misery and pain. Third, this view confuses the good of creatures with the highest good of God's own essence and being—treating the good of creatures as an end in itself that God is constrained to pursue. What such

taught in traditional Christian theology.

an expectation misses is that God himself is always the highest good and all "minor goods" (such as creatures and their actions and experiences) are always necessarily ordered to God's own goodness, never their own. While creatures do experience both good and evil in the present world, there is no reason to think that their own overall well-being should be a higher priority than God's own goodness in the grand scheme of things. Thus, God is right and just to judge sin and even to inflict eternal separation and suffering from their highest good (himself) as willed by the creature. Further, the fact that some may look back at the sufferings of this world and see how they pale in comparison with the glory of the beatific vision does nothing to explain the existence of the suffering right now. As Davies explains,

> This focus, however, and whatever its merits may be, turns attention away from the less than glorious world in which we currently find ourselves. If we (as we are here and now) want credibly to claim that God is indeed good, then, it seems to me, we need to be able to point to what we can draw attention to when it comes to the here and now.[51]

Therefore, the eschatological theodicy seems to function more as a distraction from the problem of evil rather than a resolution of it.[52]

Little's Creation-Order Theodicy

One final approach to theodicy that I will here address is that proposed by Bruce Little, which he calls a "creation-order theodicy." While not a theodicy in its strictest sense, Little nevertheless poses what he holds to be an explanation of the evils in the world by suggesting that God has created a world of certain ordered principles that allow for both a genuine human freedom and the possibility of gratuitous evil.[53] As Little explains,

51. Davies, *Reality of God*, 231.

52. Eschatological theodicies also bear the additional challenges of not being accessible by direct experience, relying heavily on the tenets of particular theological traditions (such as Christianity), failing to provide any sort of similar explanation for the evils of non-human suffering (for animals that do not experience the beatific vision and have no rational concept of God or Christ, for example), and a host of other problems concerning the plight of the damned (those who never realized the beatific vision).

53. Little himself denies that his own theodicy constitutes a "greater-good" argument against evil, and unlike most theodicies, his argument allows for the possibility of gratuitous evil as a part of God's created order. Thus, unlike most theodicists, Little does not use his own argument as a means to deny that gratuitous evil exists. Little

> It appears that in order for there to be a stable created environment in which God and creation interact in a purposeful way, only two possibilities exist. Either God determines *everything*, thus assuring the order of creation based on divine predetermination, or God provides for the suitable function of creation by establishing certain moral (internal) and physical (external) ordering consonant with man's power of moral choice.[54]

Thus, for Little, an interactive world inhabited by creatures that possess free moral choice is a reasonable alternative to the unpalatable theistic determinism that most theists reject. Little goes on to explain how God's "best" in this present world extends not only to natural evils but to the moral operation of its creatures as well.

> One could argue that this is not the only logically possible created-order design. Nonetheless, given the infinite wisdom, goodness, and power of God, it is difficult to maintain (at least consistently) that this is not the best of possible created-order designs. This includes both the moral and physical ordering of creation, which is to say that creation-order optimizes the function of creation and its interaction with the Creator as well as its conformity with the counsels of God.[55]

As such, per Little, the ordering of creation, both naturally and morally, are aspects of the world that should be and are considered effectively unimprovable. The resulting world chosen by divine decree, therefore, becomes unalterable according to its creation-order once it is chosen amidst all other lesser possibilities.

> From all possible worlds, God selects the best of all possible worlds to be the world that he will actualize. Once that world is actualized, things will be as they are in that world and they cannot be otherwise. While creation-order establishes how God interacts with any and all possible worlds, the only possible world now is the one God has actualized.[56]

---

instead intends to show (given things such as the order of nature and the free will of its creatures) that gratuitous evil is possible in a world created by God (such as the present one), and therefore it does not contradict God's existence. He seems to be using the term "theodicy" in the sense of a justification or explanation of the evils in the world, however, and as such, it fits within the heading of a "theodicy" for the purpose of my argument here.

54. Little, *Creation-Order Theodicy*, 162; emphasis in original.

55. Little, *Creation-Order Theodicy*, 166.

56. Little, *Creation-Order Theodicy*, 176.

Therefore, per Little, the present world is one of a suppositional necessity such that God cannot override it or make other than it is in order to reduce or eliminate the evil that results from its natural operation. For Little, unlike most theodicists, this means that gratuitous evil can occur in the actual world on account of the authenticity of human moral freedom.

> The genius of the created-order design is that it gives man power of moral choice in a way that is authentic. This authentic power of moral choice makes it possible for man authentically to love and obey God. It also leaves the opportunity for man significantly to disobey God. This possibility of disobeying God means that such disobedience will have real consequences. The consequences of this disobedience often results in gratuitous evil. The created-order does not provide a means for God to filter out the bad choices from which he cannot bring about a greater good. Instead, the creation-order design allows for gratuitous evil as a corollary to the authenticity of the power of moral choice.[57]

Here, Little departs from many of his contemporary counterparts by affirming the actuality of gratuitous evil (evil without some concomitant greater good to justify it in a world created by God). Just such a concept of evil, per Little, is the inevitable byproduct of the creation-order established in the present world. "This seems to hold God hostage to evil in order to have the good God knows is best for man, but God is unable to create it apart from using evil."[58] Therefore, for Little, if gratuitous evil remains a possibility in the world and does not contradict or cast doubt on the existence of God, then the problem of evil is resolved. Despite his acceptance of gratuitous evil, Little considers his solution a theodicy because it ultimately presents a divine justification for gratuitous evil. "This theodicy recognizes the reality of gratuitous evil while maintaining that God is morally justified in permitting such."[59]

There is much to commend in Little's approach to the problem of evil, which bears certain similarities to my own argument. First, Little rightly eschews the traditional means of theodicy that attempt to defend against the problem of evil by finding explanations and justifications to deny the apparent gratuity of some evil in the world by hanging their success on how well some instance of evil is explained and justified. This inevitably leads the theodicist to a host of inadequate and unsatisfying

57. Little, *Creation-Order Theodicy*, 162–63.

58. Little, *God, Why This Evil?*, 77.

59. Little, *Creation-Order Theodicy*, 161.

attempts at morally justifying some horrendous example of evil. Admitting that evil can and is at times gratuitous avoids these pitfalls and shifts the focus to an *explanation* of evil in terms of God's existence and nature, as well as the ordinary operations and causal forces at work in the natural world. Second, Little rightly emphasizes the important (yet often neglected) distinction between *absolute* necessity and *suppositional* necessity, which bears weight in the evaluation of the problem of evil. Put simply, if God has suppositionally created the world in a certain manner, then it makes little sense to demand or expect God to "undo" what he has done when the natural operation of that world results in some measure of evil and suffering for its inhabitants. Third, as I have mentioned, Little emphasizes *explanation* over *justification* in his theodicy—appealing to the natural order of the world as the explanation of why some evils arise (particularly for natural evils) and the free will of creatures as another explanation (particularly for moral evils) that both operate as created and intended by a perfectly good God. Fourth, Little recognizes that God stands under no obligation to interrupt or interfere with the "good" operation of the world he has made in order to prevent its natural results (including various evils). "Given God's omniscience, it is difficult to think of a situation in which God would be required to act contrary to his established creation-order to avert some unwanted state of affairs."[60]

Suffice to say, I largely agree with Little's intuition here regarding God and gratuitous evil but not, perhaps, for the same reason as Little. The primary difference between my argument and Little's in regards to the problem of evil is that of God's moral obligations toward the world he creates. While Little rightly denies that gratuitous evil *by definition* contradicts God's existence, he does argue that God's goodness places him under certain obligations in relation to the creation-order he decided to establish upon his creation of the world. Thus, for Little, God necessarily takes steps to minimize gratuitous evil as much as he is able without violating the created order. For example, "God gives commands that govern how one treats others. When the neighbor is treated with love and respect, gratuitous evil is minimized. The moral commands are codified aspects of the creation-order by which man is instructed to live rightly in his material existence."[61] But if God can issue commands to minimize evil in this way, and this can be incorporated seamlessly into

60. Little, *Creation-Order Theodicy*, 166.

61. Little, *Creation-Order Theodicy*, 167.

God's creation-order, then why would the creation-order preclude God from acting in even more bold ways to further minimize the gratuitous evil that does occur? God could give similar commands audibly and unmistakably to every human immediately before any act of cruelty against another, for example, which would certainly go much further in reducing pain and suffering in the world. Little may argue here that to do so would threaten the balance of freedom and consequence or result in a suboptimal creation-order, but this does not seem obvious upon reflection, and God could still leave the act and its results entirely up to the creature in the end—thus preserving a meaningful sense of freedom in its own volitional acts. While it is admittedly difficult to imagine the full weight and impact of such a drastic action on God's part to reduce the impact of gratuitous evil in the world (and its full effect on the creation-order), it seems nonetheless feasible to imagine that something like this would be open to an omniscient, omnipotent God within his own creation-order.

Further, Little argues that God does in fact work *against* evil in various ways be reducing its impact in some cases. "When [a Christian suffers because of righteous living], the believer can be assured that God is at work to reverse evil intent against him and bring good to him either in this life or the age to come."[62] But if God can act in such a way in these instances of suffering without impacting his creation-order, then why not in all of them, or at least in more obvious ways towards the evils we do experience? Little is clear (and I believe correct) that such goods that may follow from evil do not constitute a *moral justification* of those evils, but if he intends to portray the creation-order as the reason why evils may sometimes be both unhindered and gratuitous, then such an explanation does not seem to comport well with instances of evil when God does in fact intervene in the ways Little suggests.

As such, for Little, God has reduced and minimized evil as much as he can because he has made the "best of all possible worlds" in his creation-order, though some gratuitous evil inevitably slips through the cracks. "The amount of gratuitous evil is at an irreducible minimum in relation to the good, because God knows all the worlds (not actual, but potential worlds—middle knowledge—assuring that the best would be actualized)."[63] Unlike Little, my argument, however, is that God does not *have* to reduce or minimize gratuitous evils in this way, even though he

62. Little, *Creation-Order Theodicy*, 170.

63. Little, *Creation-Order Theodicy*, 178.

often chooses to do so anyway (on account of his divine grace). Thus, gratuitous evil likely exists, and is arguably explained, on account of the natural operation of the world and the freedom of its creatures as Little argues, God is under no obligation to create the world in any such manner (or reject other live options from among other possible worlds), and the present world is not necessarily the "best" in any quantifiable sense (by measuring the goods and evils each world contains, for example), so long as it is essentially good as a creation of God.

A FAREWELL TO DEFENSES

Moving now from the practice of theodicy as a response to the problem of evil, another approach has been widely advocated in what has come to be known as a "defense." First coined by Alvin Plantinga, a "defense" attempts to do much the same thing as a theodicy by proposing some reason or justification for God's permission of evil in the world but with the added qualifier that the justification itself does not need to be defended by the theist as one that is actual or verifiable; rather it must only be *possibly* true.[64] As Plantinga describes, "A theodicist, then, attempts to tell us why God permits evil."[65] With a defense, however, "the aim is not to say what God's reason *is*, but at most what God's reason *might possibly be*."[66] The advantage of this approach is that one need not bother defending the truth of the theodicy itself, because its truth is effectively irrelevant to the argument. Thus, the demand for evidence to support the position of the defender is misguided and unnecessary. The aim of the defense is not to show what God's reasons are, but rather to show that the propositions "evil exists" and "God exists" do not entail a contradiction. This, of course, is a weaker approach than a full-fledged theodicy since it may yet turn out to be false upon closer examination, and what it accomplishes is generally only a minimal refutation of the stronger logical problem of evil, though it does have application to the evidential argument as well and is often addressed in this context. As Peter van Inwagen explains,

64. To further complicate matters, some philosophers use the term "theodicy" when meaning a defense. Richard Swinburne, for example, calls his own approach a theodicy, but clarifies that given the distinction mentioned here between revealing God's *actual* reasons and God's *possible* reasons, his project would actually be considered a defense. See Swinburne, "Some Major Strands," 46n2.

65. Plantinga, *God, Freedom, and Evil*, 28.

66. Plantinga, *God, Freedom, and Evil*, emphasis in original.

> The word *defense* was first employed as a technical term in discussion of the "logical" version of the argument from evil. In that context, a defense is a story according to which both God and suffering exist, and which is possible "in the broadly logical sense"—or which is such that there is no reason to believe that it is impossible in the broadly logical sense. Let us adapt the notion of a defense to the requirements of a discussion of the evidential argument: a defense is a story according to which God and suffering of the sort contained in the actual world both exist, and which is such that (given the existence of God) there is no reason to think that it is false, a story that is not surprising on the hypothesis that God exists.[67]

As such, the defense can be applied in a sense to evidential arguments by presenting a "story" that allows for both the existence of God and any evidential instance of evil in the world that is at least possible given the existence of God. Thus, van Inwagen employs the defense in much the same way that Plantinga does by avoiding the necessity to defend the story against problems it may have with only the more general aim to show that it is at least possible or does not entail a contradiction. "A difficulty with a theory does not necessarily constitute evidence against it. To show that an acknowledged difficulty with a theory is not evidence against it, it suffices to construct a defense that accounts for the facts that raise the difficulty."[68] As such, I will here evaluate two defenses as examples of the sort of responses sometimes employed in light of the nature of God and approach to natural theology I have argued for.

Plantinga's Free Will Defense

Intended initially as a response to J. L. Mackie's logical problem of evil, Plantinga's "free will defense" has garnered a wide-reaching respect and is often included and addressed in most subsequent works on the problem of evil. Plantinga begins by establishing the value of a world with free creatures as superior than one without: "A world containing creatures who are significantly free (and freely perform more good than evil actions) is more valuable, all else being equal, than a world containing no free creatures at all."[69] Further, Plantinga argues that in such a world

67. Van Inwagen, "Problem of Evil, Air, and Silence," 156; emphasis in original.

68. Van Inwagen, "Problem of Evil, Air, and Silence," 170.

69. Plantinga, *God, Freedom, and Evil*, 30.

containing free creatures, it is possible that some creatures may choose to do evil, and simply by creating a world with such creatures in it, evil may be the unavoidable result. Also, for Plantinga, it may simply be beyond the power of God to ensure that all free creatures only do good because of the nature of freedom that significantly free creatures truly enjoy. Here, Plantinga defines a concept he calls "transworld depravity" to explain a sense in which free creatures can be said to commit evil acts in *every possible world* in which they exist.

> What is important about the idea of transworld depravity is that if a person suffers from it, then it was not within God's power to actualize any world in which that person is significantly free but does no wrong—that is, a world in which he produces moral good but no moral evil. . . . And the price for creating a world in which such persons produce moral good is creating one in which they also produce moral evil.[70]

As such, for Plantinga, it may just be the case that God freely creates a world that includes significantly free creatures; it is a better world than one that does not contain free creatures; and on account of the freedom of those creatures, evil arises and inhabits the world God created. Thus, if Plantinga's approach is at least possible, then the stronger logical form of the problem of evil is refuted.[71]

While initially promising as a response to the problem of evil (particularly in its logical form), there remains a sense in which the free will defense does not fit together with the God of classical theism. While I have argued that God's omniscience does not contradict the possibility of human free will, the finer points of what it means for a creature to will something and in what sense that decision is influenced by God (if at all) are critical to understand how creaturely free will can be said to operate both under divine governance and yet independently of any coercion or influence. Per a classical understanding of natural theology, creatures are not independently free in their actions *per se*, but the will of the creature is always directed in a sense toward a specific end—what Aquinas refers

70. Plantinga, *Nature of Necessity*, 186.

71. Though Plantinga's defense aims largely at moral evils, he includes a similar explanation of natural evils as the result of free non-human beings (such as fallen angels, for example) who influence the natural world in a similar way that human moral evils result from free human actions. It is unclear if Plantinga himself holds this view, though as a reminder, the truth of his defense is not at issue, and thus he is in no need to defend it or offer evidence in support of it in order to validate his argument. See Plantinga, *God, Freedom, and Evil*, 57–59.

to as "happiness."[72] This end is directed by God as first mover and finds its ultimate realization in God himself as the perfectly good and the infinite source of all goodness. Hence, as Aquinas explains, God is always the mover of the will. "God moves man's will, as the Universal Mover, to the universal object of the will, which is good. And without this universal motion, man cannot will anything. But man determines himself by his reason to will this or that, which is true or apparent good."[73] Thus, creatures are created with their will directed toward the good, and all free creaturely choices are made with this ultimate end in mind and caused by God to act in this manner.

As such, the will of creatures—at every point—is always driven by its divine cause. In fact, per a classical view of natural theology, God's causal activity accounts for everything that exists, including free creatures and their choices. In fact, one can reasonably say that the necessary condition for there being free creatures at all is God causing them to be. Thus, it would be absurd to suggest that the very causal activity that is necessary to produce free creatures also somehow impedes or prevents that which it causes to be—namely their free acts of will. God does not have to be the author of the free choice itself in order to be the author of the creature that makes the choice, the cause of the operation and result of that choice, the final cause of the directed will that drives the choice, and so on. As Brian Davies explains,

> If God brings it about that I do something as you might bring it about that I do something, or as something else in the universe might, then he and his omni-causality would be a threat to my freedom. Yet, so I am arguing, that is not how God makes it to be that I act freely. He does so simply by making me to be a freely acting person.[74]

72. Per Aquinas, the will is moved toward the good on account of its nature and desires happiness as its end, and this comes from God as first mover, who also serves as the highest and best good toward which creaturely happiness is ultimately directed. As Aquinas explains, "In like manner neither is natural necessity repugnant to the will. Indeed, more than this, for as the intellect of necessity adheres to the first principles, the will must of necessity adhere to the last end, which is happiness: since the end is in practical matters what the principle is in speculative matters. For what befits a thing naturally and immovably must be the root and principle of all else appertaining thereto, since the nature of a thing is the first in everything, and every movement arises from something immovable." Aquinas, *Summa Theologiae*, I.82.1.

73. Aquinas, *Summa Theologiae*, I-II.9.6.

74. Davies, *Reality of God*, 127.

The free will defense portrays God's causal activity as if God were part of the same system that he is causing to be by the same causal activity—acting either in congruence or opposition with creaturely freedom—but there is no reason to think that this is so. God is not a member of a system in which his actions always tend toward necessity in the sense that Plantinga implies. God is free to act through causal means that are either necessary or contingent, and the effects of those causal means themselves are likewise either necessary or contingent in turn. Thus, God first causes the creature to act freely, and the creature necessarily does so unimpeded.

A further issue with the free will defense is how God can be said to reduce or eliminate the possibility of evil in the world without impacting the freedom of its creatures. Given the understanding of the will described above, any creature in the presence of God would always freely choose him as its most desired good. It is in the created nature of creatures to seek the good, and in the presence of the greatest and highest good (e.g., God himself), all creatures would necessarily choose God as the proper object of their will. If God intended to place creatures in a world in which they do not necessarily choose him (e.g., a world where creatures are free to either accept or reject him), God would need to be absent from such a world such that he could not be perceived directly. In such a case, creatures would be faced with a myriad of lesser goods to choose from in place of God—none of which would perfectly and ultimately satisfy the appetitive desires of the creature, though many of which would likewise serve as temporary substitutes for the highest good sought by the will, or "lesser goods" so to speak. These lesser goods themselves would not and could not fully and permanently satisfy the creature's desires. Therefore, in such a world, creatures would be able to act freely in their own capacity to choose between the lesser goods available to them because they have no direct knowledge or experience of the highest good in God himself. In this way, creatures in the present world are necessitated, in a sense, toward the objects of their will (driven by appetitive desires) because the will, by nature, is driven toward the good, and the greatest good is not directly perceived in the present world. God, therefore, both limits and necessitates the will of creatures in a sense that does not seem to fit with Plantinga's defense.[75] If God made the nature

75. Further, creatures are created with specific natures and powers that are limited in what they can choose and do, which further prescribes the choices they are able to make. A human cannot choose to fly or lay an egg, for example, and this does not "limit" their freedom, so long as their operative human nature remains functionally

of legitimate goods and evils more obvious or inescapable in the creaturely experience of the natural world, then creatures would naturally seek those goods and *freely choose them* instead of lesser goods (or evils), and this seems to be something God could certainly have done without denying or limiting the freedom of the creature. In fact, any provision of knowledge and awareness of the goods sought by creatures would "limit" their freedom in some way—including the powers of reason and awareness given to free creatures in the present world; thus, unless creatures were to act entirely in isolation with no awareness or knowledge at all of anything else (which would raise the additional question as to what an "act" of that creature could possibly be), then God has necessarily limited freedom by his creative decrees.

However, since God has suppositionally chosen to place the will and nature of the creature in the circumstances that it is presently in (with the range of limited finite goods available to it in the absence of the beatific vision), then it would be right to say (à la Plantinga) that any evil that resulted from such a choice on the part of God would be in a sense inevitable and inescapable, but this would be evil that results from God's creative decrees, and it would not serve as a moral justification of evil since God could certainly have done differently. In short, Plantinga's argument depends on the proposition that creating free creatures necessitates a world where evil is unavoidable (even among all possible worlds so long as the creature is genuinely free), but this does not appear to be the case if God were to organize the world in such a fashion where the good was more obvious to the creature in question. Thus, Plantinga seems to be saying that because God made the world the way he did (with good and evil in abundance), he could not have done otherwise—which is either a meaningless tautology or simply confuses the concepts of absolute and suppositional necessity.

Further, there is no reason to think that God could not have made the highest good of the beatific vision an object of direct access to creatures in the present world. In such a state, all creatures by nature would seek God and his divine will above all else, and they would do so freely. Such a concept does not deny or contradict free will even though all creatures would always freely choose God above all else. As Brian Davies explains,

whole and unhindered through the process of every choice they make. If God is able to limit or necessitate creaturely choices by their natures in this way, could he not do so in more restrictive ways to limit the scope of evil in the world (which is the focus of the evidential problem of evil in the first place) without violating human freedom?

> To see and know God as he is might render a human being unable not to love God. But it does not follow that the human being in question has been deprived of freedom. This person has been presented with what he or she most wants (given that God is a good to be prized above all others), and in going for it he or she is not being deprived of freedom. We are surely free in so far as we home in on what we want.[76]

In the same way, all creaturely freedom is directed toward happiness (on account of the good it seeks), without contradicting the possibility of free will. As such, a creature presented with the ultimate and highest object of joy and peace in the beatific vision of God himself would not contradict its freedom in choosing that object. A creature does not need the power to choose what it cannot choose in order to have freedom—it must only possess the range of choices available to it, according to the nature it has been given. Therefore, contra Plantinga, there is no reason to think that God could not have achieved a world without any evil whatsoever while still creating creatures with genuine freedom.[77]

Van Inwagen's Irregularity Defense

Another defense offered against the problem of evil is that of Peter van Inwagen, who aims his response particularly at Paul Draper's evidential argument. Recall that Draper offers an alternative evidential argument (distinct from Rowe's more direct syllogistic approach) that avoids claims about divine justifications for evil in favor of a direct probabilistic

76. Davies, *Reality of God*, 135.

77. While the philosophical topic of "free will" and what precisely that entails has been a critical aspect in discussions surrounding the problem of evil, it is a category with an abundance of technicality, nuance, and layers of argumentation, rebuttal, and response that would entail a work in itself. Since my argument here does not depend on any specific interpretation of free will (beyond what I have already presented here), I will not explicate or defend my own position in any further detail. Stated weakly, however, my own view of creaturely free will is that it is both an act of the creature empowered and actualized by God but also not determined or coerced in any way toward its specific end (apart from the creature's own self-determination). As such, I disagree with the kind of libertarian freedom implied by Plantinga as requiring that the creature itself act in some way wholly independently of any divine causal activity, though I also deny any sense of absolute determinism that some (such as Plantinga) often put forth as the only alternative for the theist in discussions of the will. For more on this topic, see McCluskey, "Intellective Appetite," 434–42; Pilsner, *Specification of Human Actions*; Kretzmann et al., "Thomas Aquinas on Human Action," Gilson, *Christian Philosophy*, 238–48; and Davies, *Thought of Thomas Aquinas*, 220.

comparison of theism with an alternative non-theistic hypothesis. Designed to evade theodicies altogether as a potential response to his argument, Draper proposes an alternative non-theistic hypothesis to theism (which he calls the "Hypothesis of Indifference" or "HI") and argues that the idea of an entirely indifferent universe is *more likely*—given the evidence of the various examples of good and evil that arise in the universe—than any theistic hypothesis. For Draper, the question comes down to a probability calculus pitting the evidence for good (in favor of theism) against the evidence for evil (favoring atheism). However, van Inwagen argues that such a world with sentient creatures and no possibility of suffering that Draper's argument suggests would be highly irregular and defective. The syllogism offered by van Inwagen is as follows:

(1) Every possible world that contains higher-level sentient creatures either contains patterns of suffering morally equivalent to those recorded by S, or else is massively irregular.

(2) Some important intrinsic or extrinsic good depends on the existence of higher-level sentient creatures; this good is of sufficient magnitude that it outweighs the patterns of suffering recorded by S.

(1) Being massively irregular is a defect in a world, a defect at least as great as the defect of containing patterns of suffering morally equivalent to those recorded by S.[78]

While not in the form of a logical syllogism (unlike Rowe's evidential argument), van Inwagen offers these premises to build a basis for holding that the irregularity of a world without evil precludes such a world from being a viable option for a benevolent creator. As with Plantinga, the advantage of such an approach for van Inwagen is that it does not require the theist to prove that such a hypothesis is either true or even likely true. Thus, the result is limited in that it does not completely resolve the evidential argument, but rather it puts the questioner in a state of quiescence, unable to make a judgment on the matter from an evidential basis. "Rather, the stories will, or should, lead a person in our epistemic situation to refuse to make any judgment about the relation between the

78. Van Inwagen, "Problem of Evil, Air, and Silence," 143. For van Inwagen, "S" stands for "a proposition that describes in some detail the amount, kinds, and distribution of suffering—the suffering not only of human beings, but of all the sentient terrestrial creatures that there are or ever have been." Van Inwagen, "Problem of Evil, Air, and Silence," 137.

probabilities of S on theism and on HI."[79] Further, for van Inwagen, humans simply lack the epistemic position to make value judgments in the sense that Draper's evidential argument requires.

> My position is that we cannot be sure, and that for all we know our inclinations to make value judgments are not veridical when they are applied to cosmic matters unrelated to the concerns of everyday life. But there is no *prima facie* case for the thesis that the actual sufferings of beasts constitute a graver defect in a world than does massive irregularity. Or, at least, there is no case that is grounded in our intuitions about value.[80]

As such, for van Inwagen, there is no reason to think that suffering somehow trumps a world of massive irregularity by some value-judgment, and thus van Inwagen's own alternative hypothesis is a valid rebuttal to Draper's argument. Again, van Inwagen need not prove that the value judgment is in the favor of his hypothesis of irregularity, or that it is even likely to be true; rather, he must show only that such a determination exists as a possibility to achieve a successful defense.[81] Therefore, van Inwagen concludes that his argument successfully removes any evidential argument involving pain and suffering from consideration as *prima facie* evidence against the theistic hypothesis.

> While the patterns of suffering we find in the actual world constitute a *difficulty* for theism and do not constitute a difficulty for the competing hypothesis HI, they do not—owing to the availability of the defense I have outlined—attain to the status of *evidence* that favors HI over theism. It follows that the evidential argument from evil fails, for it is essential to the evidential

79. Van Inwagen, "Problem of Evil, Air, and Silence," 142.

80. Van Inwagen, "Problem of Evil, Air, and Silence," 150.

81. Van Inwagen advocates for a commitment to what he calls "modal skepticism," which would leave such highly theoretical cosmic value-judgments as no more than mere possibilities, or at best entirely undetermined. As he explains, "I have urged extreme modal and moral skepticism (or, one might say, humility) in matters unrelated to the concerns of everyday life." (Van Inwagen, "Problem of Evil, Air, and Silence," 151.) Further, van Inwagen insists that this position is not an *ad hoc* response to the evidentialist argument but more like a foundational position from which to develop one's own philosophy in the first place. "I have not accepted the extreme modal skepticism that figures so prominently in the argument of this section as a result of epistemic pressures exerted by the evidential argument from evil." Van Inwagen, "Problem of Evil, Air, and Silence," 152.

> argument that those patterns of suffering be evidence that favors HI over theism.[82]

Hence, for van Inwagen, if the knowledge and experience of pain and suffering in the world cannot serve as evidence against theism, Draper's evidential argument fails.

While van Inwagen is right to cast doubt on the level of confidence one can portray in an evaluation of highly theoretical "possible worlds," and he is also correct to deny the idea that the evidence of pain and suffering in the world somehow serves as positive evidence against theism, there nevertheless appears to be some concern about the success of van Inwagen's approach. First, addressing van Inwagen's own hypothesis of irregularity directly, it is not obvious that God could not prevent at least some terrible suffering without invoking massive irregularity in the world. As Bruce Russell explains,

> Van Inwagen has no adequate response to someone who says that, if God exists, he would be obligated to reduce to some extent the level of terrible suffering that exists in the actual world. Neither the violation of the laws of nature nor the interference with people's freedom that would be required would be so great as to justify God's failing to intervene.[83]

Thus, van Inwagen's approach relies on the idea that the God of theism should be expected to prevent or counteract *all* accounts of evil and suffering in order to be consistent, while a quick rejoinder would claim that God could prevent at least *some* suffering and pain without upsetting the balance of order present in the world to any significant degree. Further, considering the classical understanding of "goodness" as described in this work, it is difficult to see why the "intrinsic or extrinsic good depends on the existence of higher-level sentient creatures" in the world, as van Inwagen suggests. In fact, the goodness of a world does not depend on the existence or non-existence of anything at all (save God himself), and the good of sentient beings is only good insofar as they exist and are created. One cannot judge a world with created beings against a world that has none and come to any value-judgment whatsoever about which is better than the other. Similarly, it is difficult to see why "massive irregularity" in a created world would be a *prima facie* defect in that world (so long as the irregularity in question does not somehow entail a contradiction, which

82. Van Inwagen, "Problem of Evil, Air, and Silence," 161; emphasis in original.

83. Russell, "Defenseless," 201.

it would be effectively impossible for God to create). Insofar as a world with massive irregularity existed and operated as such with evils often or most often overwritten or prevented by God, then that world would be existing and functioning as created and would therefore be "good" in that respect. One can only hold that such a world would be defective if compared to the standard of the present world; if the other world existed, then the present world would be the one that is defective. As such, there is no reason a theist holding to a classical natural theology should have any need to employ a defense along the lines of what van Inwagen suggests.[84]

A FAREWELL TO SKEPTICISM

One final approach to answering the problem of evil that is distinct in significant ways from either a theodicy or a defense is what has come to be known as "skeptical theism." This approach does not attempt to provide direct answers to the problem of evil in the same way as a theodicy or defense, but rather it seeks to show that whatever the answers may be to the problem of evil, there is no reason to think that a finite human intellect would have any reason to know or understand what those answers might be. Per the skeptical theist, "We ought to be skeptical about our ability to make the relevant judgment about whether or not it is likely that there is a justifying reason for the evil we observe."[85] This approach has the advantage of avoiding some of the pitfalls of theodicists and defenders mentioned above while seeming to simply skirt the issue altogether by claiming a blanket ignorance of God's justifying reasons for evil, whatever they may be. Critically, the skeptical theist is able to accept Rowe's second premise that God must have some justifying reason to allow evil, and they are able to deny Rowe's first premise without any

84. Other potential issues exist with van Inwagen's argument, even if taken at face value without invoking classical theology. For Paul Draper's own response to van Inwagen's defense, he proposes a handful of criteria that van Inwagen fails to meet in providing a "story" for the theist to employ as a counterpoint to Draper's formulation: 1) it must be antecedently aprobable given theism, 2) it must be good in the sense of being just as likely or probably given both theism and HI, and 3) it must be "undefeated" or immune to what Draper calls a "counterdefense," which would be a sort of opposite-premise that claims the opposite of the story and turns out to be just as likely as the story itself given the prior conditions of aprobability and goodness. Draper holds that van Inwagen's approach fails in various ways in each of these respects. See Draper, "Skeptical Theist," 175–92.

85. Ganssle and Lee, "Evidential Problems," 22.

evidential support given. As such, per the skeptical theist, God certainly does have reasons that would be sufficient to us if we were in an epistemic position to identify or understand them, but we simply are not in such a position, and the flaw of the problem of evil is that it is trying to make us what we are not. As explained by Rowe himself,

> So, according to the skeptical theist, we simply are in no position to *reasonably judge* that God could have prevented the fawn's five days of terrible suffering without losing some outweighing good or having to permit some equally bad or worse evil. Our limited minds are simply unable to think of the goods that the mind of God would know. And since we are simply unable to know many of the goods God would know, the fact that no good *we know of* can reasonably be thought to justify an infinitely good, all-powerful being in permitting the fawn's terrible suffering is not really surprising.[86]

Here, Rowe refers back to the example of natural evil from his original formulation of the evidential problem of evil—the burning fawn—and illustrates the argument of the skeptical theist in that God's justifying goods are beyond our range of perception and simply stretch the limits of human understanding. In fact, some philosophers hold that the skeptical response has definitively defeated any point to the evidential argument putting forth examples of apparently gratuitous evil altogether: "There is a point worth noting here: the role of apparently pointless evil has lost its importance in the argument from evil. It is admitted that our failure to see the point of certain evils is at least as likely on the theist's hypothesis that there is a reason for it which is beyond our ken as it is on the hypothesis that there is no reason for it."[87] For Russell, the skeptical theist has succeeded in arguing that the apparent gratuity of evil is irrelevant and shifted the argument to a sort of probability calculus that supports the position holding the most evidential support.

In this section, I will focus chiefly on two prominent proponents of theistic skepticism who have advanced just such a position in response to the problem of evil: William Alston and Stephen Wykstra.[88] I will also

86. Rowe, *Philosophy of Religion*, 122.

87. Russell, "Defenseless," 196. Here, Russell is referring to Draper's evidential argument, which relies on the competing hypotheses of theism and any nontheistic position (such as Draper's hypothesis of indifference).

88. The skeptical theistic response is certainly not limited to Wykstra and Alston, though theirs are two of the more prominent voices in defense of this approach. For other philosophers who hold similar views, see Ahern, *Problem of Evil*; Fitzpatrick,

address an argument from Alvin Plantinga in defense of Wykstra, as well as Rowe's response to Plantinga and Rowe's reformulation of the evidential argument as a means to illustrate his own objection and sustain his original argument. I will conclude with my own analysis of the skeptical theistic approach and conclude that skeptical theism does not provide an adequate response to the problem of evil, though it does offer an important lesson of perspective in an evaluation of the problem that should not be neglected by the theist.

Skeptical Theism

William Alston lays the base framework of the skeptical position first by acknowledging the validity of Rowe's second premise of his argument that God must have justifying reasons for the things he does and does not do in regards to the presence of evils that arise in the world. Echoing the view that God holds certain moral obligations toward the creatures he created, Alston argues,

> Any plan that God would implement will include provision for each of us having a life that is, on balance, a good thing, and one in which the person reaches the point of being able to see that his life as a whole is a good for him. . . . So long as the sufferer is amply taken care of, I can't see that this violates any demands of divine justice, compassion, or love.[89]

Here, Alston proposes that God owes to creatures a life that is "on balance a good thing" to anyone able to see it as such, and so long as God is able to do this (even in the midst of ongoing suffering), then he is morally justified in allowing evil in the world. However, Alston explains, the ability to see the overall good of every life is something known only to God. As Alston argues, "It would be exceedingly strange if an omniscient being did not immeasurably exceed our grasp of such matters. Thus there is an unquestionably live possibility that God's reasons for allowing human suffering may have to do, in part, with the appropriate connection of those sufferings with goods in ways that have never been dreamed of in our theodicies."[90] Thus, for Alston, the possibility remains that all

"Onus of Proof," 19–38; and Reichenbach, *Evil and a Good God.*

89. Alston, "Inductive Argument from Evil," 111.

90. Alston, "Inductive Argument from Evil," 109.

instances of evil may be justified in just such a manner that the limited human intellect and perception cannot grasp it.

> Perhaps, unbeknownst to us, one or the other of these bits of suffering is necessary, in ways we cannot grasp, for some outweighing good of a sort with which we are familiar, e.g. supreme fulfillment of one's deepest nature. Or perhaps it is necessary for the realization of a good of which we as yet have no conception. And these possibilities are by no means remote ones.[91]

Toward this end, Alston identifies six categories of human cognitive limits that prevent humans from adjudicating the matter of whether evil exists that God is able to prevent without sacrificing a greater good: lack of data, complexity greater than we can handle, difficulty of determining what is metaphysically possible or necessary, ignorance of the full range of possibilities, ignorance of the full range of values, and limit to our capacity to make well-considered value judgments.[92] Given these inherent limits to human understanding, it should not be surprising to a human observer that a great deal of incongruity and confusion may seem apparent to us in the natural world that all actually have justifying reasons for their existence. As such, per Alston, arguments from evil on the basis of gratuitous evil fail to establish any evidential support for their positions.

Another more extensive explanation of skeptical theism comes from Stephen Wykstra, who characterizes evidential arguments as what he terms "noseeum" arguments. Following from Swinburne, Wykstra builds on the question as to whether a human observer is in a sufficient epistemic position to see some God-justifying reason for evil if such a reason were actually there.[93] Wykstra refers to this as what he calls a "Condition for Reasonable Epistemic Access" (CORNEA). He defines this as follows: "On the basis of cognized situation s, human H is entitle to claim 'It appears that p' only if it is reasonable for H to believe that, given her cognitive faculties and the use she has made of them, if p were not the case, s would likely be different than it is in some way discernable by her."[94] In other words, Wykstra argues, an observer cannot claim that something appears to be the case (such as that there are no

91. Alston, "Inductive Argument from Evil," 109.

92. Alston, "Inductive Argument from Evil," 120.

93. For the original argument that Wykstra means to expound upon in his own skeptical theistic position, see Swinburne, *Existence of God*, 254–55.

94. Wykstra, "Humean Obstacle," 152.

God-justifying reasons for the quantity and severity of evil in the world) unless one has reason to believe that the opposite (that there are in fact God-justifying reasons for evil) would be obvious to the observer given their own cognitive qualities and epistemic position. One cannot claim, for example, that there appear to be no fleas in one's garage because one cannot see them while standing in the driveway; if fleas were there, the observer would not be in a position to see them anyway, so a failure to see fleas from the driveway is not evidence that they are not there, and it does not increase the likelihood that they are not there for the observer. Per Wykstra, the same is true for any justifying goods associated with the evils one discovers in the world—there may be a whole host of goods that are intimately connected with the evils in question in ways humans cannot hope to identify or comprehend, and thus, argues Wykstra, humans are not able to infer that such goods do not arise simply from the fact that they are entirely unknown.

However, a number of objections have arisen against Wykstra's proposal that undercut his basic premise. Rowe, for example, argues that the inference from evidential evil to no justifying goods is still valid because there are a great deal of goods we do recognize in the world—none of which come close to justifying certain extreme instances of suffering.

> For if we divide the possible justifying goods into those that fall within our intellectual grasp and those utterly beyond our ken, and then discover that none of the goods in the first category are justifying for God with respect to such horrendous evils, we significantly lower the likelihood of God's existence. This is particularly so if our antecedent expectations are that the justifying goods are as likely to fall in the first category as in the second.[95]

In other words, if we have no reason to think that the associated goods that justify instances of evil would have to be hidden in some way *by necessity*, then we can be confident that finding no associated goods *at all* (hidden or not) is a valid inference to the fact that they do not exist—or at least this raises the probability that they do not exist and makes such an inference reasonable. Further, Bruce Little argues that particularly egregious acts of evil (such as those most often favored by evidential arguments) are so massive and obvious to the observer that one would expect an outweighing good to be also massive and obvious on a scale that would make a flea look more like an elephant, so to speak. "In addition, it

95. Rowe, "Evidential Argument from Evil," 282.

would seem that if the evil was a really big evil, then in order for the good to outweigh the evil, it too would have to be a rather large good, in which case one wonders how it could be missed."[96] Taking the Holocaust as an example, an act of such immense evil that caused untold suffering on an enormous scale measured in the millions of lives would need a justifying good, equally as impactful (or more so) in a way commensurate to the evils it justifies; given this expectation, the fact that no such obvious goods arose from the imprisonment, torture, and murder of millions of victims is enough to bring one to the reasonable conclusion that those evils were and are entirely unjust and gratuitous. Per Brian Davies, "If we are reasonable in believing anything, we are reasonable in believing that there are instances of evil which are not morally justifiable in terms of good brought about or evil prevented."[97]

In a later formulation of his own CORNEA principle written to shore up some of these weaknesses, Wykstra (largely replying to Rowe's criticism) admitted to "infelicities" in his original argument as he "went for the knock-out punch" by presenting his argument that one could establish with relative certainty that there were "good reasons for thinking" that God's reasons for permitting many evils is beyond our ken. He adopts instead a more modest approach, arguing that any evidence of "noseeum" evil in the world is unsurprising given a theistic context, even if it would be fully expected under an atheistic context. Thus, for Wykstra, the evidence of "noseeum" evil in the world does not help the probability of the atheist's position. He writes,

> Rowe's central objection was that Core Theism gives 'no reason whatever' to think that the goods served by current evils would often be either in the distant future or for some other reason beyond our grasp. I have argued that this is false. Accepting Core Theism greatly increases our reason to think such goods would often be in the distant future; it does give us a great deal more than 'no reason whatever' to think these goods would be 'deep' goods, often beyond our ken.[98]

Here, Wykstra shifts his focus to more of a probability argument with the intent of showing that the absence of concomitant goods is "unsurprising" given theism and thus offers little in evidential support for atheism.

96. Little, *God, Why This Evil?"*, 65.

97. Davies, *Reality of God*, 157.

98. Wykstra, "Rowe's Noseeum," 145.

Further, others have argued that unexplained evil is actually what theism would predict and expect if it were true, and thus evil in this respect actually offers support for theism. "The existence of some evil that cannot be fully explained is just what we should expect if theism were true."[99]

However, Rowe once again criticizes Wykstra by pointing out that the mere assertion of God's existence does not itself entail that goods beyond our ken of which only God is aware necessarily obtain and remain unknown to us.

> But the mere assumption that [God] exists gives us no reason whatever to suppose *either* that the greater good in virtue of which he permits most sufferings are goods that come into existence far in the future of the sufferings we are aware of, *or* that once they do obtain we continue to be ignorant of them and their relation to the sufferings.[100]

Thus, Rowe here identifies a critical flaw in Wykstra's approach—simply that God's existence does not itself imply that his justifying goods should be unknown or remain hidden, and thus the inference to atheism on the basis of gratuitous evil remains valid. Per Rowe, "So I conclude, contrary to Wykstra, that the mere hypothesis of [God]'s existence gives us no good reason to think that things would appear to us just as they do so far as the sufferings of animals and humans in our world are concerned."[101] In order to defend his argument from Rowe's criticism, Wykstra would need to explain how theism somehow necessitates or implies that human observers of suffering in the world should remain largely ignorant of God's justifying goods.[102]

In defense of Wykstra, Plantinga emphasizes the assumption that God's justifying reasons must be known by humans in order to be valid. In evaluating Rowe's claim that "many cases of evil are apparently pointless," Plantinga considers what this could mean:

> But how shall we understand Rowe here? Shall we see him as holding that in fact there are many cases of evil such that it is apparent that an omnipotent and omniscient God, if he existed, would not have a reason for permitting them? But this is much

99. Ganssle and Lee, "Evidential Problems of Evil," 19.

100. Rowe, "Evil and the Theistic Hypothesis," 164–65.

101. Rowe, "Evil and the Theistic Hypothesis," 165.

102. For more on various objections to Wykstra's CORNEA argument and a critical evaluation of his argument in light of his ongoing interactions with Rowe, see Trakakis, *God Beyond Belief*, 77–124.

> too strong; as Stephen Wykstra points out, we could sensibly claim something like this only if we had reason to think that if such a God did have a reason for permitting such evils, we would be likely to have some insight into what it is. But if theism is true, then this is false; from the theistic perspective there is little or no reason to think that God would have a reason for a particular evil state of affairs only if we had a pretty good idea of what [that] reason might be. On the theistic conception our cognitive powers, as opposed to God's, are a bit slim for that. God might have reasons we cannot so much as understand; he might have reasons involving other free creatures—angels, devils, the principalities and powers of which St. Paul speaks—of which we have no knowledge.[103]

Thus, like Wykstra, Plantinga stresses the epistemic limits of human perception as a critical element in the evaluation of evidential arguments, though God's justifying reasons would have no need for consideration of human cognitive limitations as a condition of their own validity. Rowe, however, readily admits that he does not mean to communicate epistemic certainty with his claim: "And what I'm saying about certain evils is that there is something about them and the situation in which they occur that makes it reasonable for us to believe that they are pointless."[104] For Rowe, similar to a theistic defense, it is enough that the inference is reasonable in order to sustain his evidential argument—not that he has conveyed a level of certainty that escapes the mere possibilities that arise when considering the skeptical theists' response. As such, Rowe modifies his argument to a position of inference to illustrate this emphasis and avoid Plantinga's critique. He organizes his new argument as follows (taking E1 and E2 to represent particularly heinous evidential examples of evil that appear to have no justifying goods):

> P: No good state of affairs we know of is such that an omnipotent, omniscient being's obtaining it would morally justify that being's permitting El or E2.
>
> Q: No good state of affairs is such that an omnipotent, omniscient being's obtaining it would morally justify that being in permitting El or E2.[105]

103. Plantinga, "Epistemic Probability and Evil," 73.
104. Rowe, "Ruminations About Evil," 71–72.
105. Rowe, "Ruminations About Evil," 72.

Rowe's new approach becomes one of an inference from the entirely human perspective of P to the conclusion about God and his motives in Q. In defense of his inference, Rowe argues:

> For the question can be raised: How can we have confidence in this inference unless we have a good reason to think that were a good to have J it would likely be a good within our ken? My answer is that we are justified in making this inference in the same way we are justified in making the many inferences we constantly make from the known to the unknown. All of us are constantly inferring from the A's we know of to the A's we don't know of. If we observe many A's and note that all of them are B's we are justified in believing that the A's we haven't observed are also B's. Of course, these inferences may be defeated. We may find some independent reason to think that if an A were not a B it would likely not be among the A's we have observed. But to claim that we cannot be justified in making such inferences unless we already know, or have good reason to believe, that were an A not to be a B it would likely be among the A's we've observed is simply to encourage radical skepticism concerning inductive reasoning in general.[106]

Thus for Rowe, absent any defeaters, his inference is valid for the same reason humans often go about making similar inferences, and unless the entire practice of inference is to be abandoned, the inference to God's likely non-existence is valid given the evidence of evil in the world. "Until we are provided with some reasons for thinking that if there were an omnipotent, omniscient, wholly good being who created our world, then the goods in virtue of which he permits El and E2 would be undetectable by us, we certainly are within our rights to infer Q from P and conclude that it is likely that there is no such being."[107] As such, the position of the skeptical theist appears to have achieved at best a stalemate in the evidential argument from evil, though given Rowe's weaker argument, it seems that the bar he sets rises above the range of the skeptical theist, who must now deny Rowe even the inference of no justifying goods on the basis of human ignorance of those goods, which is more difficult to achieve.

106. Rowe, "Ruminations About Evil," 73.

107. Rowe, "Ruminations About Evil," 79.

A Critique of Skeptical Theism

There is much to be commended of the position of skeptical theism. First, it avoids the practice of theodicy altogether and rather embraces the unfathomable and unknowable ways of God as a critical aspect of the theistic response to the problem of evil. Given the classical view of God and his nature and attributes, it should be unsurprising that a comprehensive understanding of the infinite, omniscient creator of the universe (which arguments from evil seem to demand) would rise well above the cognitive limits of finite human creatures. As such, if direct access to the divine councils of God truly lies beyond the reach of human epistemic limits (which most theists readily admit), then one should be willing to embrace these limitations and evaluate any challenges against God and his nature accordingly. Whatever arguments purport to contradict what can clearly be known of God through our observation of the natural world on the basis of a lack of epistemic access to the knowledge and councils of God should be treated with a healthy dose of suspicion and skepticism. Likewise, there is much that *can* be known and deduced about God from a knowledge of his effects in the world with a certain level of confidence that serves at least as much importance in an evaluation of the problem of evil as the evidential support for the evil itself. In other words, one need not know the actual explanation of evil to know that it is fully explained on the basis of what can be known of God and his nature and attributes.

However, theistic skepticism falls short of a sufficient resolution to the problem of evil for a few important reasons. First, it does not explain how some evils *can* or *could* be morally justified by the one who arranges things in such a way to bring about those evils (or one with the power but not the will to prevent them). Davies observes, "We may not know how things fit together as God does, but we can be pretty sure when someone is in agony, and we can sensibly resist the suggestion that anyone (even God) is morally justifiable for *arranging* this, however it fits in with the entire history of the universe (whatever that is and regardless of our ignorance concerning it)."[108] The skeptical theist generally holds that God—on account of his perfect goodness—must have a moral justification for every evil that occurs, even if that justification remains unknown to the theist. Thus, it is difficult to see how the skeptical theist resolves the moral dilemma that befalls other greater-good theodicies by arguing that God therefore arranges things in such a fashion that brings

108. Davies, *Reality of God*, 133.

about horrendous evils *on account of* achieving goods for other beings (or creation as a whole) as if the goods achieved are the ends and the evils the means. Adopting such a view leads to a range of unpalatable conclusions about God and the nature of morality that do not fit well with basic human moral proclivities.[109]

Further, such an approach raises additional concerns regarding whether a human observer of evils in the world should interfere with evil that occurs if God means to use those evils for some good purpose that the human cannot see or know. Bruce Russell presents such a case study where neither God nor a human onlooker intervenes in a brutal rape and murder:

> The question at issue is whether we must be unable to judge that there are no *justifying* reasons for human nonintervention if we are unable to judge that there are none for Divine nonintervention. I have argued that we must. Moral skepticism about God's omissions entails moral skepticism about our own omissions.[110]

As Russell observes, if I am skeptical about God's reasons for permitting some instance of evil that I observe, it seems to follow that I should also be skeptical about my own reasons for intervening to prevent that evil, for each set of reasons would seem to be grounded in the same assumption—that all evil that arises in a theistic world is necessarily justified in a moral sense on account of the good it brings about, even if I have no direct knowledge of what those goods could possibly be. For example, if I see a child stepping out into traffic and about to be crushed by a bus, given the skeptical theist's reasoning, I should also be skeptical about whether I should reach out and pull the child back, lest I unintentionally thwart God's efforts to bring about some unknown good from the child's death.

109. This particular critique of skeptical theism focuses on the general assumption by the skeptical theist that is akin to other greater-good theodicies in that God is a type of *moral being* who must have a moral justification for the things he does and does not do in the face of the evil that arises in the world. If the skeptical theist were to affirm that God (on account of his divine nature and attributes) is in no need of any such justification, then this critique would be avoided. However, without any need for a moral justification for God's actions, it is difficult to see what sort of skepticism the theist is expected to have that would advance a resolution to the problem of evil. However, I am sympathetic to the skeptical theist's position, and I will adopt a similar approach to a general theistic skepticism in chapter eight below toward a resolution of a new approach to the problem of evil, which takes what can be known of God through natural theology and applies that as a *prima facie* reason to hold that all evil is necessarily explained in a universe created by God—even if God is in no need of a moral justification for that evil.

110. Russell, "Defenseless," 198.

Ganssle and Lee argue that this sort of skepticism only applies when considering whether *others* have cause or not to stop some instance of evil and does not apply when considering whether I myself have cause. "This objection rests on a confusion. Being in doubt whether here exists a good reason for someone else's nonintervention is not the same as positively *having* a good reason for nonintervention."[111] However, the point of the skeptical theist's argument in the first place is that a theist can remain confident that God in fact *does* have justifying moral reasons for every evil observed—even if those reasons are entirely unknown or beyond our ken. This commits the theist to hold that literally *every* instance of evil—no matter how horrendous—has an unknown or even unimaginable associated greater good that depends on that evil, and as such any evil is always a means to a greater good, which is exactly what justifies God in allowing some evil to go on unimpeded. Thus, for the theist, the child stepping out into traffic certainly has a justifying reason for his pending demise, and by extension, anyone who interfered with that course of events would be acting against the greater good that God intends for this instance of evil to facilitate. It becomes problematic for the skeptical theist to conclude that the goods associated with evil should be treated with skepticism while any efforts to prevent or mitigate evil should not. In short, if God does not want to prevent some horrific evil from occurring for some reason only he knows, then neither should we. The central point here is that it is not enough for the skeptical theist to simply say that one cannot or does not know God's reasons for allowing horrific evils—the skeptical theist must also affirm that such a justification does in fact exist in the realm of what is unknown *to the human observer* and as such, in order for evil to be sufficiently justified for God to allow it, some greater good—even if unknown—must necessarily arise. As such, the skeptical theist would seem to have a *prima facie* reason to allow evil in the same way God apparently does (not to directly "cause" evil necessarily but at least to avoid intervening to prevent or reduce it). The consistent skeptical theist, therefore, in this situation must find himself in the precarious position of either doubting theism altogether or allowing the child to be crushed.[112]

111. Ganssle and Lee, "Evidential Problems of Evil," 25.

112. Another factor that plays a relevant role in this particular critique is that of a human's moral obligations to stop or reduce such evil whenever it is possible to do so. One could argue, for example, that God has commanded humans to act in defense of a child that is about to be crushed by a bus, and thus the human should not consider any divine reasons at all in their decision to act in defense of the child. However, this approach seems to deny the very premise that the skeptical theist relies upon in the first

Another concern for skeptical theism is the inherent danger in utilizing a position of blanket skepticism (or literally the absence of evidence) as the basis for a resolution to evidential arguments. If one relies primarily on what is indirectly unknown or unseen (such as God's divine reasons for allowing evil) as the basis for a critique of what can be attested by direct evidence (that horrendous and gratuitous evils apparently occur *en masse*), then one is in the precarious position of denying evidence on the basis of non-evidence. In order to respond to the actual evidence of gratuitous evil in the world, it would seem that one would require at least some contrary evidence of their own that the evil is not actually gratuitous to resolve the issue at hand. Appealing to what simply cannot be known or seen as an explanation of what is known or seen is actually no explanation at all. As Draper argues, "Indeed, the skeptical claim that we can't directly assess the probability of there being such a reason [for God to permit evil] sounds more like an admission that theism is doomed to explanatory inferiority than like a powerful retort."[113] Given this, the skeptical theist must at some point strive to overcome his skepticism in order to draw at least some reasonable conclusions about God from what can be known as a basis for arguing that the unseen is necessarily there. For example, one could begin with a position of natural theology and demonstrate that God exists and is necessarily perfectly good, and thus all evil is necessarily explained in a theistic universe so long as it does not entail a contradiction. However, this is not the typical approach of skeptical theism, which relies instead on the fact that humans simply lack the epistemic vantage point to recognize and identify the goods that justify evils. In order to utilize this approach, one must first establish with certainty how one can know that the unknown goods actually do occur. As Mark Scott explains, the theist must remain committed to reason:

> Theodicy cheats if it begins by playing by the rules of reason only to discard them once the going gets tough intellectually, once it comes up against evils that do not fit neatly into its theoretical system. The appeal to mystery, then, obfuscates the

place to argue that God is morally justified in allowing the child's death—that God's own moral obligations are excused on account of the good that comes from such a tragedy, and thus it would seem—if one is consistent—that the human's moral obligations (as given by God) are excused as well. For more on this particular critique of skeptical theism (as well as an interesting additional claim that skeptical theism also undercuts teleological theistic arguments), see Sehon, "Problem of Evil," 67–80.

113. Draper, "Skeptical Theist," 178.

> problem rather than illuminates it. It defers the problem of evil rather than solves it with the intellectual tools at its disposal.[114]

For Scott, when faced with an objection like the problem of evil, one must not abandon the tools of reason and turn to some sense of imaginative speculation regarding what *cannot be known* rather than seeking conclusions based on what *can be known*. Whatever conclusions can be drawn from reason must form the basis for a reply to the problem of evil. Thus, for both theist and non-theist alike, one must rely on the evidence available to support one's conclusions.

> Similarly, once we have conducted the relevant search for moral reasons to justify allowing the relevant suffering (thinking hard about how allowing the suffering would be needed to realize sufficiently weighty goods, reading and talking to others who have thought about the same problem), we are justified in believing that there are no morally sufficient reasons for allowing that suffering.[115]

As Russell explains, after some consideration of the matter, it is reasonable to draw conclusions about what one observes in the natural world regarding evil and its causes and to hold those conclusions with some level of confidence. Thus, a position of general uncertainty or blanket skepticism invoked *without a sufficient evidential or philosophical basis* toward a resolution of the problem of evil is an inferior position to conclusions one can draw from a basis of sound philosophical reasoning (such as a process of natural theology, for example).[116]

114. Scott, *Pathways*, 207.

115. Russell, "Defenseless," 197.

116. Most skeptical theists seem to take an approach more akin to a *defense* by simply arguing that it is *possible* that God's reasons are obscured from the human perspective, and so long as this were the case, then the evidential problem of evil would be unable to conclude that gratuitous evil actually occurs. What is most often lacking from such an approach, in my view, is any *prima facie* reason why such goods should be concealed in the first place or how one can be confident that these unseen goods actually exist given what is known of God and his nature and attributes. Were the skeptical theist to ground their assumptions regarding God's reasons for evil or the good that necessarily follows from evil in prior philosophical reasoning regarding God's nature and attributes, I will concede that this particular criticism would be avoided. However, such a process would hardly be "skeptical" in its strictest sense if one begins with what is clearly known (as with a process of natural theology).

GOD AND GRATUITOUS EVIL

After considering the various ways that theists have attempted to resolve the evidential problem of evil on account of denying Rowe's first premise (regarding the existence of gratuitous evil), I will conclude this chapter with a look at vulnerabilities in Rowe's second premise instead (regarding God's obligations to prevent gratuitous evil whenever possible). Such an approach has a number of advantages for the theist, such as the freedom to readily affirm that what is evil truly is evil and may even in some cases be genuinely gratuitous. This approach, however, is not without its own challenges—namely, it seems to go against the theist's natural instincts as to how one might expect a perfectly good, loving God to behave toward creatures that live in a world he has created. Here, I will examine a method of denying God's obligations toward gratuitous evil while maintaining a sense of God's perfect goodness that transcends the bounds of human morality.

As stated, the evidential problem of evil poses a challenge to theism on the basis of instances of evil identified in the world that appear to have no concomitant greater good associated with them—in other words, the existence of *gratuitous evil.* Therefore, as Rowe defines it, let "gratuitous evil" refer to any evil that God could have prevented without sacrificing a greater good or preventing a greater evil, and let "God" represent the omniscient, omnipotent, perfectly good creator of the universe in terms of the approach to natural theology and classical theism discussed in this work. Given this, the most common approach to the evidential problem of evil can be simply restated in the following *modus tollens* syllogism:

(1) Gratuitous evil exists.

(2) If God exists, gratuitous evil does not exist.

(3) Therefore, God does not exist.[117]

The most common response from theists to this particular argument is a generally assumed acceptance of (2), which necessitates a denial of (1) in order to avoid the conclusion. In order to deny (1), theists most often seek to develop a theodicy or defense that explains how evil that appears to be gratuitous has actually facilitated a greater good or prevented a

117. While it is more standard in a *modus tollens* syllogism to begin with the conditional premise followed by the negation of the consequent in the second premise, I have structured this simplified argument in this manner so that each numbered premise corresponds more closely with Rowe's original evidential argument.

greater evil, thereby justifying God in his refusal to intervene or prevent the instance of evil in question. However, as I have previously argued in this chapter, the prospects of theodicies and defenses presented in defense of theism have been largely unsatisfying and leave the problem of evil unresolved. Further, the approach of the skeptical theist that argues for the general epistemic impotence of a human to be able to adequately identify an instance of gratuitous evil in the world (a denial of (1) from an epistemic standpoint) seems to struggle as less of an explanation of evil and more of a lack of explanation.

As I have formerly argued, no example of theodicy of which I am aware adequately achieves the level of confidence and widespread acceptance necessary to categorically deny the truth of (1). Swinburne's greater good theodicy, for example, fails to adequately explain how the existence of evil is required for creatures to gain a proper knowledge of evil, and he also fails to establish sufficient cause to think that the limited good of human freedom (benefitting humans specifically) would be sufficient to justify the wide range of suffering and evil experienced by other sentient non-human creatures. Further, his own view of God represents a misguided view of divine personhood that seems alien to the God of classical theism. Hick's soul-making theodicy likewise fails to address a wide range of evils experienced in the world that seem to have little impact on developing the moral character of sentient creatures, and it also exacerbates God's supposed moral failures by suggesting that he wills evil itself as a means to an end; as such, it would seem that evil should be something celebrated and even arguably encouraged. Thus, it is difficult to see how any moral being could be justified in using evil in a manner such as Hick suggests. Further, eschatological theodicies fail to address how the distant future goods of the beatific vision or the seemingly unconnected goods of divine relationship in the present world can sufficiently justify the evils experienced by creatures—especially since the beatific vision or a perfect divine relationship could be achieved just as well without any evil at all.

The prospect of "defenses" (as opposed to theodicies) seems equally grim as a means to resolve evidential arguments from evil. Plantinga's free will defense presents a confusion between God's causal activity and creaturely freedom such that the range of options available to God are somehow limited upon the creation of free creatures. Plantinga's position on freedom implies that God is a part of the system he is causing to be and that genuine freedom requires a certain range of divine inactivity that

that does not appear to be the case (at least in terms of classical theology). Further, Plantinga seems to confuse absolute and suppositional necessity in the sense that God is said to be beholden to the world as it is because he could not have done better (with less evil, for example) out of an absolute necessity, but this depends on the level of freedom (or creaturely ignorance of the highest goods) instantiated in the present world, which God could not have been necessitated to choose. Either way, Plantinga's argument encounters difficulties when posed as a resolution to the evidential problem of evil. Considering van Inwagen's irregularity defense, it is not obvious that God could not have prevented at least some evil in the world without upsetting the regularity of the natural world to any significant degree, and it is not obvious why the goodness of the created world should depend on the existence of free creatures in the way van Inwagen's argument requires.

Finally, the offer of skeptical theism (as per Stephen Wykstra, Robert Alston, and others) raises the question of skepticism to an unpalatable level in consideration of other aspects of theism that would naturally follow from adopting such an approach as a solution to the problem of evil—such as skepticism surrounding a human's obligations toward the evils that arise in the world and skepticism regarding other widely-accepted theistic claims that seem to follow from their argument. Further, it is difficult to base any conclusions on an account of one's judgments about observations in the present world that are entirely unknown and unknowable.

Considering the problems associated with these various theodicies and defenses in light of classical theism, it seems prudent to consider the possibility that a resolution to the evidential problem of evil rests instead on the denial of (2). The question that follows is what additional conclusions or problems may arise for theism if gratuitous evil is affirmed as a real possibility in a world created by God. Plantinga, addressing specifically the probabilistic problem of evil and taking a position akin to the skeptical theist, poses just such a question:

> Clearly, the crucial problem for this probabilistic argument from evil is just that nothing much follows from the fact that some evils are inscrutable; if theism is true we would expect that there would be inscrutable evil. Indeed, a little reflection shows there is no reason to think we could so much as grasp God's plans here, even if he proposed to divulge them to us. But then

> the fact that there is inscrutable evil does not make it improbable that God exists.[118]

Here, Plantinga asks whether anything follows from the existence of inscrutable evil (or some instance of evil such that humans cannot discover or even imagine a justifying greater good). While not the same as gratuitous evil *per se*, the question is just as relevant when considering (1) as to what exactly follows from the fact that gratuitous (or inscrutable) evil exists. If one accepts both premises (1) and (2), then it follows necessarily that God likely does not exist, but if (2) is mistaken and God is under no obligation to prevent instances of gratuitous evil from occurring, then it is possible that gratuitous evil could exist in a world created by God.

The Reality of Gratuitous Evil

Due to the relative weaknesses of theistic attempts to discredit Rowe's (1), I am sympathetic to other theistic attempts to resolve the problem of evil on the basis of a denial of (2), such as those offered by theistic philosophers I have addressed above, including Herbert McCabe, Brian Davies, and Bruce Little. Given the understanding of God as *ipsum esse subsistens* from a position of natural theology, it is evident that God stands under no *moral obligation* toward the world he creates and the creatures it inhabits beyond what God himself freely and independently chooses (in a suppositional sense) given the creation he does in fact actualize—though never of any *absolute* necessity on account of some *a priori* requirement of his own perfect goodness. God is obliged on account of his nature to create only what has "being" and is therefore "good" metaphysically speaking, though this would not prevent him from creating good things that are not as good as they could be—such as creatures who do not yet fulfill or embody the full potential of their created natures (creatures in a state of privation, for example). Hence evil can rightly exist in a world created by God and, by extension, even evil without any moral justification for its existence. God has no obligation on account of his nature to allow evil only when it is necessary for the achievement of some greater good (or preventing some greater evil), and as such, gratuitous evil is also possible in a world created by God.[119]

118. Plantinga, "Epistemic Probability and Evil," 75–76.

119. This does not of course mean that God cannot or does not bring good out of evil or use at least some evil as a means toward a greater good. In fact, Christian

Further, the classical view of God described in this work denies that God is a moral being at all—at least in the same way that creatures are considered moral beings. It seems to me that God holds no moral duties and obligations in the same way creatures do, and thus God acts freely and can actualize any world he wants—even one "inferior" in a sense to other theoretically possible worlds that may contain more goods or less evils—so long as the world he actualizes has "being" and is therefore good on the whole.[120] Whatever God creates in such a world, he does so freely, and the sorts of things he makes and the natures they may possess are all made by God in whatever fashion he may choose—including the capacity to perform and experience evil in the world they inhabit. The creation of such a world does not place God under a new relationship or other sort of moral obligation to the good and well-being of the sorts of creatures he has chosen to create. Rather, God is only suppositionally necessitated to the existence of things to which he has already granted existence in exactly the fashion and nature of the things that they are (once again, as designed and decreed by God himself). He does not owe to creation a perfection of natures that would preclude the possibility of defect or privation. Thus, evil can and does occur in the actual world, and the sorts of evils that do occur could be gratuitous without threatening the omnipotence, omniscience, or perfect goodness of God.

Still, one may argue that these ideas (as defended by philosophers like Davies and McCabe) are mistaken and that the God of classical theism is in fact described in such a fashion that would place him under a moral obligation of sorts to prevent gratuitous evil—even if only suppositionally. For example, the capacity to sin belongs to creatures due

theology holds that God does at times incorporate evil acts and purposes into his divine plan and for his own good purposes. Further, it may even be true that God does in fact bring good out of evil in many disparate circumstances. The point I am making here, however, is that God is not *obligated* to do so in a moral sense (or in any necessary sense required by his divine nature and perfect goodness). Whenever God incorporates the evil acts of creatures into his divine plan or brings good out of evil when it occurs, it is because he freely chooses to do so—often as a demonstration of his compassion, grace, and provision for his people, though never because he was somehow necessarily constrained to do so on account of his moral perfection.

120. When I say that creation must be "good on the whole," I do not mean that it must contain more good than evil or that it would have some sort of appropriate balance of good and evil that would justify God in permitting the quantity and prevalence of evil in the world. Rather, I mean "good" in the metaphysical sense as that which is synonymous with the "being" or existence granted by God. A world is "good on the whole," therefore, when it has being and contains things that exist and persist in a sense of suppositional necessity as the sorts of things they are.

to their lack of sight of the proper goods they seek by nature, thus God cannot sin.

> And sin as we properly speak of it in moral matters, and as it has the nature of moral wrong, comes about because the will by tending toward an improper end fails to attain its proper end. And in the case of God, the causal source cannot be deficient, since his power is infinite, nor can his will fail to attain its proper end, since his very will, which is also his nature, is the supreme goodness that is the final end and first rule of all wills. And so his will by nature adheres to, and cannot defect from, the supreme good, just as the natural appetites of things cannot fail to seek their natural good. Therefore, God cannot cause sin because he himself sins.[121]

Here, Aquinas illustrates that God's will cannot fail to achieve its proper end, and God's perfection precludes any possibility of failure or deficit in his acts, and thus God cannot fail in the same way creatures fail to achieve their own proper ends due to deficiencies in their own finite perceptions. However, one may argue that this seems to be precisely the point of the problem of evil in the first place. God, by definition, cannot "sin" as per classical theism; thus, any evidence that seems to indicate a sin (or moral failure) on the part of God becomes evidence against the existence of such a being. In fact, I do agree that this is a possible path available to the non-theist to revive the problem of evil in light of the view of God I have thus far endorsed. If one could demonstrate through some sort of evidential demonstration that God has in fact "sinned" in a way that his own divine nature and perfect goodness precludes, then one would have grounds to doubt that such a being was in fact the God of classical theism. However, this could not be accomplished as easily as identifying gratuitous evil in the world. A "divine sin" would necessarily involve a great deal more to count for such an argument. For instance, one may propose some instance where an act of God has failed to choose the good of his own being as its proper end in favor of some lesser or counterfeit good. As such, in order to identify such an instance, one would have to have some insight into the divine mind or explain why some act of God (or effect created by him) failed to achieve his own proper ends or was somehow directed toward a lesser good other than the good of God's own perfect nature and being (or even perhaps some act or end directed toward evil as an end in itself). Such a task would be admittedly difficult

121. Aquinas, *On Evil*, 143–44.

to achieve, and I cannot begin to imagine how it could be accomplished or what it would look like, though it is a possibility open to the non-theist and would, if successful, present a valid argument against God's existence.

Resolving Rowe's Evidential Argument

Considering Rowe's evidential argument in light of the foregoing analysis, one must dispute at least one of Rowe's premises in order to defeat his evidential problem of evil. Keep in mind, of course, that Rowe is not seeking a deductive logical argument meant to achieve absolute certainty; he instead presents a process of inductive reasoning, where the weight of evidence is said to favor atheism over theism. Hence, Rowe does not believe that he can sufficiently *prove* the truth of his premises beyond a reasonable doubt, though his argument does still depend on the success of his premises to make his evidence persuasive. Rowe holds that God's moral obligation to prevent gratuitous evil can be taken for granted, and the evidence in favor of gratuitous evil is greater than its negation—thus, for Rowe, the evidence in favor of God's nonexistence is also greater than its negation. As we have seen, however, given the perspective of natural theology developed in this work as applied to Rowe's evidential argument, it is evident that Rowe's second premise ("An omniscient, wholly good being would prevent the occurrence of any intense suffering it could, unless it could not do so without thereby losing some greater good or permitting some evil equally bad or worse") is false. Given the view of classical theism, I have advocated (as derived from a particular focus on a Thomistic natural theology), there is no reason to think that God would always prevent gratuitous suffering. It is clear that God would not cause such suffering directly as an end in itself, but there is no reason to think that any suffering that occurred as a result of the operation of the natural world—however gratuitous it may be—should be such that the perfectly good God of classical theism would prevent it if he was able to do so. This does not mean that God is a moral monster or that he has morally failed in some way. In fact, it means that God has upheld the creation he has made according to its own natural order and that it is functioning precisely as intended.[122] If evil and suffering are the occasional byproduct of a good

122. By claiming the world "functions as intended," I do not mean to imply that God has made the world *for the purpose of* bringing about suffering and pain and that the world functions "as intended" in this respect—that would be something more akin to God seeking evil as an end in itself, which is something God cannot do. Rather, God

creation that was created by God and directed toward him and his goodness as its proper end, then the evil experienced and witnessed in such a world would not be evil as an end in itself, and God would not be violating any principles consistent with his divine nature. As such, evil could exist and persist without any "greater good" associated with it in the way Rowe's argument demands, and thus Rowe's argument is resolved.

Resolving Draper's Evidential Argument

Further, in consideration of Paul Draper's approach to an evidential argument from evil, Draper suggests that his alternative hypothesis must be *serious* and it must *explain* the data better than the alternative. He defines these requirements as such:

> Specifically, one hypothesis is a 'serious' alternative to another only if (i) it is not *ad hoc*—the facts to be explained are not arbitrarily built into it—and (ii) it is at least as plausible initially as the other hypothesis. And one hypothesis "explains" certain facts much better than another if those facts are much more to be expected or much less surprising (in the epistemic sense) on the one hypothesis than on the other.[123]

However, given my analysis and the view of God presented as *ipsum esse subsistens*, Draper's alternative non-theistic hypothesis (HI) does not meet the criteria he prescribed. First, the plausibility of Draper's "indifferent creator" is questionable when compared to the explanatory scope and plausibility of an understanding of classical theism developed through natural theology starting from our observations of the natural world and reasoning from effect to cause.[124] Further, it is difficult to see what facts

created the world for certain good purposes that theists have proposed (such as to display his majesty, for example), which always conclude in the goodness of his own being, and the evil and suffering that results from such a world are a byproduct of its natural operation and the acts and wills of the creatures it contains. In this sense, it "functions as intended" by accomplishing his divine purposes for his creation while also resulting in instances of evil as the natural world and its creatures interact with one another.

123. Draper, "Probabilistic Arguments," 316.

124. Of course, the general plausibility of theism is widely debated and not widely accepted among philosophers of religion once arguments for and against its veracity are considered. However, I mean to address here what Draper himself refers to as the initial condition of his own HI. As such, Plantinga clarifies Draper's plausibility requirement: "How are we to understand 'plausibility' here? I think Draper means to abstract from specific epistemic situations: the plausibility of a hypothesis depends not on considerations such as the specific evidence (propositional and non-propositional) I may

about the world (if any) could be said to be "more expected" or "less surprising" when compared to theism—particularly if God stands under no moral obligation to behave in a certain way that humans would be able to predict or prescribe in his actions. As such, unless Draper means to offer evidence of things God literally cannot do (such as logical contradictions) or instances where God has directly lied or failed to do what he promises, then any other attempt at "predicting" God's behavior would be inherently futile. Gratuitous evil, for example, is not good evidence for HI over theism.

Peter van Inwagen offers an additional path open to the theist in resolving Draper's argument: "If one could successfully argue that one simply could not know whether to expect patterns of suffering like those contained in the actual world in a world created by an omniscient, omnipotent, and morally perfect being, this would refute the evidentialist's case for the thesis that there is a *prima facie* reason for preferring HI to theism."[125] As such, I believe that the approach to natural theology I have endorsed accomplishes exactly this. Specifically, as with the analysis of Rowe's argument above, the accepted possibility of gratuitous evil in a world created by God—which is no more likely to include gratuitous evil or not given theism—resolves any probabilistic weight that gratuitous evil may offer between Draper's alternative non-theistic hypothesis and theism itself. Much like Rowe, Draper argues, "Since God is morally perfect, He would have good moral reasons for producing pleasure even

---

have for or against it (else HI might not be nearly as plausible, for me, as theism), but on more general considerations such as its scope, how it fits in with what is generally known, and the like." (Plantinga, "On Being Evidentially Challenged," 247.) Thus, as Plantinga explains, the explanatory scope and how it addresses the facts of the known world seem to make classical theism more plausible *on its surface* than Draper's HI—at least without a great deal of additional explanatory effort on Draper's part than what he has provided thus far in favor of HI.

125. Van Inwagen, "Problem of Evil, Air, and Silence," 155. In his analysis of Draper, van Inwagen offers additional methods open to the theist as well: "The theist may argue that S is much more surprising, given HI, than one might suppose. The theist may argue that S is much less surprising, given theism, than one might suppose. The theist may argue that there are reasons for preferring theism to HI that outweigh the prima facie reason for preferring HI to theism that we have provided." (Van Inwagen, "Problem of Evil, Air, and Silence," 153–54.) In my view, the existence of gratuitous evil is certainly less "surprising" on theism than originally thought, and there are certainly reasons for preferring theism to HI that outweigh a preference for HI over theism—mainly those provided in a method of theistic argument and natural theology such as what I have presented in this work. Thus, considering additional paths toward a resolution and barring any additional work from Draper to shore up these difficulties in his presentation, I hold that Draper's evidential argument has been sufficiently resolved in favor of theism.

if it is never biologically useful, and He would not permit pain unless He had, not just a biological reason, but also a morally sufficient reason to do so."[126] Here, Draper presents a case for God's moral obligations in that he means to discredit God on moral grounds with his probabilistic evidential argument that holds God to be morally indebted to his creation in a sense that pain should be minimized as much as possible. By identifying gratuitous pain and suffering, therefore, Draper has provided evidence in favor of HI over theism, which he believes shifts the weight of probability to his non-theistic hypothesis over theism.

However, once again, the God of classical theism is not a moral being beholden to providing a certain life (of sufficient goodness and pleasure that outweigh the pain or suffering one may experience, for example) to creatures he creates. He loses no amount of goodness in his own nature if the world he creates occasionally results in bouts of unjust evil and suffering faced by its inhabitants. Thus, in the analysis of Draper's probabilistic argument, God would need no "good moral reasons" for doing what he does or not doing what he does not do. As such, any evidence of evil that seems to be unjust or gratuitous in the world offers nothing in weight of probability favoring Draper's HI or theism. The existence of gratuitous evil becomes meaningless in the probability calculus that Draper's argument requires, and it is therefore entirely beside the point in any debate over the existence of God on that basis.

What, then, can be said of God and gratuitous evil? If gratuitous evil can (and likely does) exist in the world, how does this fit with the perfectly good, loving, compassionate God that is so often espoused by theists? It is to these questions that I turn in chapter eight.

126. Draper, "Pain and Pleasure," 336.

8

The Problem That Persists

In the foregoing chapters, I have illustrated how a careful examination of the nature of God (by way of a largely Thomistic natural theology) can help to resolve the evidential challenge of the problem of evil. If God is not a moral being in the same way that creatures are moral beings (holding to certain moral duties and obligations toward other created beings), then there is no reason to think that God must prevent gratuitous evil whenever he is able to do so, and thus the evidence of gratuitous evil in the world provides no support for God's nonexistence. If the position I have defended is correct, then the challenge that gratuitous evil poses to the possibility of God's existence in the actual world has been sufficiently resolved.

To this point, the evidential problem of evil has been considered largely from a *macro perspective*—as an argument that proceeds by a process of inference from individual examples of evil to a set of universal implications that follow as applied to reality as a whole. Of course, this is generally the aim of evidential arguments in the first place (and many other philosophical arguments as well, for that matter)—to discover truths about reality as a whole (such as the existence of God) on the basis of one's observations and discoveries about the natural world. Therefore, since a proper understanding of God's existence and nature (as gained from natural theology) reveals that gratuitous evil stands in no contradiction with God's existence, then the problem of evil (as a means of denying God's existence) is robbed of its persuasive potential.

However, I will now propose a modified argument from evil designed to survive the foregoing analysis by relying on more of a *micro perspective* of evil and its causes—what is sometimes referred to as the "why" problem. This question asks how evil comes about in the first place and why there should be any evil at all. The relevant consideration is how God and evil are said to "fit together," so to speak. Addressing an apparent gap in his own response to the problem of evil, Brian Davies observes, "If I am right, evil does not render God's existence impossible or unlikely. To say only that, however, is not to give any particular answer to the question 'How do God and evil fit together?'"[1] Therefore, it may not be a logical contradiction for God and evil (even gratuitous evil) to both exist in the actual world, but this does not help with the question as to why such evils exist in the first place or what sort of reason there might be that would explain how and why horrendous evils occur. Likewise, Bruce Little speaks to this open question that naturally arises when theodicies fail and the possibility of gratuitous evil is acknowledged: "Some events beg for some answer, an answer that neither minimizes the horrific nature of the evil, nor simply ignores it by suggesting things like this have always happened. The human heart will not be silent forever on such matters."[2] Thus for Little, the question arises from the "human heart" in a distinct examination of evil and its causes specifically from a human perspective. Unlike the evidential problem of evil *per* se, this question seeks more of an *explanation* of evil rather than a *justification* for it.

Taking this into account, there remains an approach to the problem of evil that presents a new challenge for theists even if the question of God's existence is resolved. The question as to why God should create a world rife with evil and remain (according to some) absent or ambivalent in the face of it remains open. Such a question may not entail a logical contradiction that rises to a philosophical challenge against the existence of God, yet while questions such as this remains unresolved, it can nevertheless be confusing and unsettling for either the theist or the seeker. After all, it is the human belief in God as a loving, compassionate creator that is the primary target of arguments from evil in the first place, and it is on that basis that the problem carries the weight that it does. As Rowe explains, "The existence of evil in the world has been felt for centuries to be a problem for theism. It seems difficult to believe that a world with such a vast amount of evil as our world contains could be the creation of, and under the sovereign control of, a supremely good, omnipotent, omniscient being."[3] The difficulty, as Rowe here describes, is one's *belief* in a

1. Davies, *Reality of God*, 229.
2. Little, *God, Why This Evil?*, 2.
3. Rowe, *Philosophy of Religion*, 112.

God who would create a world teeming with evil and yet does seemingly little to stop or prevent it—even though it seems that there is much that he could do if he were willing and able to do so. In this chapter, I will consider first the proper perspective of evil that leads to the "why" question in the first place. I will then evaluate a particular sense in which God can be said to have "reasons" for what he does and does not do—including in consideration of the existence and persistence of evil in the world. I will conclude with a look at a *new evidential argument from evil* designed to survive the position of natural theology I have here endorsed.

THE PERSPECTIVE OF EVIL

Evidential examples of evil most often advanced in defense of arguments from evil thrive on particularly egregious and horrific examples chosen to appeal to our basest moral instincts—such as the Nazi Holocaust or the abuse of a child. These arguments would arguably be just as well served by more mundane examples such as a worm that bakes to death on a slab of concrete; however, this would not appeal to our base human passions quite as emphatically or effectively as more offensive and violent examples do. The reason is that the problem of evil is about more than simply a detached philosophical question about whether or not the existence of God is consistent with the existence of evil. Rather, it appeals to our most innate feelings and ideas concerning God, evil, and goodness. Our own human passions and base instincts about right and wrong, good and evil, justice and injustice are what fuels arguments from evil—mostly because the problem for many, at its core, is more personal than logical.

The instinct toward relying on one's own individual judgments and perspective as a basis for adjudicating on the character and nature of God in view of evil is common. William Rowe, for example, relies on just such an approach as a condition for accepting his evidential argument: "To these three [grounds for accepting his first premise] I now would add a fourth: our reasonable judgments of what an all-wise omnigood being would endeavor to accomplish with respect to human (and animal) good and evil in the universe."[4] Rowe here assumes the proper position and authority to adjudicate on the reasonable expectations of God in light of evil. The conflict that follows is one of perspective—assuming or requiring a divine perspective when a human perspective is the only

4. Rowe, "Evil and the Theistic Hypothesis," 162.

one available. As Geisler and Corduan argue, "Indeed . . . total disproofs of God from evil are self-defeating, for they assume an ultimate or divine perspective in order to prove there can be no such perspective."[5] Thus, arguments from evil assume a perspective that just simply is not available to the human observer and cannot possibly be known—that of a divine perspective of evil and its various causes and reasons for being. Though we lack the divine perspective necessary to make such a judgment, our own expectations are illicitly informed by our own human perspective of evil and what we might assume a perfectly good God would do in the face of evil—even though philosophical reflection reveals that God himself stands under no such obligation. Even so, this does nothing to alleviate the initial human perspective that was assumed in the discussion—seeking and expecting a loving, gracious God to act when evils arise. As I have argued, God is under no moral obligation to prevent gratuitous evil, though certain questions surrounding God and evil are left seemingly unresolved—specifically an *explanation* of evil (where it comes from and how it arises in a world of things always ordered toward the good) that remains properly grounded in a human perspective without illicitly seeking or assuming what properly belongs only to God. As Bruce Little explains, the challenge of the problem of evil has always been a personal one in this respect: "It is the human experience that begs for some answer, some meaningful clarification. It is the pervasiveness of evil and the personal affliction from evil that causes the heart to cry: 'God, why this evil?'"[6]

To be clear, the question of perspective in this manner is not centered on whether or not God exists, or even whether one should believe in him or not, but rather one of searching and grasping for an explanation of evil such that it "fits" in a theistic universe from a human perspective. After all, if it is true that God exists as an omnipotent, omniscient, perfectly good creator, and all of creation is necessarily ordered toward the good in a teleological sense, and yet evil persists that is utterly horrendous and gratuitous, then how is it that evils such as this come about? What is the *reason* for evil? While we can confidently and reasonably affirm that God exists (on the basis of natural theology, for example), and God is in fact consistent with all of his classical divine attributes (including omniscience, omnipotence, and perfect goodness), we are nevertheless confronted with this largely unresolved question—not because we have

5. Geisler and Corduan, *Philosophy of Religion*, 342.

6. Little, *God, Why This Evil?*, 11.

cause to doubt God's existence but because what we know of God does not seem to fit with what we know of evil. Little offers a similar explanation of the significance of the "why" question: "I do not ask the question because I doubt, but quite the contrary, because I believe. I ask the question of God, not because I think I have found God to be guilty of moral lapse in permitting evil to persist, but precisely because I believe there are answers—answers consistent with everything else I believe about God."[7] Here, the "why" question is not so much about one's intellectual knowledge of God's existence and nature; rather, the "why" question is centered on how evil is ultimately explained in a theistic universe—if God and evil do coexist, then the answers to these questions must also exist in some fashion to be discovered or revealed. Thus, the theist can be confident that God does exist, evil does exist, and there are in fact answers to the "why" question.

Returning once again to the Thomistic approach to natural theology I have thus far defended, it is worth considering exactly how Aquinas might resolve this question. According to Davies, Aquinas himself offers no such solution.

> So one might be naturally suspicious of someone who regards himself as having gotten his or her mind around both God and evil. Is Aquinas such a person, however? Some people seem to assume that he is, that he takes himself as having neatly tidied up anything that we might think of as the mystery of God and evil. Yet such a view of him is deeply misguided, for, in a serious sense, Aquinas has no solution to the problem of evil and does not think of himself as being able to explain the occurrence of evil in the world.[8]

As Davies here explains, Aquinas offers no explanation that would seem to satisfy the "why" question (or even arguably the problem of evil itself). In fact, Aquinas does not directly consider what contemporary philosophers would call the "problem of evil" at all, for Aquinas (via natural theology) begins from the idea that God clearly does exist, and his analysis of things such as evil in the world are undertaken on this basis. However, Aquinas does briefly consider one possible counterargument when addressing his own arguments for the existence of God that seems to mirror the problem of evil. The argument he poses is, "It seems that God does

7. Little, *God, Why This Evil?*, 11.

8. Davies, *Thomas Aquinas on God and Evil*, 129.

not exist; because if one of two contraries be infinite, the other would be altogether destroyed. But the word 'God' means that He is infinite goodness. If, therefore, God existed, there would be no evil discoverable; but there is evil in the world. Therefore God does not exist."[9] Here the argument Aquinas considers is specifically aimed at God's infinite goodness, which would seem to preclude even the possibility of evil as properly considered. Aquinas's reply, however, addresses only the apparent contradiction and suggests that God can and does bring good from evil, which emphasizes that God's infinite goodness nevertheless persists in the face of evil without any apparent contradiction. He simply writes, "This is part of the infinite goodness of God, that He should allow evil to exist, and out of it produce good."[10] As such, Aquinas holds that no contradiction is apparent, though he stops short of explaining exactly how or when God brings good from evil. For Aquinas, God's reasons and motives are simply beyond the pale of human perception. "He [Aquinas] thinks that God might have made a world with no evil in it and that even the world as it is reflects God's nature is good. But he does not claim to fathom God's motives in bringing things about as they exactly are."[11] While Aquinas holds that humans can certainly discover that God exists (via our observations of the world through natural theology and theistic arguments, for example) and likewise hold (absent any contradiction) that evil also exists, it is clear that God's ways are simply unfathomable and unsearchable for the finite human intellect.[12] As Davies explains,

> Aquinas is convinced that sober reflection ought to lead us to see that "God exists" and "evil exists" are not logically incompatible statements. . . . But he does not take himself to have searched the mind of God so as to be able to come up with an intellectually satisfying ("Ah, now I see") answer to why there is evil at all or why there are particular evils that have occurred and do occur. And, indeed, one would not expect him to, given his fundamental conviction that we are seriously in the dark when thinking of God.[13]

9. Aquinas, *Summa Theologiae*, I.2.3.

10. Aquinas, *Summa Theologiae*, I.2.3.

11. Davies, *Thomas Aquinas on God and Evil*, 129.

12. Aquinas approaches questions of God's existence and the existence of evil from a position of natural reason and philosophical inquiry, though he recognizes the cognitive limits of finite humans to fully comprehend the full essence and nature of God. Thus, some things in this sense for Aquinas are simply left unexplained.

13. Davies, *Thomas Aquinas on God and Evil*, 130.

Thus for Davies, there is no direct explanation of evil nor answer to the "why" question in Aquinas, which leaves the question seemingly unresolved.

However, the theist can draw on certain facts and principles that may be clear on reflection regarding the existence of evil and the nature of God that can help to progress one toward a possible resolution of the "why" question. Though humans cannot hope to attain a divine perspective on evil given our natural cognitive limits, we are still driven to make sense of it in some fashion—at least from a finite human perspective, and one hopes to draw on examples and evidence in the world to come to at least some understanding toward the explanation of evil. It is here, after all, that the problem of evil has its greatest impact, and on account of the elusive nature of any obvious answer, it may seem at a glance to present a real problem for the theist—a sort of internal contradiction in which the theist must exist. As such, even taking the Thomistic approach and beginning with a confidence in God's existence (by way of natural theology) seems to yield limited results for the theist. As Davies observes, "For these reasons, therefore, I take it that the 'We Know that God Exists' Argument yields limited results. At any rate, it certainly does nothing to explain how evil and God fit together."[14] The question follows as to what God's reasons might be (if any) for the evil that permeates the world. This is the basest challenge of the problem of evil, and even if God is not morally obliged to prevent evil, and the existence of evil does not contradict God's nature (as I have argued), one may still postulate that there must be some *good reason* as to why evil exists in the first place. I will thus consider what it means for God to have "reasons" in this respect.

THE REASON FOR EVIL

As I have argued, the problem that persists beyond my own analysis of the problem of evil in light of God's nature and attributes is the "why" question, which seeks to discover why there should be any evil at all, or what the "reason" for evil could possibly entail. If God is the first efficient cause of all that exists—including things that suffer and experience corruption and privation—then one may assume that God must surely have good reasons as to why things exist as they do and why he did not or could not have made things at least a little better than they are now.

14. Davies, *Thomas Aquinas on God and Evil*, 228.

Such an inquiry does not necessarily assume that God is under any sort of *obligation* to make the world some other way or to prevent evil from occurring as much as it does—though it does assume that there must be at least *some* reason or explanation for why there is as much evil as there is and why God has not yet done something about it. To be clear, it would not need to be a reason that *justifies* God's permission of evil in a moral sense; it would rather simply be a reason that *explains* why evil arises as much or as often as it does as an aspect of God's own creation-order.

The theist may assume at first that God must have reasons for what he does in a similar way to humans.[15] Little, for example, patterns this assumption on the idea that humans are made in God's image: "Part of what constitutes the image of God in man is that man is a moral being with a mind capable of moral judgment. In this way, man is not only an expression of the mind of God but given a mind patterned after God's mind. . . . Although man's mind is inferior to God's mind, it nonetheless is capable of processing in a manner similar to the mind of God."[16] For Little, a human can have at least some idea as to how God's own mind operates based on how human minds operate, and it is clear that humans come to decisions on how to act based on a discursive reasoning process—taking the information we have about the world and deciding on a course of action on that basis. As such, if Little is right, we should be able to investigate or inquire—at least to an analogical degree—as to the mind and motives of God and his actions.

Not all philosophers would agree that God has "reasons" for what he does in this respect. For example, Brian Davies holds that God does not act for reasons at all, in any sense that comports with how humans act. Davies suggests that seeking reasons for God's acts commits the same category mistake as one does when treating God as a moral agent. First, Davies points out that one cannot suggest that God acts (as humans do) to fulfill some need that he has.

15. By using the word "reason" in reference to God, I mean an explanation as to why God has done something (or not done something) with respect to the causal relationships involved (including its ends and means). A reason in this sense (as applied to God) would entail an explanation as to what specific ends God's act is ordered toward and how those ends are achieved by the causal operations involved. Further, the reason for some indirect effect of the natural world is explained by its own causal operations that bring it about and direct it to its own ends. Thus the "reason for evil" in reference to the acts and decrees of God would entail an explanation as to what brought that evil about, what ends it is ordered toward, and God's own causal relationship with the evil and its own causes.

16. Little, *Creation-Order Theodicy*, 137–38.

> If God is the source of all that exists (the reason why there is something rather than nothing), then he cannot have a need that would be met by how things go in the created order. For how things go there will be his doing, not something he waits on or desires to help him on his way. . . . For these reasons, therefore, I think that we should back away from the suggestion that God acts for reasons as people do.[17]

Here, Davies stays true to the concept of God as *ipsum esse subsistens* and correctly observes that such a being would be in need of nothing at all—even in terms of what he has created. Davies's argument here is that God does not engage in the same sort of discursive reasoning process that creatures do when we identify or recognize a need or desire, determine how best to achieve it with the means available to us, and go about a series of steps or actions to obtain the desired outcome. For Davies, humans act for reasons because we understand the world in many different ways and under many different descriptions—unlike a cat, for example:

> One might well speak of the reason why the cat chased the mouse. But "reason" here has nothing to do with framed intentions. There may be reasons why the cat chased the mouse. But they are not the cat's reasons. In Aquinas's opinion, however, human action is precisely a matter of things acting with reasons of their own. And, he thinks, with the ability to act with reasons of one's own comes an understanding of the world under many different descriptions. Or, rather, as Aquinas sees it, the ability to understand the world under many different descriptions is why people have the ability to act with reasons of their own.[18]

Here, Davies lays out the factor that distinguishes the human from the cat, and this is precisely the factor that distinguishes the human from God as well. For Davies, at least as far as he takes Aquinas, God simply cannot act for reasons in any kind of comprehensible sense because "acting for reasons" as humans do requires a multitude of varied perceptions about the world—specifically, that the good humans seek is at times unknown or obscured, and thus humans are faced with myriad lesser goods with which to seek fulfillment for some need or desire, and this multitudinous perception of the world is what requires humans to make decisions and reason to conclusions as to what should be done in some given circumstance. God, however, understands all aspects of the world perfectly. God

17. Davies, *Reality of God*, 216.

18. Davies, *On Evil*, 37.

does not develop rival interpretations of the world in the way humans do, and thus God has no need to construct any sort of discursive reasoning process that leads from one point to another in the same way.

Further, as Davies explains, God has no needs to fulfill, and thus God never acts toward the fulfillment of needs, even though this is how humans act in the decisions we make.

> For Aquinas, people have freedom of choice since, unlike non-human animals, they can interpret the world in different ways (under different descriptions) and act in the light of the ways in which they interpret it. In this sense, so he thinks, their actions are governed by reasons that are fully their own. . . . On his account, we aim for what we want in a world in which we (as thinkers) can recognize different things as likely to satisfy us in different ways. And on this basis we deliberate with an eye on means and ends.[19]

Thus, per Davies, God (unlike creatures) has no needs or desires for anything he lacks; thus, God never "deliberates" in this sense and never "acts for reasons" as a means to an end that God is himself presently without. As such, while humans act to fulfill needs or obtain what we desire, God has no needs at all and desires nothing beyond the perfection of his own essence and being.

Finally, Davies's argument is not that God's reasons are simply beyond our ken. For Davies, it is not our ignorance of what God's reasons may be that is at issue—it is that God does not act for reasons at all. "It is not that God has reasons of which we are ignorant. My point is that God is not something we should think of as having reasons for acting or not acting in the first place."[20] Davies therefore concludes that it is simply a category mistake for humans to seek answers to the "why" question of evil: "So I fear that there is no intelligible answer to questions like 'Why did God do this to me?' or 'Why did God make the world as it is?' Such questions, I think, just ought not to be asked if they are requests for reasons that God has."[21] Thus, for Davies, the "why" question surrounding God and evil is basically incoherent and not a question that has any meaning or import. Such a question commits a category mistake and

19. Davies, *On Evil*, 38.

20. Davies, *Reality of God*, 219.

21. Davies, *Reality of God*, 218.

holds God to be something he is not—a being like-minded with creatures that acts toward ends as creatures do.

Davies is certainly correct that God does not act for reasons to fulfill some need or lack, and he does not engage in a discursive reasoning process, deducing truths from syllogisms or making decisions from information gleaned from a varied knowledge of the world. Whatever "reasons" one may seek from God cannot be anything like God fulfilling a need, satisfying a passion or desire, or deducing some course of action on the basis of discursive reasoning or passive observation. For Aquinas, God's will is not driven or caused by his understanding but identical to it. He does not comprehend conclusions, for example, on the basis of premises, but he knows both simultaneously—thus it is in fact a category mistake to attribute discursive reasoning to God.

> If the understanding perceive the conclusion in the premise itself, apprehending both the one and the other at the same glance, in this case the knowing of the conclusion would not be caused by understanding the premises, since a thing cannot be its own cause; and yet, it would be true that the thinker would understand the premises to be the cause of the conclusion. It is the same with the will, with respect to which the end stands in the same relation to the means to the end, as do the premises to the conclusion with regard to the understanding.[22]

Here, Aquinas illustrates what I believe Davies is driving at—namely that in such a case as one who understands both premises and conclusion (or means and ends) in one act of cognition, then the relationship of effect to cause is fully grasped and understood, even though the effect is not known *on account of* the cause (or vice versa). For Aquinas, it is in this same way that God knows both means and ends, even though he does not will the means on account of the ends.

> Now as God by one act understands all things in His essence, so by one act He wills all things in His goodness. Hence, as in God to understand the cause is not the cause of His understanding the effect, for He understands the effect in the cause, so, in Him, to will an end is not the cause of His willing the means, yet He wills the ordering of the means to the end. Therefore, He wills this to be as means to that; but does not will this on account of that.[23]

22. Aquinas, *Summa Theologiae*, I.19.5.
23. Aquinas, *Summa Theologiae*, I.19.5.

Aquinas here explains how God wills both means and ends (or cause and effect) and understands both fully in their causal relationships, though it cannot be said that God wills means *on account of* the ends he has in mind. If X causes Y to occur, then it is true that God wills both X and Y, but he does not will X *in order to achieve* Y—he wills both simultaneously in their own causal relationship. In other words, it is not *on account of* the ends that God wills the means, and not everything God wills must be a means or end in this respect. God does not come to a conclusion about what to do or how to do it on the basis of some end he has in mind, though he does and can will both the end and the means that bring it about in one eternal act.

Nevertheless, even with this in mind, it is not entirely vacuous to say that God acts for a divine purpose or toward some specific intended end in what he does and does not will. Recall that the "why" question speaks specifically to the *human perspective* of God and evil and how evil can be properly explained *by creatures* who simply lack an eternal, divine perspective. From a human perspective, causes are ordered to effects and means to ends, and even though God wills both simultaneously from his eternal vantage point (and never one on account of the other), humans can nevertheless identify and recognize causes and means distinct from their effects and ask reasonably what effects or ends those causes must be ordered toward (or caused by) from an eternal, divine perspective. In this sense, the phrase "God acts for reasons" retains at least some coherence within a Thomistic account of God's nature and will.[24]

For example, God may have brought plagues on ancient Egypt that in turn caused Pharaoh to free the enslaved Israelites, and while God does not will the plagues *on account of* the freedom of the Israelites (as if

24. Additionally, it is clear that an understanding of God as *ipsum esse subsistens* reveals that God's acts cannot be directed solely toward lesser goods as the ends toward which he aims. For example, God cannot and does not will a creature eternal happiness *for its own sake*. God can will eternal happiness for a creature, but the end toward which its happiness is ordered must always be grounded in the eternal and perfect goodness of God. Thus, in a very real sense, the goodness of God is the only proper teleological direction of anything and everything God does. However, God can will the existence of things that are themselves ordered toward his goodness (such as humans, animals, and the entire creation-order), and this is not a contradiction because God is not willing those things for their own sake but for the good of his own infinite majesty, so to speak. Per Aquinas, "Thus, then, He wills both Himself to be, and other things to be; but Himself as the end, and other things as ordained to that end; inasmuch as it befits the divine goodness that other things should be partakers therein." Aquinas, *Summa Theologiae*, I.19.2.

the freedom of the Israelites constituted some sort of *need* that God had that somehow required the plagues as the means to fulfill that need), the plagues are nevertheless ordered to that end by God in their own causal relationships. Further, the emancipation of the Israelites could not be an *end in itself* for God (again, as if fulfilling some divine need or desire) but rather an act of God directed ultimately at his own goodness as its proper end (perhaps by leading the people to a right worship of him, for example). As such, the plagues can be said to achieve a divine purpose as causes ordered toward specific ends—all of which are ordained by God in every aspect of their causal relationships, and thus the plagues can be said to be enacted by God *for a reason* in a similar (though not identical) sense that humans act for reasons. Further, God's "reasons" in this respect are not *on account of* the ends God has in mind; they speak to no lack or need in God of any kind, though they are nevertheless divinely ordered as causally operative toward specific ends simultaneously willed by God for his own divine purposes. Therefore, it seems that one can speak of God as *acting for reasons* in a distinct non-univocal sense. In fact, Brian Davies often repeats that it is only when applied in a univocal sense that concepts of God acting for reasons become muddled or incoherent: "If 'having a reason' means anything like what it means when it comes to people having reasons for acting, the notion seems inapplicable when talking about what can be ascribed to God."[25] Thus, one cannot speak of God having reasons in the same way humans do, though there is still an intelligible sense in which one can speak of God acting for reasons that remains coherent for the classical theist.

However, if God's reasons do not and cannot include a lack or need in God's own essence or nature, what could they possibly entail, and what would a divine reason actually be in reference to his acts and decrees regarding the created world? First, while God has no privations of his own in his own essence, created beings certainly do, and there is nothing in an understanding of God as *ipsum esse subsistens* that would prevent God from acting toward fulfilling or restoring a lack or privation in some other being. To be clear, God does not *have* to act for the benefit of privative beings (out of some necessity or moral obligation, for example), and God choosing to act in such a manner would not make it an end in itself if he did, but he can do so nonetheless (as an act of divine grace, for example), and supposing he did, this would serve as a

25. Davies, *Reality of God*, 218.

"reason" for God acting in this regard. Thus, referring to the specific ends toward which some divine acts are causally ordered describes (at least analogically) a "reason" for those acts—even if such reasons do not entail a discursive reasoning process or God fulfilling a need that he possesses. Returning to the biblical example of the Exodus, one could describe just such a "reason" for God to part the Red Sea. God certainly did not part the sea in order to fulfill a need in himself or uphold some moral duty he had toward the Israelites. However, the Israelites themselves were in a predicament backed up against impassible terrain, with Pharaoh's army closing in behind them, and thus the people had a rather significant need or lack that only God could fulfill. As such, God parts the sea in the biblical narrative, and by this his people are redeemed and the Egyptian army is defeated. Thus, one could reasonably say that God parted the sea *in order to* deliver the Israelites from their captors since that act was causally ordered to that end—even if God did not will the parting of the sea because he somehow *needed* to deliver the Israelites as an end in itself. Here it seems that there is an intelligible sense from a human perspective in which God may act for a reason—to bring about some end that he means to accomplish as ordered in its own causal operations.[26] As such, this act of God would have been directed toward a need or lack in the Israelites rather than a need or lack in God himself, and the parting of the sea was properly ordered to an end God intended as a causally operative factor in the deliverance of the Israelites. Therefore, it seems that God does "act for reasons" in a sense that retains at least some shared meaning with how humans act for reasons—as divine acts ordered to specific ends, even if

26. In the same biblical narrative, there is also an indication that God may have reasons for *not* doing certain things as well (or doing things differently than he may have done)—suggesting that God actively and purposefully rejects alternatives in some way, even if not discursively. The Israelites in Exodus are in the predicament they are in at the Red Sea because God decides not to lead them through enemy lands. "Now when Pharaoh had let the people go, God did not lead them by the way of the land of the Philistines, even though it was near; for God said, 'The people might change their minds when they see war and return to Egypt.' Therefore, God led the people around by way of the wilderness to the Red Sea; and the sons of Israel went up in battle formation from the land of Egypt" (Exod 13:17–18). As such, it appears that it is possible that God at times rejects alternatives for specific reasons in what he chooses to do. While such a reasoning process for God would not be a discursive one (where premises or *a priori* facts are first considered or evaluated in order to reach certain conclusions about the Israelites, for example), it is nevertheless apparent that God can and does reject alternatives in some way as ordered toward the ends God means to bring about, and thus it would seem once again that God may even have "reasons" for what he does not do.

those reasons are never out of an *a priori* obligation to do so or for the purpose of fulfilling some need or lack in God himself.

The question follows, therefore, as to whether God has reasons like this for *everything* he does or does not do and whether all of his acts (or "non-acts") must have some good purpose in mind that would serve as a reasonable explanation if properly understood. From a Thomistic perspective, everything God wills must be directed toward the ultimate and highest end of God's own divine goodness. "Thus, then, He wills both Himself to be, and other things to be; but Himself as the end, and other things as ordained to that end; inasmuch as it befits the divine goodness that other things should be partakers therein."[27] As such, everything in existence as created by God is ordered toward the good to varying degrees, even if some things are "more good" or "more perfect" than others. Further, God cannot will evil or corruption as an end in itself, though evil and corruption can result as accompanied by other goods. "Now God wills no good more than He wills His own goodness; yet He wills one good more than another. Hence He in no way wills the evil of sin, which is the privation of right order towards the divine good."[28] Thus, God cannot will "the evil of sin" so to speak, which is a privation of right order as an end in itself, though he can will goods that are attached to evils on account of punishment or the regular operation of the natural world. "The evil of natural defect, or of punishment, He does will, by willing the good to which such evils are attached. Thus in willing justice He wills punishment; and in willing the preservation of the natural order, He wills some things to be naturally corrupted."[29] Hence, it seems that all instances of evil that arise in a world created by God would be such that they are attached to some good in that same world, either as an aspect of the regular operation of the natural order or as an aspect of moral consequence or moral failure ("punishment" in Aquinas's terms). If such an attachment is necessary in anything willed by God, which includes every evil that occurs in the world, then it would seem that there would be some *reason* or *explanation* for every instance of evil in this regard—even if it is not a reason that fulfills a need in God, represents some moral obligation or duty on God's part, or specifies some means enacted *on account of* some desired end that God intends to accomplish.

27. Aquinas, *Summa Theologiae*, I.19.5.

28. Aquinas, *Summa Theologiae*, I.19.9.

29. Aquinas, *Summa Theologiae*, I.19.9.

Therefore, if God can be said to act for reasons in the analogical sense described above, and everything that occurs in the world is willed by God as ordered toward a specific end (even the goodness of God himself), then there must remain some meaningful sense in which questions like "God, why this evil?" can be legitimately posed. If every evil and privation—in order for it to arise in a world created by God—must be "attached" in some way to a good and not be willed as an end in itself, the question remains as to what good some instance of gratuitous evil may in fact be attached to and how it "fits together" so to speak with the goodness of God in that respect.

Further, if God can and does act at times toward the benefit of some creatures (such as the Israelites in the biblical narrative), then it would seem that deliverance from evil (at least in those instances) fulfilled some divine purpose in some way that other instances do not. Thus, one could reasonably ask why the Israelites warranted deliverance at the Red Sea while they did not warrant deliverance from Roman occupation, for example. While such a question would not imply that God has a lack in himself that must be fulfilled or that he is under some divine obligation to act when gratuitous evil occurs (as the problem of evil suggests), it is nevertheless a meaningful question in that God does seem to act for reasons as ordered to specific ends in the analogical sense described above, and seeking divine reasons for why God does or does not act in some specific circumstance would not be a meaningless or vacuous inquiry. If this is a legitimate question, therefore, then it seems that an argument from evil could be reframed in such a way that admits to the logical compatibility of both God and gratuitous evil and yet seeks to identify some instance of evil that lacks a sufficient explanation for how and why it came about as an aspect of God's creation (as resulting from or ordered toward some otherwise-good operation of the natural world). As such, a reframing of the problem of evil in this sense would not seek a divine *justification* for evil (in a moral sense) but would rather seek a divine *explanation* of evil, such as why and how some instance of evil arises and the causal explanations involved.

Further, it is reasonable to conclude that God acts in some circumstances and not others because some may be ordered toward (or lead to) some divine purpose (as distinct from the divine purpose inherent in the natural order of God's creation) while others do not. In a world where evil runs rampant, therefore, it is not meaningless to inquire as to why divine deliverance from some instance of evil does not or would not be associated with some good purpose that would warrant that deliverance from God's perspective. Such would not imply a divine moral obligation to prevent evil in some circumstance—though it would constitute at minimum an understanding of the causal operations in the world that might help to explain why God may intervene in one case and not another. Further, every evil that arises in the world must have a "reason" associated with it, in reference to the acts and decrees of God that would entail an explanation as to what brought that evil about, what good causes were operative, what good ends its causes were ordered toward (if any), and God's own causal responsibilities surrounding the evil and its explanation. Since all of creation is ordered toward the goodness of God and all evil exists only as a privation of the good, then every instance of evil must be associated with some good—both as the cause of that evil and the end toward which its cause is ordered.[30] As such, a new evidential argument from evil could be proposed that seeks to identify some instance of *unexplained evil* that is not causally ordered in the manner I have described, and if such an example were evident, one would arguably have cause to deny the existence of God.

A NEW EVIDENTIAL ARGUMENT

From the perspective of classical theism and the approach to natural theology I have thus far defended, a possible path forward for the nontheist is to seek an explanation or "reason" for the evil in the universe (or some specific instance of evil). Toward this end, one may propose a new evidential problem of evil in a such a manner that raises this question without ascribing moral duties to God or committing the sort of anthropomorphic category mistakes common to other arguments from evil. Here I will propose just such an argument and consider whether it bears weight in the discussion of the existence of God. For the purpose of this argument, let *S* be some likely instance of gratuitous evil that is

30. Note that the "associated good" in question here does not speak to the "greater good" of certain theodicies that attempt to justify God's permission of that evil in a moral sense. Rather, the associated good that must be linked in some way with every instance of evil only serves an explanatory role that helps to determine how and why some instance of evil came about and what goods were involved in its causes. This speaks directly to the "why" question of evil, which becomes relevant when God's moral obligations are denied. Thus, some instance of evil could be genuinely gratuitous and yet still have an "associated good" that sufficiently explains that evil.

discovered in the actual world with no morally justifying good associated with it.

(1) There is no explanation for *S* such that *S* is caused by (or results from) some associated good.

(2) If God exists, there is an explanation for *S* such that *S* is caused by (or results from) some associated good.

(3) Therefore, God does not exist.

Here, the argument follows a familiar pattern as typical evidential arguments from evil, though with some significant differences. First, this argument does not imply, require, or suggest that God is under some moral obligation to stop or prevent evil whenever he is able to do so. As such, there is no indictment against God on a moral basis that commits the sort of category mistake that most evidential arguments fall prey to. Second, given what I have argued concerning the nature of God as revealed through a Thomistic natural theology, the theistic response to this syllogism must focus on a denial of (1) rather than (2). The result, for the theist, may appear to be directed back to the practice of theodicy to resolve this form of the argument.

To illustrate the challenge this new argument brings, consider that premise (2) speaks to the *explanatory goods* that must necessarily be in operation in a world created by God in order for any evil to arise in such a world. In other words, gratuitous evil may not be valid evidence against the existence of God because of some absent or unknowable "greater good" to justify the evil in question. However, this evil must still be such that it can be sufficiently explained in a privative sense as an aspect of a theistic world. Recall that evil is by definition a privation of the good, and thus evil cannot and does not exist (especially in a theistic universe) apart from the good causes associated with it, according to the natural operations of the world (and the natural and proper teleology of those goods as directed toward some higher good). If this is so, then one should expect to find some explanatory goods that either cause some evil to take place or explain that evil in terms of the goods it affects and is effected by. Here, premise (2) holds that God—on account of what we know of his nature and creative works, as well as the natures and causes of good and evil in the universe—creates only what is good and permits evil only in a privative sense as caused by (or resulting from) some associated good—thus all evil must have a "reason" for its existence in this regard. Again, this does not suggest that the evil in question cannot be gratuitous. Further, the reason for *S* must exist in some explanation of the causal operations at play such that it explains the evil in question in terms of the goods associated with it—including the causes of *S* and the goods those causes were ordered toward in a teleological sense.

Premise (1) holds that some instance of *S* can be proposed that does not have an obvious explanation in this regard—such as an instance of evil that does not appear to arise in association with what is good in this way. Such would be an example of *excessive* or *unexplained* evil, so to speak, such that its emergence occurs beyond any reasonable explanation or that it somehow undermines the very creation in which it exists in violation of the good of the natural order itself. In pursuit of this argument, it seems premise (1) is the more difficult premise for the non-theist to defend, because the burden is on the non-theist to propose an evidential example of *S* that either establishes the truth of (1) or illustrates that (1) is likely to be true given the evidential examples of unexplained evil one may identify available in the world. However, this may not be as difficult as other arguments from evil—such as identifying gratuitous evil.

In order to demonstrate that some evil exists that is neither ordered toward nor results from some associated good, one must begin with an instance of evil and examine it in all of its causal operations to see what possible goods may be involved that brought that evil about and the teleological direction of those goods that caused that evil. Taking Rowe's fawn trapped in a forest fire as an example, it is not difficult to see that the suffering of the fawn is simply a description of the natural world functioning as its nature requires. The fire begins and grows naturally, the forest itself is consumed by flames in the manner one would expect given the laws of physics and how fire naturally interacts with a forest, the fawn is trapped and burned given the way fire interacts with flesh, the fawn's pain receptors fire as per their proper natural function, and so on. In the end, the regular operation of the natural order results in the fire and the fawn's suffering exactly as one would expect given the sort of world that exists, and thus the suffering of the fawn follows naturally from the good of the created order and the proper function of things like fire and pain receptors—all of which are "goods" as considered in terms of things that exist and function toward their own good and proper ends. Using Rowe's example, therefore, it is difficult to see how the non-theist could proceed with an argument to support premise (1) with an example such as this. As such, in this instance, the *reason* for the evil of the fawn's suffering is readily apparent in that it is caused by (or results from) an associated good—the good of the order of nature and the natural function of fires and fawns. While this arguably says nothing about "why" God made the world in such a manner where fire interacts with fawns as it does, it nonetheless explains the suffering of the fawn in the context of the actual world in which it exists and the operative causal interactions that brought it about. Again, the fawn's suffering is not *morally justified* on the basis of the good of the natural order and the various elements involved, but it is certainly *explained* by it. Given this analysis, it is difficult to see how Rowe's fawn (or any natural evil for that matter—at least one sufficiently explained by natural operations such as this) may be considered as an example of some evil *S* that satisfies the conditions of premise (1).

In order to proceed, therefore, it seems that one must propose some instance of "non-natural evil," so to speak, that occurs beyond the realm of the natural order and would be "excessive" or "unexplained" in that regard. If a fawn in a forest were to be inexplicably and suddenly wracked with searing pain for a time and then fall over and die with no natural causes or explanation of its agony apparent to a human observer, then it would seem that one would have cause to affirm the likelihood of premise (1) and thus also have cause to assent to the conclusion that God (at least as understood from natural theology) does not exist. To my knowledge, however, I am unaware of any instance of evil that would meet this criteria as a definitive example. Even evil committed by free creatures on account of their own moral failures has a perfectly reasonable explanation if creatures are created with self-directed wills aimed at the good while lacking a perfect vision or knowledge of the goods that they seek, and as such evil acts by creatures (so long as they intend the good in a teleological sense, even if their efforts produce evil accidentally) would not constitute an example of (1).

One may yet seek another method of affirming (1) by suggesting that some instance of evil *S* is *excessive* or *unnecessary* (and by extension without sufficient reason for its existence) if some other world could be proposed that exists with all the same goods though without the particular evil in question. In other words, one may argue that there is no *possible reason* why the world exists as it does with the quantity and severity of evil that it has, even if the evil that does obtain does not directly contradict God's existence and is fully explained by the natural world in which it occurs. Putting aside problems with using inaccessible, non-existent possible worlds in philosophical arguments involving the actual world, this approach would fail because even if another world were possible with as much (or more) good and less evil than the present world, such an argument says nothing about the explanation of evil in the actual world, which is all that is needed to show that (1) is false. Even if another world would be possible without *S* altogether, there is no reason it should be excluded from the present world so long as it is sufficiently explicable; thus the present world would remain a possible world with *S* in no need of further clarity. The same holds true for any question as to whether God could not have "done better," so to speak, and allowed less evil and more good than what he has—so long as the actual world is a possible world where all that exists is good (in that everything that exists does in fact exist with the nature and being that belongs to it) and is teleologically ordered toward the good as its proper end, then God can be its creator. Further, since God could create any possible world at all, the present world would remain one that could be created by God so long as *S* is explained, and as we have seen, God is under no obligation to create only the "best" of all possible worlds or to minimize evil in some respect as if he had a moral obligation to do so. Thus, if the present world remains *possible* (even if another world without *S* would also be possible), then the present world is one that is able to be created by an omnipotent, omniscient, perfectly good creator.

However, even if the truth of (1) cannot be established with a strong sense of logical certainty in this regard, there remains a question as to whether the evidence of unexplained evil in the world would serve as a sufficient basis for making a *reasonable inference* to its actual inexplicability, given our lack of knowledge of what goods each instance of evil may be teleologically or causally associated with. In a world created by God, all evil that occurs must be such that it arises from some good that is teleologically ordered toward the good, and thus evil arises only accidentally or on account of some defect in the operative agent-cause of that evil. Here, it is helpful to consider ways in which evil observed can be readily explained. For Aquinas, the explanatory good involved in most suffering just is the order of the universe: "Now, the order of the universe requires . . . that there should be some things that can, and do sometimes, fail. And thus God, by causing in things the good of the order of the universe, consequently and as it were by accident, causes the corruptions of things."[31] Thus, God can be said to be the cause of evil but only in

31. Aquinas, *Summa Theologiae*, I.49.2.

the sense that things are corrupted in terms of the formal process of the natural order as created by God. Hence some things are corrupted for the sake of the good of other things, and this concomitant good is sufficient to explain the presence of at least some evil in a world created by God. Such an approach is easy to see in the case of a lion devouring a lamb, for example, as the evil of the lamb's death is ordered toward the good of the nourishment of the lion (as addressed above in chapter six). "Aquinas' view is that God cannot make lions and lambs without the lambs having something to worry about."[32] Thus "teleological evil," so to speak, reveals how some acts are ordered toward the good (such as the good of nourishment for the lion), while the evil of suffering follows accidentally (the death and consumption of the lamb); the lion does not *intend* the suffering of the lamb as an end in itself even if its actions in fact bring about that very suffering.

One possible objection here is that teleological evil such as this actually presents a *challenge* for theism rather than a sufficient theistic explanation of evil. Felipe Leon, for example, argues that teleological evil is one reason to doubt that the world might have been created by a perfectly good God. "To put it crudely, the problem of dysteleology is the problem of stupid design; the problem of teleological evil is the problem of malevolent design. Perhaps the most obvious example of teleological evil is the evil of predation."[33] Leon goes on to explain how the very design of certain carnivores (as well as other predatory organisms) lends itself to the inevitable and unnecessary suffering of its victims—such as how a lion is given claws, teeth, and a ravenous hunger (and physical need) to rip apart and consume the flesh of other creatures for its own survival. Thus, a lion is teleologically ordered to *cause suffering* as part of the natural operation and teleological direction of its own design plan—as determined by its creator. However, this example from Leon is a poor example in defense of (1) because the nourishment of the lion itself is a *good* toward which its predatory behavior is ordered—not evil or suffering as an end. The suffering caused by the lion is certainly an evil *for its prey*, though one that only arises accidentally on account of the properly functioning natures of the lion and its prey. Further, there is no reason to think that God should be obliged to reduce or avoid this sort of suffering

32. Davies, *Thomas Aquinas on God and Evil*, 70.

33. Leon, "Perfectly Good," 210.

in his creation on account of a minimization of evil, for example. Thus, teleological evil is not a successful example of (1).

However, not all evils encountered in the world have such obvious goods associated with them and may yet provide cause (at least evidentially) to the observer to question whether or not some instance of evil is or can be sufficiently explained in a similar way. Thus, some instance of evil may be sufficient at a minimum to provide an evidential basis toward an inductive argument in support of (1) if that evil can be shown to have no apparent goods that are causally associated with it. For example, a massive tsunami caused by an offshore earthquake may flood a heavily populated coastal region and cause a staggering level of destruction of life and property on a tremendous scale, yet it may be difficult for an observer to see what "good" such an evil would be associated with such that its existence is explained in a theistic universe—in other words, something "thriving" on account of some good that causes the tsunami in an accidental sense. For example, nothing seems to be "nourished" by this tragedy—the offshore earthquake gains nothing from the activation of the tsunami; the creatures, plants, and structures along the shoreline certainly gain nothing from the crash of the giant tidal wave; and even the wave itself is destroyed when it makes landfall. Nothing in such a complex interaction seems to "thrive" by this causal exchange (even if only from the vantage point of an immediate observer), even if it is all perfectly explicable by the regular operation of the world as created by God, according to its physical laws and natural operations.[34]

One may argue that such an example is no problem for the theist because every evil involved in the tsunami is only an evil that exists because something good exists first; a human infant that drowns along the shoreline, for example, is a human infant that has the good of existence

34. It is possible that the earth somehow "thrives" on account of the tectonic activity that causes this event, and tsunamis may be the unfortunate byproduct of this necessary geological operation. The operative point here is that most observers of such a phenomenon (particularly those whose lives were lost or whose property is devastated by this tragedy) would have no vantage point at all to understand the causal operations involved, and thus for many observers, the tsunami would seem to be theistically inexplicable. Further, the theist must accept that every instance of evil must be associated in some way with a good such that the evil in question cannot exist without it, and the approach of a Thomistic natural theology suggests that all instances of evil must result from some cause that is teleologically ordered in some way to the good. Therefore, it is difficult to see how the good of something like a tsunami could be explained as the byproduct of a world of interactions where some things thrive on account of others when nothing at all seems to "thrive" in any meaningful sense by the onset of the tsunami.

prior to the tragedy that took its life—as do the water, the wave, the tectonic plates, and so on. Also, it is certainly the regular operation of the natural world that defines how earthquakes come about, how they affect the tides, the behavior of water striking land, the results of human bodies thrust into a sudden flood of water, and so on. Hence, the question here is not that good is not involved *in some way* in the operation of the tsunami or that the order of the universe is not somehow at work in such a tragedy. The question that persists here involves the teleological ordering of the universe in such a manner that an evil such as a destructive tsunami may seem—as far as we know—to be an unnecessary or excessive evil.[35] To be clear, it is not that evil must somehow be ordered to "the good" in a moral sense or morally justified as other evidential arguments suggest. However, the good that produces evil must nevertheless be ordered to "the good" in a metaphysical sense such that the evil that arises accidentally from the operation of its causes is entirely explicable in a way that lies beyond the realm of a world ordered toward the goodness of God in its natural operations. Hence, the force of the new evidential argument lies in what the *human observer is able to ascertain* regarding the causal operations and teleological ordering of some evidential example of evil. Thus, if the human observer is unable to ascertain at least some possible explanatory good in the face of some example of evil such that its emergence in a theistic universe seems somehow excessive or unexplained, then that human would have reason to consider (1) as possibly or even likely true.

It is in this position of ignorance of some good involved in the face of evil (in a privative sense) *from a human perspective* that such an argument has its greatest force. As with Rowe's original evidential argument,

35. It is worth noting here that the example of the tsunami may be a poor example for some human observers. A credentialed geologist or seismologist, for example, may propose a detailed explanation as to how different aspects of the complex geological interactions involved that result in the tsunami perfectly illustrate something thriving at the expense of something else even in the midst of the accidental tsunami (perhaps the earth itself benefits in some remarkable way by the release of force that causes the tsunami, for example). I am willing to admit that these are possibilities within this example, and perhaps the example is a poor one for some. However, most observers are not geologists. The point here is not to propose the tsunami as a *bona fide* instance of S in premise (1) and defend it on a universal basis but to illustrate how one may go about proposing such an example that *for all we know* counters the idea of concomitant goods in the sense of explanatory gratuitous evil specifically from a human perspective when considering the new argument here proposed. So long as an instance of S is *apparent* from the perspective of some observer, it remains a possibility to pursue in the problem of evil.

it is difficult to establish the truth of (1) definitively simply on the basis of one's own observations of the causal operations and teleological direction of some instance of evil. For all we know, there may be some unknown cause or explanation at hand of which only God is aware and humans are not. As such, it would seem one would have to be omniscient in order to verify with any certainty that (1) is true. Thus, any unexplained evil should be taken on an evidential basis purely from a human perspective, saying nothing of what God does or does not know about some instance of evil.

In order to affirm (1), one must consider whether or not it is reasonable for a human observer to conclude—on the basis of one's own limited observations—that some instance of *S* serves as a successful example of (1). As such, one begins by considering the causal operations involved and any associated goods that may help to explain why some evil *S* came about. While not necessarily a morally justifying good, all evil must be nonetheless associated with the good in some way, and the good involved must always be ordered toward a higher good (or perfect goodness itself) as its proper end such that the evil that arises is not itself an end and exists only as an accidental byproduct of the natural operation of the world or the moral failure of free beings. However, when the natural interactions of the universe that produce evil do not appear to be ordered toward (or caused by) some explanatory good that would sufficiently explain the evil that arises, then evidence of this sort of evil as such serves as a reason to doubt that such evil is always naturally explicable, and by extension (at least on appearance) reason to doubt the existence of God as the creator of such a universe.

As such, an argument remains open to the non-theist akin to the evidential problem of evil that considers evil in its causal operations (specifically from a human perspective) as a factor considered in a reasoned position on the existence of God. If natural theology reveals that all evil in a theistic universe must be associated with some good in both a privative and teleological sense (as arising accidentally or on account of some defect in its agent-cause), as I have argued, and no such associated good is obvious to a human observer as far as one knows in light of some instance of unexplained evil, then it would seem that this would provide a basis for denying God's existence for that observer. As such, applying this aspect of proper perspective to the new evidential argument, the modified argument would look something like this:

(1) There is no explanation for *S* such that *S* is caused by (or results from) some associated good *as far as I know*.

(2) If God exists, there is an explanation for *S* such that *S* is caused by (or results from) some associated good.

(3) Therefore, *as far as I know*, God does not exist.

To be clear, this approach is not a logical argument that considers good and evil *per se* in any sort of universal application, and the argument as such makes no prediction as to whether or not God truly does exist. The focus here is what can be reasonably concluded regarding evil specifically from a human perspective. It is important to note that one can sometimes reasonably believe X to be true even if one is unable to observe or explain *how* X could be true; thus, even if the syllogism above is sound, one might still profess a belief in God on other grounds—such as that of natural theology. For example, I am typing this sentence on a computer, and I see the words appear on my screen as I type, and yet I cannot explain the process involved and how this is actually accomplished *from the perspective I currently have*—nevertheless, it is reasonable for me to believe that what I am doing is actually occurring, and it is also reasonable to believe that there is certainly *some* reasonable explanation as to how keyboards and computers actually work and the mechanical and electrical operations involved (even if I do not know what it is). Thus, I need not be required to explain every detail of some aspect of reality (such as the existence of God and the explanation of every instance of evil) in order to affirm that God does exist.

The point of this new evidential argument is not to establish that God does not (or likely does not) exist—rather the point is to illustrate how God's existence could be *reasonably doubted or denied* on the basis of a lack of apparent explanation for some evil S. In fact, it could be true that God does in fact exist, and yet the conclusion of this new argument could still be true *for some particular observer*. To be clear, any difficulty one may have in resolving some question about evil from a human perspective has little bearing on the truth of the matter being considered, and one may yet have reason to believe in God even in the face of a difficult challenge or problem such as the one proposed in this argument. As Davies argues, "Yet the fact that people find something hard (or easy) to believe is surely neither here nor there when it comes to what is actually the case."[36] Thus, the fact of the matter at hand is not decided by the diffi-

36. Davies, *Reality of God*, 156.

culty of belief or the sum of unresolved challenges to that belief. Humans may find it difficult to deny (or accept) the existence of God on the basis of sound theistic arguments, for example, and yet find it challenging to affirm a *belief* in God simply on the basis of the apparent incongruity of God and evil from a human perspective. Thus, the target of such an argument is not God's existence *per se* but rather the question of one's *belief* in God's existence and whether unexplained evil presents a sufficient rational basis for denying God's existence. The new evidential argument I have proposed holds that the consideration of evil from a human perspective should lend itself to a denial of God's existence on the basis of inexplicable or excessive evil in the world. This returns the burden of proof to the theist—and that to a high degree—by providing that the theist must argue either that the lack of explicatory evidence for evil *necessarily* lies beyond one's own epistemic limits for some reason or that the fact of God's existence is simply beyond what a human can reasonably conclude when such an explanation for some evil *S* is not readily apparent.

However, even if one could successfully identify an instance of unexplained evil in the actual world from a human perspective, a solution remains for the theist that sufficiently circumvents the problem—specifically as given from a human perspective. The nature of the new evidential argument involves the *human perspective of evil* concerning the possible range of causes and ultimate teleological ordering involved in some instance of unexplained evil. As such, a solution remains open for the theist that itself considers one's own human perspective about God and evil, and it is here that I will turn in the final chapter.

9

The End of Evil

CONSIDERING GOD FROM A perspective of natural theology, as I have argued, it is apparent that God is not a moral being in the sense that his actions are governed by a set of moral duties and obligations that limit or determine his actions in relation to the world and the evil it contains. As such, the evidential problem of evil is resolved on a denial of the premise that God must mitigate or prevent evil whenever it is possible for him to do so. However, a new problem arises as a result of this approach that seeks not a *justification* but an *explanation* of evil such that some proposed instance of evil must be sufficiently explained as an aspect of the created world. The search for an *explanation* of evil involves any possible goods that are associated with that evil in their own causal operations or teleological direction, which would constitute a "reason" that some evil arises in a theistic universe. As such, an explanation of evil in terms of the goods involved that bring it about accidentally and are teleologically ordered toward the good must be apparent given what is known of God from the perspective of a Thomistic natural theology. Further, any explanation must be apparent from a human perspective of the evil in question and its causal operations (since this is all that is available to the observer), and thus the result of the argument defines what should be concluded of God's existence specifically from that human perspective. Hence if any instance of evil seems difficult to explain or without sufficient reason for its existence (considering the range of possible goods involved in the causal operations that brought it about), then it seems that one would have reason to doubt the existence of God.

This approach speaks directly to the "why" question of evil—such as the reason some evil came about or what possible goods may have been involved that resulted in that evil. Often instances of evil in the world seem excessive or unnecessary such that they may lack any obvious explanation to human observers, and to establish some legitimate example of inexplicable evil, one must only identify some evil *S* that is unexplained from a human perspective. If this is accomplished, then the observer has cause to deny God's existence *so far as one knows*. As such, there are all sorts of possible examples of instances of evil that may seem unexplained to those who witness or experience them, such as violent natural disasters that appear to emerge out of nowhere, mysterious injuries or diseases, unexplained disappearances, phantom memories of trauma or abuse, bad dreams or hallucinations, and so on. The point here is not that these examples always or actually lack natural causes or reasonable explanations—rather, in many such instances, an explanation of evil is not forthcoming *from a human perspective*, and the "why" question of evil is thus effectively unresolved. In such instances—given what is known of God—one should expect all such instances of evil to have at least some explanation in the causal operations and teleology involved that brought that evil about. When there appears to be no such explanation, then that evil may seem effectively inexplicable and suggest a contradiction to the God of classical theism—as allowing evils to occur that are either somehow beyond the scope of the causal operations of the natural world (or the acts of free moral agents) or without explanation in terms of the teleological ends involved (such as evil willed as an end in itself).

However, an option remains open to the theist to resolve this challenge that affirms both what can and cannot be known from a human perspective concerning good and evil and a reasonable basis for a committed belief in God. In short, the option available is a denial of premise (1) of the new evidential argument on the basis that *given any reasonable evidence or argument for God's existence*, there is necessarily sufficient reason to the same degree to hold that every evil *S* is in fact ordered toward (or results from) some associated good—even if one cannot and does not know what the explanation of *S* actually is from a human perspective. In other words, if there is any good reason whatsoever to think that God exists and is in fact omnipotent, omniscient, and perfectly good as classical theism affirms, then there necessarily is in fact good reason to hold that all instances of evil are necessarily explained even if it is not obvious to the observer. With this considered, anyone who has sufficient reason to believe that God exists also has sufficient reason to believe that premise (1) is false and all apparent evils in the world—however inexplicable they may *seem*—are entirely resolved in a theistic universe.

In this final chapter, I will consider this proposed solution to the new argument from evil from the perspective of a Thomistic natural theology. I will consider how reasonable evidence and arguments for God's existence offers the theist a rational basis to conclude that all evil (however gratuitous or excessive it may seem) can be and necessarily is fully explained in a theistic universe. I will follow with a consideration of God's goodness in the face of evil as a rejoinder to the objection that associated or explicatory goods may be logically impossible for some instance of evil followed by a reconsideration of other theistic efforts often employed in defense of the problem of evil that can play an important role in understanding a range of possible explanations of evil as found in a theistic universe. I will conclude by considering some possible objections to this approach, and I will show that any apparent gratuitous or excessive evil does not provide a sufficient reason to deny God's existence.

CONFIDENCE IN THE FACE OF EVIL

I have shown how a theistic foundation in natural theology renders the problem of evil unsound when considering that the God of natural theology holds no moral obligation to minimize or eliminate evil in the world. While a definitive, deductive argument therefore may be beyond the reach of the problem of evil, evidential arguments nevertheless do not depend solely on the logical certainty of their premises (as logical arguments from evil generally do) but also on the persuasive power of the evidential evils presented toward an inductive approach. The target of such arguments is the reasonable and rational basis for a human belief in God, which is arguably undermined by the severity and seeming inexplicability of the evils seen in the world. As such, the evidential argument from evil aims more to *persuade* rather than *convince*, and to whatever degree one considers the examples of evil offered by evidential arguments as particularly egregious and inexplicable, to the same degree one may be persuaded to abandon belief in the God of classical theism—or at least treat such a belief with a degree of suspicion.

Premise (1) of the new evidential argument from evil (as proffered in chapter eight) asserts, "There is no explanation for some evil *S* such that *S* is caused by (or results from) some associated good *as far as I know*." The argument here is that, on the evidence and understanding of the human observer, some instance of evil may appear to be without a sufficient explanation as to how and why it arises in a universe created by God, as considered from a human perspective. However, there is no reason to think that one's knowledge of evil and its concomitant causal operations are not or could not be likewise also informed by what one understands about the existence and nature of God as deduced from sound theistic arguments, and this presents a path forward for the theist in light of this new evidential argument.

A detailed discussion of human epistemology and how one's own inherent beliefs and knowledge of the natural world are properly obtained and shaped in the human mind is a work in itself and beyond the scope of the present project.[1] Thus, I will state only weakly here that I believe that much of what humans generally understand and interpret in light of our interactions with the world are informed in various ways by the foundational understanding we hold of the nature and causes of things observed. Also, what humans come to know and believe about the origin, purpose, and meaning of the world has a significant impact on how humans perceive the various aspects and effects of the natural world—including instances of good and evil.

Therefore, given the understanding of God presented in this work from the perspective of a Thomistic natural theology, how one interprets the general causes and teleology of good and evil would be (and should

1. Aquinas himself has a great deal to say on the process of human cognition and how it proceeds from the data of sensible reality to the creation of phantasms and an understanding gained in perception of the quiddity of things known (and so on). However, says Aquinas, the intellect can be deceived when the definition of a thing is considered in relation to other things or contains a contradiction within itself. He writes, "The intellect, however, may be accidentally deceived in the quiddity of composite things, not by the defect of its organ, for the intellect is a faculty that is independent of an organ; but on the part of the composition affecting the definition, when, for instance, the definition of a thing is false in relation to something else, as the definition of a circle applied to a triangle; or when a definition is false in itself as involving the composition of things incompatible; as, for instance, to describe anything as 'a rational winged animal.'" Aquinas, *Summa Theologiae*, I.85.6. Here, Aquinas illustrates what he considers is involved in the process of error or deceit on the part of the knowing subject—namely an error in relative concepts made by comparison between two things or within the definition of a thing itself. Considering knowledge of good and evil in the world, when evil is seen as uncaused because the explanatory scope of God's existence (as evidenced through natural theology) is omitted or neglected, for example, then the process for error in the knowing subject takes root. For more on a Thomistic account of human epistemology, see Wilhelmsen, *Man's Knowledge*; and Feser, *Philosophy of Mind*.

be) informed by this understanding. As such, the fact that all evil exists in a privative sense as linked (by their causal operations) to at least some good that itself exists by the will and power of God reflects an inescapable certainty that all evil (not evil as such but evil as a privation of the good it inhabits) is somehow explained on account of the acts of its agent-cause and the teleological ordering of those acts toward some good—even if that good is not immediately obvious to the observer. Further, there is no reason to think that the goods involved in association with some evil must of necessity be causally directed only toward goods that can be discovered or understood from a human perspective. Thus, the human observer can be confident (on the basis of God's existence, as evidenced by theistic arguments and a process of natural theology) that all evil is necessarily fully explained in a theistic universe, even if all of its explicatory goods are not immediately observed or known. The confidence that follows is a confidence grounded in natural theology that God exists in spite of the apparent inexplicability of at least some evil encountered in the world.

Therefore, if any basis for natural theology is accepted on its merits (such as the *intellectus essentiae* argument I have presented in this work), then the theist has *prima facie* reason to conclude that all evil is necessarily explained without contradiction in a world created by God. As Geisler and Corduan similarly argue, "Indeed, if there is an all-good and all-powerful God, then there is automatically a solution to the problem of evil. . . . Hence, whatever evidence favors the existence of such a God also favors the theistic solution to the problem of evil."[2] On this basis, one can likewise conclude that all evil must exist only in a privative sense and only as the result of some teleologically ordered good, either by or to some concomitant good that fully explains that evil's existence. Barring some evidence for evil that exists in and of itself (in some sort of non-privative sense), or some evidence that an instance of evil arises as an end in itself (absent any possible teleological order to the good), the theist can hold that both God and unexplained evil exist without contradiction. Further, the theist can exhibit confidence that despite one's perception of evil in the world, God nevertheless remains fully omnipotent, omniscient, and perfectly good, and there is no reason for the theist to treat this idea of God with doubt or suspicion on the basis of evil.

2. Geisler and Corduan, *Philosophy of Religion*, 314.

Given this approach, the ultimate solution to the evidential problem of evil (and the new evidential argument proposed in the previous chapter) becomes one of a committed belief in God on the basis of what can be known through the effects of the natural world (as well as potentially other forms of more direct divine revelation, if accepted in a particular theistic tradition). While natural theology itself does not explain evil in such a way that one could offer reasons *why* the world was created as it was with the quantity and severity of evils it contains, it does at least provide reason to accept that: God and evil both exist without contradiction, God never acts with evil as an end in itself, and God is directly and necessarily responsible for all that is good in the world. With this in mind, the theist can draw on what is known of God from a knowledge of the world and its causal operations and conclude—even from a limited human perspective—that God exists, one should believe he exists, and one can have a level of confidence in God and his divine goodness even in the face of evil. As such, the "why" question may not have the sort of direct answer or explanation that one desires or seeks (at least in terms of a strict natural theology), but the absence of such a direct answer from a human perspective does not imply or suggest that there is in fact *no answer*; given what is known of God through natural theology, one can be confident that there is inevitably a sufficient and reasonable answer to the "why" question, even if one does not know what it is.

A further consideration of value is that of *faith* in God, which generally entails not only a basic belief and confidence in God's existence and attributes but also a commitment and assent to what God has revealed about himself from not only his effects in the natural world but also other potential means of divine revelation—such as perhaps by authoritative prophets and apostles, for example. Up to this point, I have not invoked any specific religious doctrine or dogma in my argument and have relied solely on the evidence provided from a purely natural theology to unravel the problem of evil. However, many theists hold to specific religious traditions and additional evidence of more direct divine revelation, and it is important to illustrate how faith in these traditions may offer additional confidence and comfort for the sufferer.

Faith in this sense is an act of will grounded in what can be reasonably and rationally ascertained from a foundation of evidence and argument concerning God, his nature, and his various commands and decrees. Taking what is known of God by means of his divine revelation, the possibility of faith arises as a human act of reliance on God and his

Word as a means to combat the doubts and emotions that may arise when one faces inexplicable or gratuitous evil. Notably, it is the reliability of reason here in the face of evil that gives faith in God its greatest force when arguments from evil arise. As Edward Feser explains,

> In any event, it is precisely because of the abstraction and coldness of reason that a kind of faith is needed where evil is concerned. Not because faith is emotional. Faith is *not* emotional; it is rather an act of the will. And again, not because faith contradicts reason, for it doesn't. Rather, faith in God in the face of evil is nothing less than the will to *follow* reason's lead when emotion might incline us to doubt. . . . Hence reason tells us: have faith in God.[3]

Here, Feser lays out what I believe to be a critical aspect of the ultimate and final resolution to the problem of evil—that of a rational, committed faith in God on the basis of reason and reflection from a position of natural theology, as well as consideration of God's direct revelation. This act of faith is an act of the will on the basis of what is known about God as the perfectly good creator and sustainer of all that is—it is nothing like a "blind leap" from a ledge where nothing can be clearly seen or known (as faith is sometimes defined). It is a faith supported by reason and evidence. As Geisler and Corduan explain, "An unjustifiable and/or unverifiable faith is not worth believing, if it is believable at all."[4] Furthermore, this belief and trust in God is grounded (at least in part) in knowledge achieved by reason from the natural world, so it is not *ad hoc* or begging the question to exhibit confidence in God in the face of evil on the basis of one's natural theology or an appeal to divine revelation, for example.

Nevertheless, despite one's confidence in God in the face of evil, one may still be plagued with uncertainty as to how God's goodness could *possibly* be evident in the face of inexplicable or gratuitous evil as seen from a human perspective. It is possible, of course, that in some instances, the causal interactions that bring about some instance of evil may not be immediately accessible or knowable, and in such instances, one's belief and trust in God can still thrive while remaining grounded in a knowledge of God gained by a process of natural theology and assent to the authority of divine revelation, for example. However, the "why" question of evil still lingers for the theist (the question as to "why" some instance of evil

3. Feser, *Last Superstition*, 164; emphasis in original.

4. Geisler and Corduan, *Philosophy of Religion*, 311.

came about or what good it could possibly be ordered toward—if any), and sometimes such a question could become a threat or counterpoint to one's faith if left unresolved. As such, it is of value here to consider at least some ways that God's goodness can be clearly seen in creation and understood *even in the face of evil* purely from a human perspective.

GOOD IN THE FACE OF EVIL

The evidence for God's existence and nature in natural theology gives the theist a confidence in God and his perfect goodness even in the face of evil, and this natural theology (by means of human reason) reveals that no contradiction exists between gratuitous or inexplicable evil and the existence of an omniscient, omnipotent, perfectly good God. However, some evil may remain yet *unexplained* as a matter of its causal operations and teleological ordering, and certain examples of gratuitous evil specifically can be nevertheless difficult to accept as an aspect of a theistic universe without such an explanation. Thus the "why" question (as to why and how some instance of gratuitous evil may arise in the world) remains unanswered for the theist—even if the answer can be reasonably assumed on the basis of what is known of God by means of natural theology. As such, it may seem to an observer that the evidence of evil yet outweighs the evidence of good in the universe, and while one may not have good reason to doubt God's existence on this basis as either logically impossible or even improbable, such a conflict can nevertheless provide a challenge to one's confidence in God's existence and goodness strictly as considered from a human perspective.

With this in mind, I believe it is both possible and reasonable to say something positive about God in the face of evil. To be clear, such an attempt does not seek to provide a *justification* for evil (since no divine moral justification is necessary); neither does it seek to provide an exhaustive *explanation* of evil (since much about good, evil, and the causal operations involved may lie beyond human epistemic limits or even entirely within the hidden councils of God). However, finding at least some good in the face of evil can help to illustrate how it is *possible* that at least some instances of evil can or could be related to the various goods that exist as ordered toward the highest good in God himself. This approach is not meant to present any sort of *theodicy* as a means to justify God's permission of evil in the world. In fact, this approach takes on more the character of a *defense*, for I only intend to consider the *possibility* of certain related goods that are sometimes evident by an examination and observation of the natural world.

There is much good one can recognize in the world as associated with evil in various ways—either as a cause of evil (directly or indirectly) or something that follows from it. While the specific answer to the question of why God allows some evil may remain ultimately elusive to the theist, nevertheless a consideration of the various ways that at least some evil is and can be linked to the good in its causal and teleological operations can help to illustrate *how it is possible* for the "why" question to be resolved.[5] This is not to say that *whatever the actual reason for evil may be* that humans would (and should) be in a position to discover it. In fact, it may be so that if humans could examine the infinite reaches of the divine mind in an evaluation of all instances of evil in all of their causal relationships that humans would at once see how such an explanation would be entirely sufficient not only to explain the existence of those evils but also to explain God's permission of them to our complete and unquestioned satisfaction. In other words, God may in fact have "reasons" in mind for the evils in the world that would "justify" those evils to all human moral sensibilities if only they were known. Per Ganssle and Lee:

> For example, God may allow some evils to help develop the character of the people involved. Some he may allow so people will turn to him and experience answers to prayer. Some evil may contribute to the good of others. It is also reasonable that some evil may allow for free choices. These suggestions, and

5. In keeping with my prior analysis on the subject of God and his "reasons," I do not here mean to imply that God must have reasons for whatever he does or does not allow in the same way that humans have reasons for what they do. God cannot be said to have desires to fulfill or needs that must be accomplished in what he chooses to do. God is the ultimate metaphysical origin of both cause and effect for everything that comes to be—good things that exist with whatever perfections they possess and whatever perfections they lack. However, I hold that one can speak of God's "reasons" in a meaningful analogical sense to reflect the ordering of some things to others in a cause/effect relationship that brings some things about through intermediate causes, with the end always in mind. Thus, any effects that humans recognize in the world (particularly those associated with evil for our present purposes) must arise from some process that is itself good as created by God that includes at least some suffering or corruption as a facet of its teleological ordering in the universe. As such, one can speak of "reasons" why something occurs in an explanatory sense by understanding the causes and teleological direction of any instance of evil.

more, may provide some reasons that God may allow particular cases of evil.[6]

Here, Ganssle and Lee illustrate what most attempt to achieve by proposing a theodicy toward the justification of evil, but such an observation is not necessarily limited to that application. As I have shown, there is no need to *justify* God's permission of evil as long as the evidential evil in question is explicable in the natural world and does not entail a contradiction. The application of such an observation in this sense, however, is not toward a *justification* but an *explanation*—to scratch the itch of the "why" question, so to speak.

This pursuit of the "why" question may be of help to those struggling with an explanation for evil in light of one's confidence in God and his perfect goodness. Nevertheless, such a pursuit is not intellectually necessary to achieve a belief and trust in God in the first place. Given what can be known about God and his nature in terms of natural theology (and divine revelation), an exhaustive explanation of evil can be reasonably assumed to exist even if it is not immediately forthcoming on analysis and reflection from a human perspective. If one can know of God with certainty that he exists as an omnipotent, omniscient, perfectly good creator of all that is, then one has no need of justifying or explaining evil in order to affirm a committed belief in God—even if one naturally desires and seeks answers for those questions. In other words, one need not resolve the "why" question in order to develop a rational belief and trust in God.

Even though a committed belief in God is intellectually sound in spite of the existence of gratuitous evil, there remains some value in the intellectual pursuit of answers to the "why" question. In other words as I have argued, one can remain committed to a belief in God in the face of gratuitous evil, and yet one may still struggle in search of answers as to why some evil occurred or what good it could possibly be associated with in the grand scheme of things such that it would be fully understood and explained *from a human perspective* as an aspect of a world created by an omnipotent, omniscient, perfectly good God.[7] Perhaps it should

6. Ganssle and Lee, "Evidential Problems of Evil," 18.

7. It may be that the answers one seeks to the "why" question are not immediately forthcoming for other reasons as well. In other words, it may be that God has orchestrated things in such a fashion to deliberately obscure a fully complete and satisfying explanation of evil from a human perspective for some other purpose. For example, it may be true that if God's "reasons" for evil were fully known from a human perspective,

be sufficient to see only that it is not impossible for God to bring good from evil or allow at least some evil for the sake of good—even if it is not necessary for him to do so or if some evil is truly gratuitous. In this way, a demonstration of at least the *possibility* of an explanation of evil would preclude one from refusing belief in God on that basis. In this way, seeing how at least some evil is either caused by or leads to some good can help to foster and support an intellectual assent to God's existence and nature as revealed by natural theology.

The Greater Good

Recall that "greater good" theodicies seek to identify some greater good involved in each instance of evil such that the good in question justifies one in a moral sense in allowing that evil to arise and persist in the world. While God is in no need of this sort of moral justification, as I have argued, this approach to theodicy is largely misguided in pursuit of a resolution to the problem of evil. However, it may yet be helpful to illustrate how certain instances of evil in the world can be (and sometimes clearly are) associated with great goods—either occurring as a result of some great good or allowing some great good to emerge specifically on account of that occurrence of evil. This is not to say that all (or even most) evil must necessarily have some great good attached to it—or even to say that some good that does follows from some instance of evil is in fact *the explanation* of why that evil occurred. It is simply to say that *much good can and does emerge in the face of evil*, and such can be of value in consideration of how good and evil fit together from a human perspective. For example, it may be that the kidnapping and murder of a certain young woman becomes a catalyst that galvanizes a society in support of sweeping social changes that in turn protects countless potential future victims and brings even more perpetrators to justice. If this were the case, it would not necessarily suggest that God is the one who somehow orchestrated things in such a way to directly *cause* the woman's kidnapping and murder toward this end (as a sort of "means-end" justification)—or even that God allowed the crime to occur *for the sake of* the good that followed from it. However, one could reasonably affirm that God may

---

such knowledge would prevent creatures in some way from a natural dependence on their creator as their proper end. Even if this were so, it would not preclude a human observer for seeking answers or struggling with the question at hand. As such, it would still be of value to inquire and investigate the "why" question in the face of evil.

have used this apparent act of gratuitous evil to bring about something good. It is not that God is under a mandate of sorts to bring a good like this out of every instance of evil, but it can be helpful to recognize that he is at least able to do so and sometimes does.

Further, understanding the causal factors at play in some instance of evil helps to explain that act of evil and why it occurred. In the case of the kidnapping and murder of the woman, for example, the immoral acts and corrupted will of the perpetrator explains the evil in question because both the perpetrator and the victim exist within the context of a natural world of causal interdependency such that the actions of one being (in a corrupted pursuit of some perceived "good" for his own sake) at times intersects and affects the good of others—causing the privation of evil and suffering for his victim. Upon reflection, it is evident that a world of meaningful interaction and interdependency among its creatures is an overall good for those creatures in most cases—even if sometimes the evil acts of one such creature can have and does have a devastating impact on another. This does not in any way excuse the moral failure of the perpetrator, nor does it imply that God is somehow *morally justified* in allowing the murder of the woman *for the sake of* some good that explains her suffering in this regard (such as the good of the natural order). However, it does help to provide at minimum an *explanation* of the causal operations that led to the crime and how at each step along the way, there is always something "good" in operation (as a thing that exists according to the kind of thing that it is) that seeks the "good" in some way.

In addition to understanding the goods associated with at least some instances of evil (both causally and teleologically), it is also of value to recognize the vast quantity and quality of various goods that make up the daily world in which we live. As John Hick observes:

> It is certainly a great mistake to underestimate the extent of human suffering, which indeed exceeds the wide scope of our imagination. But it is also a great mistake to underestimate the extent of human contentment and happiness and hope. Life can be gray and grim; but it can also contain great and wide pockets of light and happiness, of beauty and charm. There are many joys within the world of persons—love and courting, parenthood, the fun of family life, friendship and loyalty, the service of stirring human causes. There is the world around us, the trees

> and clouds, mountains and lakes and valleys and seas and flower and grass and animals . . .[8]

Here, Hick illustrates the value in recognizing the good in the world as a help toward explaining the evil it also contains. Evidential arguments from evil often focus on some instance of horrendous evil as apparently *unjustifiable*, and while I have held that there may in fact be instances of genuinely unjustified horrendous evils that occur, it is also of note that the vast majority of the life and experiences of most creatures in the world involves a significant measure of things like joy, peace, contentment, happiness, fulfillment, and so on—in most cases to such a degree that these various goods experienced by creatures *far outweigh* the sum total of whatever evil and suffering those creatures may experience. This is not to say that a world created by God *has to be this way*, or that God (as creator) somehow owes his creatures a certain balance of pleasure and happiness to offset the evils they experience. In fact, the God of classical theology is a debtor to none and could have created the world *far worse than this one*—with vastly more suffering than it presently contains. Therefore, the fact that it contains such an abundance of goods for creatures to witness and experience is directly attributable to God as its source (since God is the cause of all that is good). Such does not provide a *justification* or *explanation* as to why some things go bad and some creatures at times experience apparently unjustified suffering, despair, and agony. However, it does illustrate the goodness of God in more evidential and practical ways that intersect well with one's knowledge of good and evil from a human perspective. Thus, seeing how the goods and evils of the world interact in complex ways (such as described in these few examples), with many great goods associated with various instances of evil, helps to illustrate how such an explanation for evil could possibly be achieved.

The Natural Order

Another facet of the world that many theodicists often invoke toward a justification of the evil it contains is the good of the natural order. Aquinas himself makes just such an argument when considering whether God can be attributed as the cause of evil: "Now, the order of the universe requires, as was said above, that there should be some things that can, and do sometimes, fail. And thus God, by causing in things the good of

8. Hick, "Soul-Making and Suffering," 176.

the order of the universe, consequently and as it were by accident, causes the corruptions of things."[9] Here, Aquinas illustrates what some theodicists suggest when invoking the natural order as an explanation of evil. Again, Aquinas does not here mean to *justify* God's permission of evil *on account of* the good of the natural world. Rather, Aquinas simply shows how the evil of corruption that results from the natural operation of the world he has made can be rightly attributed to a perfectly good God who causes the natural world to exist and operate as the natural law requires. The existence and consistent function of the world under a set of consistent, predictable natural laws (as decreed by God) is a good, and the evils that result from its regular operations are fully explained on that basis. Further, the evils that result from corruption, as Aquinas argues, are evils caused not for their own sake (or for the sake of evil itself, so to speak) but for the sake of the good of the natural world. Once again, this good is not a *moral justification* of evil, but it is nevertheless a perfectly reasonable and consistent *explanation* of evil such that it is entirely consistent with an omnipotent, omniscient, perfectly good God.

In further consideration of this approach, it is important to recognize that the world God has created is one of a complex system of interdependence and change where many created things do not or cannot achieve their own perfection or highest good without consuming or corrupting other things along the way. A human who eats a potato, for example, destroys the potato while gaining the good of nourishment. A fire that consumes a fawn is nourished and fed, so to speak, by the flesh of the fawn. This does not entail some sort of cosmic value-judgment in the relation of good and evil in the natural world by suggesting that fires are better than fawns, for example, but it does reveal that the perfections of at least some things depend on the corruption of others, and this is simply the way the natural world and the creatures it contains operate according to their created natures and the sorts of things they are.

Some argue that a perfectly good God should prevent evil whenever he can, though when the good of the natural world is also considered in such an argument, such a suggestion seems to be misguided. Putting aside for a moment the problems with attributing moral obligations to God, the challenge to the existence of God on the basis of natural evil remains puzzling and problematic when properly considered. As the argument goes, God has the power to override the natural order to prevent

9. Aquinas, *Summa Theologiae*, I.49.2.

suffering and death whenever it occurs. As such, the inherent suggestion in such an argument is that in order for God to make a natural world where some things thrive at the expense of others, God must also use his power to prevent any such negative consequences that arises from the operation of such a world. In other words, the argument is that in order for God to make a world like this with a regular natural order, God must prevent the world from having a regular natural order. Such an argument on its face is plainly absurd. If God creates a world such as this one, the good of its regular operation is sufficient to explain any suffering and evil in that world that may arise from its natural operations; God cannot be faulted for upholding the world he has made exactly as he has made it.

One may yet argue that God could have made the world some other way—such as a world where nothing depends on the corruption of other things to achieve their own perfections, but such an argument would entirely miss the point. First, it is true that God could certainly have done things differently, though the fact remains that he simply did not do so—God made the world as it is, it was entirely within his power to do so, and the world now possesses a sort of suppositional necessity to function exactly as it was made to function. Second, as I have argued in chapter seven, there is no basis to suggest that some other non-existent *possible world* is "better" in any meaningful sense since all possible worlds are necessarily good. Third, even if another world were objectively "better" than the present world in some way, it seems that humans would have no way to determine this since humans have no direct epistemic access to any world other than the present one. Fourth, there is no reason to think that God *should* or *must* create one world over another—any possible world is within the power of God to create, and there is nothing in the nature of God to suggest that God must limit himself on the basis of a sort of cosmic value-judgment between possibilities open to him in whatever he chooses to do. All possible worlds exist in tandem with the infinite goodness of God himself, and thus there is no more or less good in any world whatsoever so long as God is its creator (or even no world at all if God chose not to create). So long as any possible world is good (and does not contain contradictions or evil for its own sake, for example), then every possible world is equally good on the whole—regardless if some world contains "more good things" than another.

To be clear, my argument here by invoking the good of the natural world as an explanatory asset in the evaluation of the "why" question is not meant to suggest a sort of theodicy toward a moral justification for evil. The natural operation of the world may be a great good worthy of its own creation and preservation, but this does not imply that the good of the natural world somehow justifies the evils it contains (at least in a moral sense). The good of the natural world is, however, helpful to explain the reasons that evil emerges when it does, as considered from the perspective of its own natural operations. As I have argued, God makes the world as it is and upholds it according to its nature, including the natural laws that cause some things to thrive and some things to fail. The creator of the world cannot be held accountable for its continued regular operation or expected to somehow override or contradict that which he has already created for its own sake. As such, one can have absolute confidence in God's existence and certain facts about his nature while also recognizing that a great deal of evil and suffering do emerge in the world God has made without any need for additional moral justification. Nevertheless, understanding how the world works can help us understand why some evils may emerge, how these evils are not caused by God, and that God is not obliged to prevent or hinder those simply on account of the nature of the world he has already made. While this stops short of fully answering the "why" question of evil, it does nevertheless help one understand (at least from a human perspective) why and how at least some evils do occur.

Free Will

In nearly every treatment of the problem of evil, the concept of free will is often proposed as a possible reason why the evil in the world may be beyond God's power to prevent. So the argument goes, if God creates a world where creatures with genuine freedom must choose between good and evil, then God cannot manipulate the will of those creatures to ensure a world without evil. Therefore, the creation of free creatures "risks" the possibility of evil, so to speak, and the evil that results in such a world is the natural byproduct of a world that contains free creatures. As such, it is said that God could not prevent evil in such a world without also preventing free will. Since genuine human freedom is considered a great good, then the evil that results cannot be attributed to God as its cause and cannot count against God's perfect goodness (on account of the great good of human freedom that justifies the evil in question).

As I have argued, I do not believe that human freedom justifies the existence of evil in the way many philosophers suggest. For one, the exercise of the human will cannot be something that occurs entirely apart from the creative decrees of God, for God is the "first mover" of the will and responsible for the existence of both creature and will in every aspect of its existence—including the creature's nature, the operation of its mind, its judgment and will, and its perception of the good that it seeks on account of the sort of creature that it is. Further, it does not seem wrong or oppressive for God to deny an ignorant creature the exercise of its own freedom for the sake of its own good or well-being. After all, parents do this all the time: a young child wants to play in the street, but her parents—knowing the danger at hand—will invariably revoke their child's free will and prevent her from charging out into harm's way. Why then would it be overstepping his bounds for God to do the same for us—particularly when the consequences of poor moral choices are often extremely severe? A loving God who recognizes the foolish choices of creatures who reject their own highest good to the detriment of their eternal well-being (as per Christian theology, for example) would certainly be within his rights to take more aggressive measures toward constraining the human creature from harming itself in this way—either by preventing the creature from engaging in its own destructive behavior or making the highest goods it seeks more obvious to its immediate perception. Additionally, much of the suffering that flows from acts of human freedom impacts others at least as much (or far more) than the culprits themselves, which does not seem particularly reasonable as a point of justification for God to allow evil in this way. A parent may allow a child to pick what toy she want to play with, but when she tries to snatch a toy from her brother, they would likely intervene. Finally, much of the evil in the world seems to have little or no bearing on human freedom at all in any obvious causal relationship—such as disease, cancer, earthquakes, hurricanes, tsunamis, and other natural phenomena that leave untold devastation and suffering in their wakes. As such, arguments from freedom seem generally incomplete or inadequate as a response to the problem of evil from a perspective of moral justification.

However, the argument from freedom as a justification for evil is not the only way that human freedom can be invoked as a help to the problem of evil—especially when considered from a human perspective. If God exists as the creator of all humans, then he is the architect of human nature, and the highest good for the human is found in God himself—specifically to freely know, love, and honor God (as is commonly understood in most theistic traditions). Further, if creatures are created with the freedom to choose or reject God in this life, then it should be no surprise that the supreme goodness of God himself would be obscured at least to some degree as an object of immediate assent and recognition, and creatures would be left with myriad lesser goods in the place of God—thus being able to accept or reject higher goods for lesser goods as an act of the will. As such, it should be unsurprising that a rejection of God in such a case would carry consequences that stand in direct contrast to the various perfections sought by those creatures—which gives rise to evil in a world filled with significantly free creatures. Further, it seems that such evils would also become a necessary point to distinguish higher goods from lesser goods and further direct creatures to their highest good in God himself. Even suffering resulting from the natural world (or the actions of others) would serve as evidence of the overall brokenness of the world and a general separation from God caused by human moral failure. This would not suggest that God allows evil (or even causes it) *for the sake of* drawing creatures to himself in this way or even for the provision of consequences for wrongdoing, and it likewise would not justify God in a moral sense for allowing evil to persist. However, such an explanation can nevertheless be helpful *from a human perspective* to see how the prevalence and experience of evil could have its ultimate explanation in the moral failures of free creatures (and at least one possible way God could bring good out of evil). Here, the experience of evil (at least for the theist) would denote powerful evidential support for the brokenness of the world and its need for God—rather than evidence for God's nonexistence.

Christianity and Evil

A final perspective to consider is that of Christian theology and evil. For the most part up to this point, I have largely considered the problem of evil from the perspective of a Thomistic natural theology that does not presume or require any specific theological framework. As such, I have largely avoided arguments from the perspective of any particular faith tradition—that which would rely on more direct divine revelation to at least some degree and cannot be deduced from reason alone. However, I do believe that Christianity in particular offers some additional insights that may be helpful in consideration of the "why" question concerning the problem of evil from a human perspective. Here, I will briefly present just a few ways in which Christian theology addresses the philosophical problem of evil, particularly the *teleology of evil*, as in what good (if any) follows from evil such that evil itself fits within a world created by God as considered from a human perspective.[10]

One chief concern inherent in many approaches to the evidential problem of evil is why God at times seems so distant or silent and does not appear to do anything in the face of much horrendous evil in the world. From the perspective of Christian theology, however, such an assumption is entirely unfounded. In fact, as Christianity explains, evil (particularly moral evil, though also certain aspects of natural evil as well) is the byproduct of the moral failures of free creatures, and rather than entirely abandoning those creatures to their own self-destruction and eternal damnation, God has gone to great lengths to overcome the terminal nature of moral evil. Classical Christianity teaches that God has freely chosen to intervene in the world in such a way that the moral failures of creatures are provided a means of redemption and restoration—all through the work of Jesus Christ, the Son of God. Such an offer of salvation is not done out of necessity or obligation on God's part (as if to fulfill some innate moral obligation to redeem his creation), but as an act of divine grace, and the creatures to whom it is offered are freely given the choice to respond or not. In short, God did not *have* to offer salvation to those who have chosen and deserve eternal separation from God—rather he did so freely out of love for his creatures, though without violating their own freedom of will.[11]

10. One aspect of Christian theology that I will not here address is the concept of the origin or cause of evil (particularly moral evil, though also to a subsequent degree a cause of much natural evil as well) as traditionally ascribed to the "fall" of mankind through the sin of Adam—as well as the ongoing moral failures of many creatures since on account of sinful natures passed down from Adam across all of humanity. Despite the fact that an analysis of Christian theology on the fall of mankind can certainly be helpful toward a resolution of the "why" question of evil (specifically concerning its primeval origins and its subsequent effect on the natural world), an expansive discussion of the fall simply runs too far afield of the overall philosophical argument I am making here. Suffice to say from a philosophical perspective, it is enough to affirm (as I have already argued) that the cause of moral evil cannot be ascribed to God as its direct cause, and thus God cannot be responsible for the onset or persistence of moral evil. The origin of evil in the nature and actions of free creatures is nevertheless a philosophical possibility that places the responsibility of all evil squarely on the shoulders of culpable creatures and never God himself.

11. An additional aspect of the problem of evil unique to Christianity is introduced

Further, Christian theology teaches that not only does God offer salvation to creatures who commit evil acts, but he also offers hope to those who suffer by the evil acts of others (or by other natural causes) by promising and providing for a complete and final end to suffering once and for all. As such, the fact that God has provided for the salvation of the world is not meant to constitute a *moral justification* for God allowing evil to exist in the universe. God is not obliged to act on behalf of rebellious creatures or to provide any means of redemption whatsoever for either sinner or sufferer. However, per Christian theology, God has chosen to do so freely. One may argue that God should have ended suffering sooner or that he could have or should have done it some other way, but such an argument misses the point. It is not within the scope of a finite human perspective to consider how God could have or should have done anything at all—it is simply enough that he has in fact acted to end sin and evil once and for all, and on that basis it is clear to the Christian believer that a full and complete resolution to evil is forthcoming and can be reasonably accepted by faith. To whatever degree a human accepts such a concept of the divine solution for and ultimate end of evil, to the same degree that human has reason to trust in God in the face of however much unanswered evil the world may contain.

Another aspect of Christian theology that has direct impact on the philosophical problem of evil is that of the suffering of Jesus Christ. In Christianity, it is not just that God has forgiven or resolved sin safely from a distant divine vantage point without any "skin in the game" himself, so to speak. In fact, as Christianity teaches, Jesus Christ is God in the flesh, and Jesus suffered tremendous agony (both physically and spiritually) specifically for the benefit of those who have sinned and those who suffer

---

here, and that is the "problem of hell." Specifically, the existence of a loving, perfectly good God is said to be incompatible with the existence of the traditional view of hell as an eternal state of torment reserved for unbelievers (or those who reject the saving grace of Jesus Christ). Since addressing this particular aspect of the problem of evil runs too far afield from my general aim in this work to focus on and address the evidential problem of evil, I will not address this particular problem at length. Suffice to say, however, that I believe the traditional view of hell is in fact compatible with the God of classical theism as I have thus far defended, and this for a number of reasons—not the least of which is that hell is what divine justice simply requires on account of the natures of those who are ultimately damned, and there does not appear to be anything unjust or unexplained when many receive what they ultimately deserve. For philosophical arguments that deny the compatibility of God and an eternal hell, see Adams, "Problem of Hell; Spiegel, "Hell," 239–48. For an argument in favor of an eternal hell from a Thomistic perspective, see Macdonald, Jr. "Hell," 603–28.

on account of sin. As Peter Kreeft explains, "We begin with the mystery, not just of suffering but of suffering in a world supposedly created by a loving God. How to get God off the hook? God's answer is Jesus. Jesus is not God off the hook but God on the hook."[12] This concept is an aide to the Christian toward seeing suffering and pain in a different light—as something not faced alone but with Christ at one's side. This does not explain or resolve any challenge from the problem of evil that places the burden on theists to explain *why* God allows suffering in the first place, but it does help specifically from a human perspective to see that God is present in one's suffering and that God's intervention was at great personal cost to himself in the person of Jesus Christ. One may ask why it was necessary for Christ to die on behalf of sinners or suggest that God should have provided redemption some other way, but once again such a suggestion misses the point. The fact remains *from a human perspective* according to Christianity that God did choose to intervene in the manner he did, and at great personal cost, for the sake of restoring the damaged human/divine relationship. As Kenneth Surin explains, it is the identity of Christ as God in the flesh who shares in the suffering of creatures that is key to providing a solution to the problem of evil.

> Standing within the circle of the Christian *mythos*, one can affirm that the God who shares the sufferings of his creatures to the point of death is the God who is incarnate in the person of Jesus of Nazareth. Or more simply: the 'practical' approach to the 'problem of evil,' presupposing as it does the atonement wrought on the cross of the Son of God, rests finally on the principle that the God who saves is the God who is incarnate in his creation.[13]

Per Surin, God's role as the one who redeems both sinner and sufferer in this regard fosters a response to the "why" question from a human perspective largely because of God's personhood in Jesus Christ. Thus, the Christian has a means for understanding at least something about her own suffering (and that of others) on the basis of the work of Jesus Christ and his divine nature. For the Christian, suffering in this sense is

12. Kreeft, *Making Sense*, 140.

13. Surin, *Theology*, 137; emphasis in original. Surin distinguishes between the philosophical problem of evil and what he here refers to as the "practical" problem of evil—which is largely synonymous with what I have described as the "why" problem—the problem of evil specifically from a human perspective that seeks answers to why evil exists and why it so often seems unresolved.

related to a divine relationship such that it affects the very inclinations and instincts that a believer has toward suffering.

> You see, the Christian views suffering, as he views everything, in a totally different way, a totally different context, than the unbeliever. He sees it and everything else as a *between*, as existing between God and himself, as a gift from God, an invitation from God, a challenge from God, something between God and himself. Everything is relativized. I do not relate to an object and keep God in the background somewhere; God is the object that I relate to. Everything is between us and God.[14]

Here, as Kreeft explains, the Christian believer is affected to the level of her own natural instincts and inclinations such that suffering is seen in a different light altogether—as something that impacts the relationship between God and mankind in a positive and significant way. To whatever degree a Christian believer is impacted by the act of Christ—as God in the flesh—in his own suffering on the cross toward a solution to sin and human separation, to the same degree that believer develops a new perspective on her own suffering such that it not only fits together in a world created by God, but it also stands in relation between the believer and God himself.

Along the same line of argument, another significant aspect of Christian theology in consideration of the problem of evil is that of "co-suffering" with Christ. As Paul explains, "For just as the sufferings of Christ are ours in abundance, so also our comfort is abundant through Christ" (2 Cor 1:5). Here, the suffering faced by believers stands in a meaningful relation to Christ's own suffering, who in turn provides comfort for the sufferer on that basis.

> First, because God in Christ participated in horrendous evil through His passion and death, human experience of horrors can be a means of *identifying* with Christ, either through *sympathetic* identification (in which each person suffers his/her own pains, but their similarity enables each to know what it is like for the other) or through *mystical* identification (in which the created person is supposed literally to experience a share of Christ's pain).[15]

14. Kreeft, *Making Sense*, 137.

15. Adams, "Horrendous Evils," 218–19; emphasis in original. Adams here suggests that God in some way comes to "know" the depths of human suffering by his own experience, which bears a great deal of theological disagreement with the traditional view of an impassable God as revealed by a Thomistic natural theology (as I have espoused in this work). Suffice to say, I do not agree with Adams on this point, though

Here, Adams makes the case that suffering for a believer involves an enhancement to the human/divine relationship by the experience of something akin to what Christ endured for our own sake on the cross. Once again, Kreeft:

> What then is suffering to the Christian? It is Christ's invitation to follow him. Christ goes to the cross, and we are invited to follow to the same cross. Not because it is the cross, but because it is his. Suffering is blessed not because it is suffering but because it is his. Suffering is not the context that explains the cross; the cross is the context that explains suffering.[16]

As such, for Kreeft, all suffering (for the believer) is explained in a meaningful way by the suffering of Christ on the cross—such that our own human suffering is a form of participation in Christ's own work. Such a perspective engenders a natural faith and trust in God in the face of suffering unlike anything available to the non-believer. "For if we have reason to trust in God in the face of suffering, how much more ought we to trust in a God who so loves us that He became flesh, to suffer with us, and for us?"[17] Thus, on account of the sufferings of Christ, the believer has reason to trust in God even in the face of one's own suffering.

A final aspect of Christian theology that is of value in consideration of the problem of evil is that of the eschatological hope for the redemption of the sufferer and the end of all evil and suffering. Such a hope serves to encourage believers mired in suffering and despair in the present world to long for a newer and better world where the proper end of all redeemed creatures is realized in a direct relationship with God himself for all eternity. As the apostle Paul explains, "For I consider that the sufferings of this present time are not worthy to be compared with the glory that is to be revealed to us" (Rom 8:18). It is here that Aquinas identifies a stark disparity between one's hope for prosperity and justice in the present world and one's hope in a world to come. The issue at hand reduces to how one sees their own proper end. Per Aquinas,

> Note first that different people have different relationships to the prosperity of this world. Some men have it as an end because

I do believe that the relationship of human suffering to the sufferings of Christ bears a real and meaningful position that enables comfort on the part of the human when facing suffering.

16. Kreeft, *Making Sense*, 137.

17. Feser, *Last Superstition*, 165.

> they hope for nothing beyond this. This seems to be the opinion of those who declare that all rewards and punishments are in this life. Such men do not go beyond the prosperity of this world but the prosperity of this world escapes from them when they lose it. Some, however, among whom Job was included, do not place their end in the prosperity of this world, but aim at another end. They pass up the prosperity of this world more than they are passed up by it.[18]

Such a perspective effectively enhances one's general perspective toward evil and suffering in the present world such that however bad things may seem, they only pale in comparison to the immanent glory that awaits all who place faith in Jesus Christ. As Peter Kreeft observes, "Because of resurrection, when all our tears are over, we will, incredibly, look back at them and laugh, not in derision but in joy."[19] For Kreeft, suffering for the Christian is only temporary and will be reduced to an insignificant afterthought in the presence of the joys of an eternity restored to a right relationship with God. As such, many Christian philosophers have latched on to eschatological thinking as a critical aspect of considerations involving evil and suffering from a human perspective. As Ed Feser explains, one can reason to the conclusion that we were created for a life beyond this one and that God is fully capable of restoring us to such a state:

> Hence reason tells us that there is a God who created for us a destiny beyond this life and who is fully capable of guaranteeing that the good we attain in the next life outweighs the evil we suffer in this one to such an extent that the latter, however awful from our present point of view, will come to seem "not worth comparing" to the former, and indeed if anything will even be seen to have been worth having gone through from the point of view of eternity. And therefore, reason itself tells us that there is simply no reason to believe that even the worst possible sufferings of this life constitute any evidence whatsoever against the existence of God.[20]

As such, when one occupies their attention and focus with the present world and looks for a justification of evil (as per justice, reward, and punishment) as well as one's own prosperity, they find themselves at a loss. However, if one recognizes one's proper end in a world to come and

18. Aquinas, *ad Iob*, 9.4.
19. Kreeft, *Making Sense*, 139.
20. Feser, *Last Superstition*, 163–64.

forsakes things like justice and prosperity in the present world, one finds that the answer or explanation to present difficulties does not necessarily lie in this world. As Eleanor Stump explains, "It certainly does seem true, at any rate, that there is a correlation between the degree to which we associate human good with things in this world and the extent to which we see the problem of evil in its contemporary form."[21] As such, the problem of evil is addressed in this way not solely on evidence in the present world but on the hope of a world to come.

In a similar vein, Norman Geisler holds that the resolution of the problem of evil itself rests on the very idea that evil will *one day* be defeated:

> [The problem of evil] wrongly assumes that since evil is *not yet* defeated it *never will* be defeated. To affirm that evil never will be defeated would assume omniscience, which only God has. Indeed, since it has already been shown that the Bible is God's Word, we have the basis for asserting that evil will one day be vanquished.[22]

For Geisler, the solution is apparent to anyone who affirms the truth of the Bible, which affirms that all evil will one day be vanquished by God. Another approach by Marilyn Adams suggests that the beatific vision speaks directly to the "why" question:

> The created person's experience of the beatific vision together with his/her knowledge that intimate divine presence stretched back over his/her ante-mortem life and reached down into the depths of his/her worst suffering, would provide retrospective comfort independent of comprehension of the reasons-why akin to the two-year-old's assurance of its mother's love.[23]

Here, Adams argues that a future experience of the beatific vision in the presence of God would inherently resolve any question as to the meaning or apparent hopelessness faced by a sufferer in their earthly life. The implication here is that the experience of suffering is resolved even if the "why" question is never answered.[24] Once more, this is not a justification

21. Stump, "Aquinas on the Sufferings of Job," 63.

22. Geisler, *Systematic Theology*, 382; emphasis in original.

23. Adams, "Horrendous Evils," 219–20.

24. One may argue that per classical Christian theology, only those who have faith in Jesus Christ (thus Christians) are able to experience the joy and redemption of heaven while others are condemned to hell; thus for the damned, the joys of the beatific vision are of no comfort in one's present sufferings, which makes the eternal reward

of God's permission of evil in the world—as if God is only justified in allowing evil and suffering if he subsequently guarantees an eternal paradise for all who suffer. Rather, the hope of an eternal state in which the sorts of evil experienced in this world are ultimately and permanently defeated is an encouragement to Christians specifically such that the disparity and hopelessness faced by suffering and evil is mitigated to a powerful degree by a hope in our ultimate divine deliverance. With these factors considered, the Christian has good reason to maintain faith in God by believing and trusting in God and his Word even in the face of evil.[25]

POSSIBLE OBJECTIONS

I have argued that traditional evidential arguments from evil rely on a concept of God that does not correspond well with the God of classical theism (as delineated by means of a Thomistic natural theology). Evidential arguments pose a problem for theism if and only if God is a moral being subject to moral duties and obligations in much the same way humans are, and thus his failure to intervene in the face of horrendous and gratuitous evil in the world would serve as evidence of either a divine moral failure or some level of divine ignorance or impotence. However, as I have argued, it is mistaken to think of God as a "moral being" in this sense with the sort of moral duties and obligations that humans themselves possess. Therefore, God is free to prevent evil or not, depending on nothing more than his own good pleasure—with no threat to his classical divine attributes—and thus, unjustified, gratuitous evil presents no problem for the classical theist in terms of an understanding of God as revealed through natural theology.

---

of the faithful an inadequate device toward the comfort of the unbelieving sufferer. However, the argument here is not that the beatific vision is or should be of help to *all* who experience suffering as if the suffering is only somehow justified for God on that basis. Rather, my argument here is that *for Christians specifically* the joys of the beatific vision are of value in considering the "why" question of evil *from a human perspective* as having been assured of an ultimate and final defeat of evil. As such, given what is known of God and Christianity as a whole, even if the damned continue to suffer for eternity by their own will, then there is nothing in such an idea that makes either the judgment of the sinner or the salvation of the faithful unjust on the part of God.

25. For more on approaches to theodicy or an answer to the "why" question of evil specifically from a Christian perspective, see Little, *God, Why This Evil?*; Fiddes, "Christianity," 210–229; and Soelle, *Suffering*.

However, as I have also argued, a possible new evidential argument arises for the theist in consideration of how evil in the world should be sufficiently explained given theism from a human perspective. From a Thomistic perspective of natural theology, evil cannot exist, except as caused by something good (specifically an agent-cause)—and only accidentally, on account of the good teleological ends of the agent-action itself—thus, every evil that arises in the world must have an *explanation in the good*—a good agent-cause (good at least as far as it has being and is in act) and a good teleological end of that agent's action that results in some instance of accidental evil. Thus, the non-theist could argue that at least some evils in the world may lack any obvious explanation in this regard, such that some evils do not appear to be associated with the good as either caused by or on account of some good agent or teleological aim in the way Aquinas suggests. Here becomes relevant any evidential instance of evil such that its causal operations are not immediately apparent to the human observer and thus appear *from a human perspective* to be without any obvious explanation in the good such that it is fully explained in a theistic universe—thus arises *inexplicable evil* as the evidential basis for such an argument.

Given this new evidential argument, there remains a response available for the theist that deals with seemingly inexplicable evil while remaining grounded in a human perspective and avoiding the sort of category mistakes sometimes perpetrated by other theistic responses to the problem of evil—simply that of confidence in God and his attributes as revealed by natural theology in the face of evil. Thus, on account of God's existence, nature, and attributes as revealed from natural theology, every instance of evil in a theistic universe is necessarily fully explained for the believer and consistent with the existence of God even when it may seem inexplicable from a human perspective. Additionally, there remains a great deal of evidential support for a wide variety and abundance of goods in the world as well as evidence of at least some evil that is clearly associated with goods in the way a Thomistic natural theology requires. As such, the human belief in God in the face of evil is grounded in not just a successful natural theology but also evidential support in the world for the fact that many evils are readily explained on account of the sorts of causally associated goods that one is able to identify as explanatory elements in the nature of good and evil. As such, any claim that purports to deny theism on the basis of *inexplicable evil* remains entirely ineffective and unpersuasive next to the theist's act of belief in God in the face of evil.

In this final section, I will consider possible objections to these arguments—first, objections to the idea that God is not a moral agent in the same way that humans are moral agents. I will consider certain criticisms levied against philosophers who have held such views (such as Brian Davies and Herbert McCabe), and I will conclude that these objections fail and there is no reason (given the natural theology I have endorsed) that God should be considered a "moral being" in the same way that creatures are moral beings. Second, I will consider anticipated objections to a persistent belief and trust in God as an explanatory means toward resolving the new evidential argument from evil. I will show that each objection fails for one reason or another, and thus the coherence of the existence of both God and gratuitous evil as well as the confidence of the believer in a reasoned faith in God in the face of evil serve as sufficient responses to the evidential problem of evil.

Exemplar Virtues in God

The first objection to be considered regarding the consideration of God as a moral being is simply that Aquinas was wrong (or my interpretation of him is wrong) and that Aquinas truly did hold that God is a being with a certain moral character subject to moral duties and obligations—even if those moral duties differ in significant ways from those of humans. For example, one may argue that God can be seen as morally good for at least one reason that he can be seen as good at all—that *effects* must resemble their *causes*. The fact that God has created creatures who are ordered toward moral virtue as their own proper end implies that something like an exemplar moral virtue must first exist in God. While I have already addressed an aspect of this objection in chapter five, I will here consider it further as a specific argument toward establishing a meaningful sense of moral obligation in God from a Thomistic perspective. Here, Brian Shanley, arguing from his own Thomistic perspective in response to Brian Davies, presents just such a case: "Davies argues that God cannot be morally good in the sense of having moral virtue and claims Aquinas' mantle in this regard. . . . This claim is not consonant with the texts, however, since Aquinas argues that the moral virtues can be attributed to God in the form of exemplar virtues."[26] For Shanley, Aquinas himself is said to endorse the idea that God has moral virtues in an exemplar sense

26. Shanley, *Thomist Tradition*, 115.

that bears consideration in terms of the definition and import of God's goodness. In fact, Shanley is correct that Aquinas does in fact speak of exemplar virtues existing in God in some way: "But since it behooves a man to do his utmost to strive onward even to Divine things . . . we must needs place some virtues between the social or human virtues, and the exemplar virtues which are Divine."[27] Aquinas continues with examples of certain virtues and whether they can be considered in God in an exemplar sense, such as God himself being the proper object of virtues in humans. "Thus prudence sees naught else but the things of God; temperance knows no earthly desires; fortitude has no knowledge of passion; and justice, by imitating the Divine Mind, is united thereto by an everlasting covenant."[28] As the proper object of human moral virtues, it is not clear how such virtues could reasonably apply to God in the same (or even similar) way that they apply to human moral agents. In fact, Aquinas himself denies that these sorts of exemplar virtues can be properly attributed to God.

> Of the virtues that deal with the active life some, likewise, direct the passions. These we cannot posit in God. For the virtues that deal with the passions take their species from the passions as from their proper objects; and so temperance differs from fortitude so far as it deals with desires, whereas the latter with fear and daring. But in God there are no passions, as has been shown, and therefore neither can such virtues be found in Him.[29]

Thus, as Aquinas explains, any virtues dealing with the passions cannot be attributed to God because God is "pure act" and not subject to passions. Being unswayed by passions of the flesh leaves God immune to the sorts of temptations that wrack human creatures and require us to be cognizant of moral obligations and duties as a means to resist those inclinations and desires. However, Aquinas argues that God does embody certain virtues in an exemplar sense, such as those which deal with *actions* rather than *passions*—those dealing with the intellect and the will, for example, which both exist in God. Aquinas lists at least some examples: "Now, there are some virtues directing the active life of man that do not deal with passions, but with actions: for example, truth,

27. Aquinas, *Summa Theologiae*, I-II.65.5.
28. Aquinas, *Summa Theologiae*, I-II.65.5.
29. Aquinas, *Summa Contra Gentiles*, I.92.9.

justice, liberality, magnificence, prudence, and art."[30] However, these exemplar virtues look nothing like the sort of human moral obligations that constrain humans to behave in certain ways in the face of evil. For example, God is said to be "perfectly just" because he gives to all things their due—willing both a thing to be and also what is necessary to it.[31] God is not "just" because he eliminates or prevents gratuitous evil, for example, but he is just in providing to that which he creates whatever belongs to it according to its nature. Thus, since the experience of evil exists in the potency of many created things, exemplar virtues in God are insufficient to establish any sort of divine moral obligation that would require the prevention of gratuitous evil.

Another objection from a Thomistic perspective (related to the consideration of God as a moral exemplar) is that if God is in fact not a "moral being" in the same way that humans are, this denial by itself does preclude the possibility that there may be at least some positive sense in which moral obligations or duties could be reasonably ascribed to God. One may argue, for example, that while moral goodness cannot be attributed to God in a *univocal* sense, there remains the possibility that it could be attributed to God *analogically*. Thus, God's goodness may not be a moral goodness *per se*, but in a strict analogical sense one can still hold that God certainly should and always does (on account of his nature) act in a manner that is always morally commendable. Here, Shanley offers just such an argument:

> Briefly, Thomists hold that certain terms signifying pure spiritual perfections, such as good, can be truly predicated of God in a non-equivocal fashion. Such terms are not predicated of God in a univocal fashion, as if the terms had the same meaning, but rather in an analogical fashion. According to this view, when we say that God is good, we mean that God is truly good, indeed the exemplar and source of all created goodness, but we do not purport to know or understand what God's goodness is. Analogy is based on a transference of terms connoting spiritual perfections, as first known in creatures, to God as their primary instance and causal source. Now since creaturely moral goodness is surely a spiritual perfection, it must have its exemplar source in God, even though God's moral goodness is not a state to be achieved through virtuous actions but rather identical

30. Aquinas, *Summa Contra Gentiles*, I.93.1.

31. For a further description of God's justice in terms of exemplar virtues in God, see Aquinas, *Summa Contra Gentiles*, I.93.6.

> with his very being. By reducing moral goodness to behavior in accord with virtue or moral obligation, Davies begs the question in favor of denying moral goodness to God.[32]

Similar to the argument considered above, Shanley takes the time to describe the process of analogical predication as one that identifies God as the exemplar source of all perfections. If God can be analogically presumed to be morally good on account of the spiritual perfection of moral goodness in created beings, says Shanley, then such an attribution would seemingly entail that God is in fact morally good in a meaningful way—even if his moral goodness (as identical with his nature) cannot be directly known.

The relevant response here is exactly in what sense creaturely moral goodness can be said to have its exemplar source in God. It simply does not follow from Shanley's assertion here that moral goodness in creatures implies moral goodness in God. Understanding what it is for a creature to be morally good is an important first step in understanding how such a characteristic could possibly be analogically attributed to God in any meaningful sense. For Aquinas, moral virtue in humans includes an appetitive aspect involving a conflict of sorts between one's intellectual reason and the lure of one's passions and desires, which at times oppose reason.

> Accordingly for a man to do a good deed, it is requisite not only that his reason be well disposed by means of a habit of intellectual virtue; but also that his appetite be well disposed by means of a habit of moral virtue. And so moral differs from intellectual virtue, even as the appetite differs from the reason. Hence just as the appetite is the principle of human acts, in so far as it partakes of reason, so are moral habits to be considered virtues in so far as they are in conformity with reason.[33]

Hence it would follow, for Aquinas, that the intellectual virtues could be analogically attributed to God but not moral virtues, as God is a being without any passions or any appetitive quality. God's understanding is always perfect, and his will is always directed perfectly, with no appetitive opposition such as humans experience. God would be the exemplar of moral virtues only as the proper end toward which all moral virtues are directed but not as one who achieves moral virtue in any analogical way

32. Shanley, *Thomist Tradition*, 116.

33. Aquinas, *Summa Theologiae*, I-II.58.2.

similar to a human. Thus, God (at least on account of a Thomistic approach to natural theology) is just not the sort of being to have moral duties.

Justice in God

According to Shanley, however, there remain cases where moral virtue exists in God—specifically, those connected with acts of will, which can be analogously attributed to God. The example Shanley focuses on is that of divine justice: "Hence there is a significant sense in which God is bound in justice to give what is due to a creature. . . . Hence it seems that Davies is at odds with Aquinas himself in claiming that moral virtue cannot intelligibly be ascribed to God, and so it would seem that God could be called morally good."[34] Thus, for Shanley, if justice can be reasonably attributed to God, then we have cause to call God not only good but morally good—since justice itself is a moral virtue. However, once again, Shanley seems to miss what it means for God to be just, and how this differs meaningfully from what we mean by human justice. For Aquinas, God is just by giving things their due: "Furthermore, it was shown above that because God wills something He also wills those things that are necessary to it. But that which is necessary to the perfection of each thing is due to it. Therefore, there is justice in God, to which it belongs to give to each one what belongs to him."[35] The sort of justice Aquinas describes here is one of a *distributive* justice but not one that somehow requires God to give to creatures "as much good and as little evil as he possibly can," so to speak. Per Davies,

> But notice how Aquinas explains what it is for God to give what is owed. He clearly does not think that God is (distributively) just because he provides for things what some moral law to which he is subject says that he should (and is, therefore, a good and just God). He says that God is distributively just by being the Creator who, by his providence, makes things to be what they deserve to be in so far as they are creatures fashioned by him.[36]

Here, Davies explains what justice means for Aquinas—the giving of what is due—which is attributed to God not on account of how much good he is able to conjure for the beings he has created but on account of the very

34. Shanley, *Thomist Tradition*, 116.
35. Aquinas, *Summa Contra Gentiles*, I.93.6.
36. Davies, *Reality of God*, 99.

essence of the created being itself and what its own nature requires for its existence as the kind of thing it is. As such, Shanley here fails to establish a sense of divine moral obligation for God. While Shanley is right that Aquinas does speak of exemplar virtues in God, what does not follow is that those exemplar virtues would oblige God toward a sense of moral behavior such that his acts or inaction can be adjudicated on that basis. If God is distributively just to his creation, for example, then it is only because he gives what is due based on the sort of things he has made. God is under no obligation to grant non-essential things to creatures such as happiness, peace, comfort, grace, forgiveness, etc. God may still freely choose to grant such things but not out of an *a priori* moral obligation to do so. Nor is God obligated in some way to grant these things equally to all creatures, for some may thrive while others suffer; whatever God gives to existing creatures (beyond what they inherently require on account of their created natures), he does so freely and not by compulsion or necessity. Also, nothing God does fulfills some need or lack in himself or accomplishes some aspect of his nature that is incomplete or undefined without it (as a moral obligation would), and things willed by God apart from himself cannot be considered necessary in this respect. As Aquinas explains, "Hence, since the goodness of God is perfect, and can exist without other things inasmuch as no perfection can accrue to Him from them, it follows that His willing things apart from Himself is not absolutely necessary."[37] Likewise, it is not condemnable for God when some creatures suffer or fail to thrive in some way—it is just simply creatures functioning as their natures prescribe and allow.

Considering justice further as a counterargument to the concept that God is not a moral being, James Sterba (in a critique of Davies) presses the argument that divine justice poses a problem for God if all it means is that God gives to creatures what they are owed. "To say that God is just simply amounts to God's giving his creatures what is owed to them . . . For Davies, this seems to involve simply sustaining them in existence, not interfering with or aiding them in the world in any way."[38] For Sterba, if all justice means is that God causes creatures to exist as the sorts of things they are, then the term "justice" seems meaningless as a means of saying something good or positive about God. Sterba goes on to reference the analogy of a parent caring for a child (which Davies himself

37. Aquinas, *Summa Theologiae*, I.19.3.

38. Sterba, *Is a Good God*, 112.

uses to illustrate his meaning of what divine justice can metaphorically represent). "So judged by Davies's own parent analogy, it would seem that a God who simply did no more for us than sustain us in existence could not be considered just."[39] However, this is not what Aquinas (or Davies) suggests when attributing justice to God. Aquinas dismisses one sense of justice which cannot be attributed to God as that of *commutative* justice (the sort of justice involved in a mutual exchange that benefits two parties in some way). However, another sort of justice (*distributive* justice) is rightly attributed to God. Per Aquinas,

> The other consists in distribution, and is called distributive justice; whereby a ruler or a steward gives to each what his rank deserves. As then the proper order displayed in ruling a family or any kind of multitude evinces justice of this kind in the ruler, so the order of the universe, which is seen both in effects of nature and in effects of will, shows forth the justice of God.[40]

Thus, for Aquinas, God's justice is far more than a mere "upholding in existence" but rather the divine provision of the entire natural order—involving both the natural interactions of non-sentient things and the acts and outcomes of the activities of sentient beings as well. All is provided by God on a constant, ongoing basis for every living thing. Without a world of natural and predictable interactions and meaningful acts and consequences, it is difficult to imagine what sort of chaotic, violent, dangerous, unpredictable world we might have. At the very least, it would be difficult to imagine such a world as somehow *better* than the present one—or more conducive as the product of an omnipotent, omniscient, perfectly good being. I can imagine, for example, evidential arguments for the nonexistence of God based on the evidence of an entirely unpredictable and unstable universe that would be far more troublesome for the theist than the present evidential problem of evil. Further, Aquinas argues that God's justice as directed toward humans specifically involves both what is ordered to creatures themselves on account of their natures and what is ordered to God (as all creatures are).

> Thus in the divine operations debt may be regarded in two ways, as due either to God, or to creatures, and in either way God pays what is due. It is due to God that there should be fulfilled in creatures what His will and wisdom require, and what manifests

39. Sterba, *Is a Good God*, 113.

40. Aquinas, *Summa Theologiae*, I.21.1.

> His goodness. In this respect, God's justice regards what befits Him; inasmuch as He renders to Himself what is due to Himself. It is also due to a created thing that it should possess what is ordered to it; thus it is due to man to have hands, and that other animals should serve him. Thus also God exercises justice, when He gives to each thing what is due to it by its nature and condition.[41]

Thus, for Aquinas, God's divine justice is not a "moral obligation" *per se*, in any sense intelligible with the idea that God must behave in a certain manner in response to evil in the world. Rather, God's justice involves a giving of what is due—ordering creatures toward both himself and the good of their being and nature and all that requires. As such, there is no sense in which God as possessing exemplar virtues (such as that of justice, for example) can be attributed any sense of moral goodness or obligation.

God as a Villain

Another argument to consider against the concept that God is not a moral being is that such a God would effectively be reduced to either a product of deistic apathy or a positively horrendous moral monster. As such, Sterba argues that it is incoherent for Davies to claim that God cannot be subject to moral requirements because God cannot be said to reasonably require moral obligations for rational creatures yet fail to uphold those same obligations as a rational being himself. "This is because the law of nature that God presumably implanted in our hearts is understood to apply to all rational beings including God himself. So it would indeed be contradictory for God to implant a law of nature in our hearts that applies to himself and then to act contrary to that very law he promulgated."[42] Here, Sterba argues that all moral requirements from God apply to all rational beings, including himself, so any claim that God is free to violate the same moral statutes he gives to creatures entails a contradiction. Sterba's argument here is puzzling. It is not clear why the creator of some rule or requirement issued to one's subordinates should necessarily apply to the creator of that rule as well. A parent may tell their teenager that they are not permitted to drive after dark, but there is no

41. Aquinas, *Summa Theologiae*, I.21.1.

42. Sterba, *Is a Good God*, 116.

reason such a rule should apply to the parent as well. After all, parents most often know more about what their child can and cannot handle and what they should and should not do than even the child herself. How much more does God know about what humans can and cannot handle and what humans should and should not do—even if those very limitations would not in turn apply to an all-knowing, all-seeing divine manager of the universe? The moral law given by God to humans applies precisely on account of the sort of beings humans are and how they must live and interact in a world *as humans*. Since God is not a human, there is no reason to think that any such moral law must apply in the same (or similar) manner to God as well.

One may argue that the nature of moral directives themselves are not or should not be limited to humans specifically but can be applied *in principle* to all rational beings, based simply on an understanding of what such directives entail. Further, it may be argued that the moral directives given to creatures must somehow reflect the goodness and perfections of God in such a way that God himself is also constrained to obey those directives in some way—at least in any sense where he interacts with humans, perhaps. Otherwise, one may argue, God would be unworthy of worship or praise as an infinitely good being. However, there is no reason to think that moral directives—*even in principle*—have application to God on a similar basis, since all moral directives are bound up with the natures and limits of humans and how humans are meant to interact with others. If God were expected on this basis to obey his own moral precepts, then it seems that such a requirement effectively anthropomorphizes God into something he is not—a being standing in a direct two-way relationship as a peer with other beings that requires a certain behavior or decorum for God to warrant the respect of his creation. God is not such a being in such a relation and thus has no need to adhere to morality toward that end.

Further, Sterba's critique does not accurately represent Davies or Aquinas in this regard. There is nothing of which I am aware in Aquinas (or Davies) that implies that God's moral directives apply to "all rational beings including God" in the way Sterba suggests. For Aquinas, there are a great deal of moral categories that simply do not apply to God in the same way as humans. The command not to kill, for example, befits humans who have no power or authority over life and death, and yet (unlike humans), God is the creator, giver, and sustainer of all life, and thus it is within the purview of God to kill as he sees fit. Further, it is simply within the mortal nature of humans to die, and thus all human death is necessarily in accord with human nature without any injustice on God's part. The same goes for anything that properly belongs to God in this way (such as a human's relationships, health, property, and general well-being); as the first efficient cause of everything that exists, God has the proper authority over literally everything in existence—including humans and their own well-being—and he can rightly do with his own creation as he pleases. Aquinas makes a similar argument in response to a question concerning God's authority to at times override the very moral directives he has also given to creatures—such as commanding one human to kill another as an act of divine judgment. Aquinas's argument is that death is part of the nature of humans on account of their current state before God, and thus God has the right to take life by any means he sees fit.

> All men alike, both guilty and innocent, die the death of nature: which death of nature is inflicted by the power of God on account of original sin . . . Consequently, by the command of God, death can be inflicted on any man, guilty or innocent, without any injustice whatever. In like manner adultery is intercourse with another's wife; who is allotted to him by the law emanating from God. Consequently intercourse with any woman, by the command of God, is neither adultery nor fornication. The same applies to theft, which is the taking of another's property. For whatever is taken by the command of God, to Whom all things belong, is not taken against the will of its owner, whereas it is in this that theft consists. Nor is it only in human things, that whatever is commanded by God is right; but also in natural things, whatever is done by God, is, in some way, natural.[43]

Here, Aquinas makes the case that God is the ultimate owner and responsible party of everything in creation—including life, property, marriage, and even nature itself. As such, even if moral precepts apply in some way to God (which I believe they do not), God's responsibilities in this regard would look nothing like what humans experience, since it is within his divine rights to do with his own creation whatever he pleases.

Sterba's main issue with Davies in this regard, however, focuses on the idea that by permitting evils that God is able to prevent, God is ultimately culpable for those evils to a staggering scale—making God the equivalent of a horrendous villain.

43. Aquinas, *Summa Theologiae*, I-II.95.6.

> . . . the real problem with Davies account is not so much with his denial that God is subject to moral requirements. Rather, the real problem is that God, if he exists, and were not subject to such requirements, would still admittedly be permitting the horrendous evil consequences of all the immoral actions in the world when he could easily have prevented them without either permitting a greater evil or failing to secure a greater good, which is far more evil than that has been produced by all the great villains among us.[44]

Here, Sterba argues that God is culpable for "permitting" the heinous acts of all of history's greatest villains (as well as every other bad thing that has ever occurred, for that matter), making God on this account the greatest of all villains. Here, it seems Sterba's objection is inherently self-defeating, since he is attempting to refute the claim that God is not a moral being by providing an illustration that is only valid if God is in fact a moral being—namely, that of God being named a "villain" on account of allowing free creatures to act freely, even when they occasionally commit heinous evil acts. God is only "evil" or a "villain" if he stands under a moral obligation to prevent gratuitous evil whenever he can and yet has failed or refused to do so. If God were not subject to such requirements, as the antecedent of Sterba's conditional premise states, then permitting the natural operation of the world and its creatures—including all of the evil that arises by its effects—would hardly be "evil" for God. Sterba here needs to explain how God could be considered morally evil if he were not subject to moral requirements in the first place if this objection were to succeed. As such, if God is not a moral being as I have suggested, then this objection simply fails.

The Incoherence of Divine Goodness

Another related argument against the concept that God is not a moral being is that a non-moral God cannot be considered "good" in any relevant or meaningful sense. As Stephen Wykstra argues,

> If we avoid these confusions, we can see the force of the claim that if God exists, there is some outweighing good related in the specified way to every instance of suffering he allows. For denying this is tantamount to saying that God could allow some intense suffering either because he enjoys the sight of occasional

44. Sterba, *Is a Good God*, 117.

> suffering for its own sake, or because he is indifferent to it. It is hard to see how such a being could be meaningfully praised as a *good* God, worthy of our worship, our obedience, and—not least—our trust. I take this to be a basic conceptual truth deserving assent by theists and non-theists alike . . .[45]

Here, Wykstra is not directly addressing the concept of non-moral goodness as applied to God, but rather he is arguing that if one rejects the idea that God must prevent gratuitous suffering (likely because he stands under a moral obligation to do so), then one loses any meaningful sense in which God can be said to be good. It is along this line of thinking that Sterba offers two arguments that a non-moral God cannot be considered "good" in any meaningful way. First, Sterba argues that the Thomistic account of God being "like" the effects he has created in some way does not lead to an idea of God as being good. Focusing on sentient creatures specifically as an operative example of Davies's argument, Sterba writes,

> Still, Davies wants to focus on the goods that all living beings seek and infer from God being the cause of all living beings each seeking its good, that God must be like the goods that all these beings seek. But given that the goods that living beings seek include [examples of natural and moral good and evil directed toward the good as either means or ends], how would it help to know that God is like this large collection of natural and moral goods and evils?[46]

Sterba's criticism here is directed at one of Davies's explanations of how God can be said to be good without being morally good—that of the Thomistic (and Aristotelian) idea that all effects must somehow resemble their causes. Sterba's basic argument is that there are a wide range of goods and evils that can all be ordered in various ways toward higher goods (as means and ends), and that if effects resemble their causes, it would seem that God must somehow "resemble" all sorts of goods and evils alike—making such a concept effectively incoherent. Here, Sterba seems to be mistaken about what is meant by the idea that effects resemble their causes. In short, Sterba confuses the immediate object of the will of a creature seeking its good with the intended aim or teleology of the will itself. Sterba suggests that this argument implies God is like goods and evils because creatures will both goods and evils as means

45. Wykstra, "Humean Obstacle," 141–42.

46. Sterba, *Is a Good God*, 118–19.

and ends, though always toward the good they perceive. But Aquinas does not argue that God is therefore like the *immediate objects* of good and evil that creatures will in pursuit of the good. Aquinas argues that it is the *natural teleology* of the creature's created will itself—the desirable "good" of perfections sought by the creature—that reflects its cause in God. "All things, by desiring their own perfection, desire God Himself, inasmuch as the perfections of all things are so many similitudes of the divine being."[47] By creating a creature that is teleologically directed toward the good, God is revealing something of his own nature—being that the things he produces by way of his creative acts are always teleologically ordered toward specific ends, which must exist in some way in God himself (since the good is the aim of the creature). The good that creatures are ordered toward is what God's created effects seek and often produce. Whether a creature wills good or evil as means toward some good they intend does not imply that God is like those *means*—but it does imply that God is like the *ends* they seek, since they seek those by nature—a nature created by God and teleologically ordered toward the good as an aspect of those created natures. Thus, God is responsible for only the good in this respect, even if some creatures will evil (indirectly or accidentally) as a means toward some good in violation of their own moral precepts.[48]

Second, Sterba argues that Davies's distinction between *malum poenae* (evil suffered) and *malum culpae* (evil done) fails on account of such an explanation exonerating not only God but sinners as well. The relevant argument he is responding to is from Aquinas in that God is not culpable for sin because God causes all things to be and orders all things to the good. For Aquinas, the cause of sin rests in the creature that perverts or

47. Aquinas, *Summa Theologiae*, I.6.1.

48. Sterba has other complaints against the idea that effects are like their causes, including that it represents antiquated Aristotelian thought (because non-sentient things cannot be said to "seek" their good) and that scientific concepts of "the emergence of greater physical complexity or higher forms of life from simpler beginnings" (Sterba, *Is a Good God*, 118) somehow refutes the idea that effects resemble their causes. I have chosen not to interact with these particular criticisms, as they invoke other concepts beyond the scope of the present project such as the reliability of Aristotelian metaphysics and the practical and philosophical viability of certain scientific models involving things like evolution and the origin of life. Suffice to say, I do believe that there is more to Aristotelian metaphysics that would support the idea of all things seeking their good (including non-sentient things), and I believe that even in consideration of the idea that complexity arises from simplicity in the scientific world (à la evolution), that effects do still "resemble" their causes in the way Aquinas (and Aristotle) suggest. As such, I do not think Sterba's other complaints are valid.

substitutes the proper object of the will for an improper one, and as such, God causes the sinner to exist, and the sinner causes sin.

> Now God cannot be directly the cause of sin, either in Himself or in another, since every sin is a departure from the order which is to God as the end: whereas God inclines and turns all things to Himself as to their last end, as Dionysius states: so that it is impossible that He should be either to Himself or to another the cause of departing from the order which is to Himself. Therefore He cannot be directly the cause of sin.[49]

Here, for Aquinas, God cannot be considered the cause of sin *in himself or in another* because God's actions cannot depart from their proper end—thus the culpability of sin rests on the sinner. Further, Aquinas argues that God causes creatures to act, but it is always the creature that sins.

> Again every action is caused by something existing in act, since nothing produces an action save in so far as it is in act; and every being in act is reduced to the First Act, viz. God, as to its cause, Who is act by His Essence. Therefore God is the cause of every action, in so far as it is an action. But sin denotes a being and an action with a defect: and this defect is from the created cause, viz. the free-will, as falling away from the order of the First Agent, viz. God. Consequently this defect is not reduced to God as its cause, but to the free-will.[50]

Per Aquinas, even though creatures who sin can only do so by being "in act"—and this on account of God's causal activity—God is only the cause of the act itself *as an act* and not the defect of the act, which is on account of the creature and considered sin.

Sterba, however, holds that given this idea of God's causal activity in this regard being devoid of the culpability of sin, it would seem that human sinners could make the same (or similar) argument in defense of themselves.

49. Aquinas, *Summa Theologiae*, I-II.79.1. Aquinas's argument here is that God as first cause cannot be responsible for what the middle cause produces itself. As such, when creatures sin, God is not the cause of that sin. "The effect which proceeds from the middle cause, according as it is subordinate to the first cause, is reduced to that first cause; but if it proceeds from the middle cause, according as it goes outside the order of the first cause, it is not reduced to that first cause." Aquinas, *Summa Theologiae*, I-II.79.1.

50. Aquinas, *Summa Theologiae*, I-II.79.2.

> Here, Davies thinks he can minimize God's involvement with moral evil by claiming that God only causes the sinner's action, which insofar as it exists is good, but not the sinner's sin, which is privation. But if this exonerates God from responsibility for the moral evil in the world, it exonerates sinners as well. This is because we could also claim that sinners cause their own actions, and insofar as those actions exist, they are good, and that sin is just a privation of moral goodness in their acts. That privation is simply a byproduct or a means of achieving the good toward which their acts are directed. It is not something that sinners ultimately will or cause.[51]

Thus, for Sterba, it would seem that sinners cause their own actions that are necessarily "good" on account that those actions exist (or are "in act" to use Aquinas's language)—thus, because the sinner aims at the good and causes something to exist, the sinner (like God) is not responsible as the cause of its own sin. Here, Sterba exhibits a number of confusions that lead his criticism astray. First, sinners do cause their own actions, but they do not cause their own actions to "exist" (or be "in act") in the same way God causes all things to exist. Existence can only come from God. Hence, creatures who sin are producing nothing good, even though the good may be precisely what they intend; the only "good" involved is the good of a creature in act as caused to be by God alone—part of the natural processes involved in the operation of the human will. Further, even though sinners do not will the evil of privation *directly* (as an end) and always in some way intend or aim at the good, this does not absolve the sinner from sin because it is still by definition a defect of the proper action toward which the creature is ordered by its creator.

Further, Sterba argues that God must be the cause of evil because God is operative as the cause of all evil acts, which cannot be excused as something "foreseen" because of his ongoing, active causal relationship with the acts themselves as they occur. "Aquinas wants to hold that God does not either will evil to be or will it not to be, but rather God wills to permit it. Yet this can't be right. This is because there are two relevant distinctions here. One is between willing something as an end and willing something as a means. The other is between intending something and merely foreseeing it."[52] Here, Sterba argues that God, in causing everything to exist, causes also the act of moral evil on the part of the creature,

51. Sterba, *Is a Good God*, 120.

52. Sterba, *Is a Good God*, 123.

and it cannot be that God is simply "foreseeing" those actions because he causes them to be as they happen; thus, God must intend moral evil when his creatures act immorally. Once again, however, per Aquinas, it is not the act of the creature itself that is willed directly by God but only indirectly as caused by the creature itself. It is not that God "foresees" evil acts and thus wills them without intending them (as Sterba suggests)—it is that God does not will evil acts directly at all. Thus, Sterba's critique here is evaded between the horns: it is not that God must either intend or foresee the immoral act—rather, God intends the creature who in turn intends the act. This leaves God inculpable as the cause of moral evil and leaves the fault squarely on the creature.

The Failure of Faith

Moving now to anticipated criticisms of a reliance on an act of faith grounded in the evidence of God's existence and his nature by way of natural theology as a reasonable resolution to the problem of evil (strictly from a human perspective), the first possible objection I foresee is that this sort of faith in God is somehow poorly placed or ineffective. H. J. McCloskey lays out a similar argument concerning the use of faith in God as a resolution to the problem of evil, which he subsequently criticizes on a basis that I will consider and evaluate here.

> Now some theists have suggested that the situation with respect to suffering and faith in God is rather like that with a friend of high moral virtue who appears to be acting badly. While inference from the facts in the world does suggest that God is guilty of evil on a vast and shocking scale, the believer is nevertheless confident that God is really good. He has a superior knowledge of God. He has faith, trust, and confidence in God, based on his experience of knowing God. Faith is explained as reliance upon God, a counting upon him which comes from personal knowledge. It is often suggested that the relationship with God is a personal one, presumably akin to that of friendship.[53]

McCloskey here offers a description of the argument that some theists put forward by invoking faith in God despite the evidence of God's moral failures. As McCloskey explains, the theist is argued to be justified in believing and trusting in God based on one's personal experiences and

53. McCloskey, "Problem of Evil," 195.

relationship with God—ultimately trusting that God is good in spite of the evil he allows in the world.[54] Per McCloskey, such an approach to faith would seem to have merit in the discussion only if it can be properly affirmed: "If knowledge of the kind that comes from long, deep, intimate friendships were possible in respect to God, such knowledge would indeed provide a basis for ceasing to regard evil as a problem."[55]

However, as McCloskey offers a critique of such an argument by highlighting certain inconsistencies and problems with using faith in this regard:

> It is significant that many who at one stage of their lives believe that they have this faith relationship with God finally come to see that they have really been experiencing something quite different. It is significant, too, that the claims made among those who believe themselves to be experiencing genuine faith actually conflict with one another. The facts that faith contains no marks of its own validity, that it is so often illusory, and that it admits of no public testing mean that it is irrational to rely on it against conclusions arrived at by rational inference. It is not to be dogmatic to insist that it is more rational to rely on the less fallible and more reliable knowledge that rational inference provides than on the sort of faith that is much confused with, and indistinguishable from, illusory faith.[56]

Here, McCloskey offers three objections to using faith as a means of responding to the problem of evil: (1) faith is often mistaken; (2) faith is

54. The argument I have put forward in this work differs in subtle but significant ways from the one characterized by McCloskey. First, I have argued that the evidence of evil in the world does not indicate a failure on God's part to live up to his divine moral goodness simply because God is not a moral being subject to moral duties and obligations. As such, the problem of evil as a logical challenge to God's existence fails, yet a similar argument persists as considered specifically from a human perspective that seeks an explanation for evil in terms of its causal relationships and the teleological good that brought it about in an accidental sense. Thus, an act of faith in God does not have to be *in spite of* any contrary evidence in this regard. Also, one's act of faith, as I have argued, is not based solely on one's subjective personal relationship or personal experience with God; rather, faith is a rational act of assent to what cannot be directly known (such as the explanation of evil) on the basis of what can be known and deduced about him and his nature from natural theology (as well as a commitment to the truth of divine revelation). However, McCloskey's criticisms of such an approach to the problem of evil, while being directed at a different but related argument, will be evaluated for merit against my argument as well.

55. McCloskey, "Problem of Evil," 195.

56. McCloskey, "Problem of Evil," 195–96.

contradictory; and (3) faith is essentially unverifiable. As such, McCloskey argues that faith is unhelpful to theist in the face of evil:

> I contend therefore that faith is not an aid to the theist in his attempt to solve the problem of evil. It would offer a way out only if it were a superior way of knowing, of the kind that may come with deep and long-standing personal friendships, and hence something confirmed by experience and knowledge of a person's actions, motives, and intentions. Faith in that sense is rarely claimed to occur. In the presence of the fact of evil it cannot occur, for it demands a previous understanding of God's purpose in allowing evil, an understanding that, by the very nature of the case, is not available. And the problem of evil is in fact aggravated by the claim that faith improves moral performance.[57]

Thus, for McCloskey, faith is not a "superior way of knowing" but is rather rife with contradictions, confusion, and other difficulties that make it inferior to the practice of basic inference that reveals evil to be a problem in the first place. Thus, for McCloskey, the theist should abandon arguments centered on faith as a response to the problem of evil.

Considering McCloskey's argument here, I do not believe that McCloskey's criticism is valid, given the argument I have presented, for a few significant reasons. First, McCloskey argues that faith is sometimes mistaken—that some who experience faith at one point in their lives come to consider it differently in light of changes or experiences that may lead them to a different conclusion at another time. However, the simple fact that someone may change his mind later in life about the object or nature of his faith (or whether what he experienced was ever faith to begin with) has no bearing whatsoever as to whether belief in God is or can be reliably and reasonably placed as a means toward the resolution of the problem of evil. People change their views and beliefs all the time, but this does not mean that the veracity of their beliefs (either prior or subsequent to such a change) is somehow called into question on that basis, nor does it imply that the abandonment of faith later in life somehow casts doubt or suspicion onto faith altogether as a possible means to discover truths about the world. For that matter, many people bear a strong commitment to natural science as the best explanation of the origin of the world, only to later abandon such a view in favor of a supernatural origin—but I doubt McCloskey would agree that this somehow casts doubt or suspicion on

57. McCloskey, "Problem of Evil," 196.

science as a way of knowing. As such, I do not believe McCloskey's first argument here has merit.

Second, McCloskey argues that differing faiths sometimes conflict and contradict one another, and this once again serves as a reason to doubt the veracity of faith as a means of knowing. Though he does not elaborate on this argument, McCloskey seems to be saying that many people have faith in different concepts of God (or gods) and that the experience of faith is held with genuine conviction—even among differing religions and worldviews where the objects of those faiths stand in open contradiction. Thus, for McCloskey, it is clear that at least some, most, or all examples of faith in God rest on objects which are necessarily errant and confused—or even entirely false. However, the mere fact that many faiths contradict each other does not itself suggest that all objects of faith are false or unreliable. The argument that "some faiths are unreliable because they contradict others—therefore, all faiths are unreliable" is a tacit fallacy of composition. In fact, even if all faiths stand in contradiction with every other faith, it could still be the case that at least one is true, verifiable, and reliable as a device to be applied to an argument from evil. The fact that other faiths exist does not make one believer's faith irrelevant—especially if that believer possesses genuine faith in a largely true and correct concept of God, as revealed by natural theology. This is in fact my argument—that the veracity of the object of one's faith should be grounded in what can be known and discovered by direct observation of the natural world and deduced by reason from there—in other words, natural theology. One may then adjudicate between false faiths and true faiths at least on this basis. Thus, McCloskey must find flaws in my own natural theology or concept of God to counter my argument; simply pointing out that others come to different conclusions or have faith in different gods is practically irrelevant on its face.

Considering McCloskey's third argument against faith, he suggests that faith as an intellectual (or spiritual) device is often illusory, unverifiable, and therefore irrational. However, McCloskey takes faith to be more of a mystical experience grounded in things like one's subjective personal experience of God. While conclusions about God based solely (or primarily) on personal experience can be valid and true, McCloskey holds that it is not a "superior way of knowing" and is rather eclipsed as an epistemological device by things like what one naturally infers from one's basic observations and experiences of the natural world. While I do agree that coming to some knowledge or conclusion based entirely on one's subjective ideas or preferences (or even one's own subjective experience) can lead to confusion and error, my own argument here does not rely on these sorts of mystical experiences of the sort that McCloskey suggests. Rather, my argument begins with one's basic observations and experiences of the natural world and draws certain conclusions about the identity and nature of its creator on that basis by means of rational inquiry and logical deduction, which would seem to fit better with McCloskey's definition of a "superior way of knowing." The act of faith in my proposal is a tertiary one that takes what is known of God and his creation and applies a necessary conclusion on that basis to what must be true of evil and suffering in the world—namely, that evil does not contradict God's existence and is always necessarily explained in a privative sense in a theistic universe. Thus, if my argument from natural theology has merit, then McCloskey's criticism on this basis does not. As such, I do not believe that McCloskey's objections to faith succeed as a means of responding to the problem of evil from a human perspective.

10

Conclusion

The evidential problem of evil (as proposed by philosophers such as William Rowe and Paul Draper) proposes to deny the likelihood of the existence of God on the basis of one's evidence for particularly horrendous, excessive, or gratuitous evil in the world. The argument relies on the premise that God—given the proper understanding and application of classical divine attributes such as God's omniscience, omnipotence, and perfect goodness—is necessarily obliged (on account of a presumed divine moral obligation) to prevent or mitigate evil whenever he is able to do so without sacrificing some greater good or causing some greater evil. As such, per the evidential problem of evil, God is said to be effectively incompatible with the existence of gratuitous evil in the world, and thus any evidence for evil in the world that appears to be gratuitous to a human observer would be *prima facie* evidence against the existence of God.

Theists have employed a variety of means to deny either the existence or impact of gratuitous evil in response to this challenge, such as proposing a range of theodicies and defenses meant to justify God's permission of evil in the world. However, as I have argued, these attempts fall short of definitively resolving the problem of evil in favor of theism. First, it is not immediately evident that God should be constrained to create the "best of all possible worlds" because all worlds that would be possible for God to create would be necessarily good, and it is difficult to see in what sense one world could be considered "better" than some other world, since the "goodness" of each world does not depend on the quantity or quality of goods it contains. Further, even if there is some sense (perhaps from a divine perspective) that one world could be considered better than another, humans would simply lack the epistemic perspective required to delineate between worlds in this way to any meaningful degree because the only possible world humans have any direct experience or awareness of is the actual one. Thus, there is no reason to think that God should be or should have been limited to only the "best of all possible worlds" upon his decision to create—such as a world with the most possible good and the least evil.

In consideration of attempts at providing a *theodicy* toward a resolution of the evidential problem of evil, some posit the goods of things like human free will, soul-making, and future eschatological rewards (such as Richard Swinburne, John Hick, Marilyn McCord Adams, and others) as sufficient to justify God's permission of gratuitous evil in the world. However, as I have argued, this approach raises apparent moral objections for God as allowing horrific evils to occur on account of some associated good as a means of moral justification for those evils. As such, this sort of means/end justification of evil simply does not comport well with one's natural moral inclinations regarding good and evil. Few would agree, for example, that someone allowing a child to get crushed by a bus (when it could have been easily prevented) would be morally justified in doing so on account of perhaps a newly galvanized community spirit that may arise in the wake of such a tragedy. On my view, this sort of argument does not improve the case for gratuitous evil in light of the evidential problem—rather, it seems to make it worse by suggesting that God engages in this sort of means/end moral adjudication that most human moralists agree would be indicative of a moral monster. Further, I have argued that the promise of the future joys of heaven (as per certain eschatological theodicies) as a means to counteract or offset the miseries of earthly life in the face of horrendous evils fails to explain why the horrendous evils would have been necessary in the first place, and it does nothing to resolve the additional problems that arise for those who may never realize such a beatific paradise (such as the damned). This approach tends to make evil either meaningless or pointless (as opposed to gratuitous), which does little to resolve the evidential problem at hand.

A further attempt to resolve the problem of evil is a *defense* (such as that of Alvin Plantinga and Peter van Inwagen), which purports to illustrate how gratuitous evil could *possibly* be answered rather than attempting to describe what is *actually* the case. The most widely recognized defense is Alvin Plantinga's "free will defense" that argues for genuine human freedom as a possible explanation of unavoidable evil across all possible worlds that contain free creatures. However, this view of creaturely freedom does not fit well with the God of classical theism as the first efficient cause of everything that exists—including the creature and its free choices. As I have argued, there does not seem to be a reason that God could not have necessitated free choices to a particular end without violating that freedom—simply by making the goods sought by creatures more clear and obvious among the range of choices available to them, for example. Thus, there does not appear to be any reason to think that God could not have made a world with free creatures and without evil if that is the sort of world he decided to create. Further, Peter van Inwagen's irregularity defense argues that frequent divine intervention toward the prevention of evil would result in a massively irregular world such that the actions of creatures would be effectively meaningless and unpredictable. However, van Inwagen fails to explain why the prevention of at least some evil would violate this principle, and he does not explain how such a "massively irregular world" would be somehow necessarily worse than the present one if it were created instead and functioned perfectly as it was designed. Thus, on my view, defenses seem to struggle in their efforts to resolve the evidential problem.

A final strategy for the theist is that of "skeptical theism" (as from William Alston and Stephen Wykstra), which advocates a general skepticism over what one can expect to recognize and know concerning God and the evil in the world. This approach argues that if God does have justifying reasons for allowing evil in the world, there would be no reason to think that humans would be in the proper epistemic position to know what those reasons truly were (or even what they could possibly be). While rightly emphasizing the epistemic distance between creatures and God, I have argued that the skeptical theist falls short of providing a sufficient response to the problem of evil because it does not explain how evil can be justified even by unseen goods, it raises objections regarding human responsibilities in the face of evil, and it relies on unknown or unknowable evidence as a factor in consideration of otherwise evident examples of evil. As such, the skeptical position by itself does not effectively resolve the evidential argument.

The proper response to the evidential argument from evil, on my view, is not a denial of gratuitous evil as most theodicists and defenders assume, but rather it lies in the denial of God's moral obligation to prevent or mitigate gratuitous evil as much as he is able to do so. Toward an evaluation of God's nature and obligations toward evil, I have advocated for building a proper foundation in a Thomistic natural theology that begins with an argument for God's existence and proceeds to a nuanced understanding of God and his divine attributes and how they relate to the existence of evil in the world. Adopting a position of analogical predication by which to approach a discussion of God and his attributes, I have proposed one such theistic argument from Thomas Aquinas that leads to all of the classical divine attributes of God—Aquinas's *intellectus essentiae* argument. This approach begins from an awareness of sensible reality shared by all humans and argues that everything we see in existence exists as a composite of *essence* (form, nature) and *esse* (act of being, existence). Given this composition, it is evident that everything that exists (or possesses an act of being) must receive that act from another, which necessarily terminates in a being whose essence just *is* its own act of being as the cause of all composite things—or an uncomposed being where *esse* and *essence* are identical. This being would be what Aquinas calls *ipsum esse subsistens*, or "subsistent being itself," which could only be the God of classical theism. Any such being would be necessarily simple, infinite, eternal, immutable, immaterial, and a host of other descriptors on account of what can be subsequently deduced of its nature, as well as the three main attributes of God that are commonly invoked in arguments from evil: omniscience, omnipotence, and perfect goodness.

Given what I have proposed on the basis of God as *ipsum esse subsistens*, God's omniscience follows from his immateriality and his causal relationship with all of creation—knowing perfectly everything in existence (as well as all potentiality or possibility) by a perfect and complete knowledge of himself. God's omnipotence follows as the cause of all being, and thus God is able to actualize any possibility or potentiality since he is necessarily identical with his own act of being. God's perfect goodness follows from God as being purely "in act" on account of his identity of essence and *esse* and thus entirely perfect and absent any potentiality. Further, Aquinas argues that goodness *per se* as an aspect of reality is really identical with being (with the added aspect of desirability), and as a being whose essence *just is* his act of being, God is necessarily perfectly good as an aspect of his own infinite, perfect nature.

As applied to the problem of evil, and on account of God's perfect goodness, I have argued that it is difficult to see in what way God should be properly considered a being who stands in any real relationship with created beings as having some moral duty or obligation on behalf of those creatures (or creation as a whole). As such, a critical premise of the problem of evil is resolved on the basis that God simply does not in fact have a responsibility to limit or mitigate evil (whether gratuitous or not) on behalf of creatures on account of his infinite and perfect goodness. This raises a possible confusion as to what exactly God's goodness would entail if he is not "omnibenevolent" in the sense that some suggest, and further it raises the question as to the relationship between God and evil.

Considering the causes and nature of evil (and following an Aristotelian/Thomistic vein), I have argued that evil is itself a privation of the good—or some lack or deficiency in some existing thing that hinders or prevents it from being everything it should or could be according to its nature. As such, evil cannot exist in God, and it also cannot exist apart from something good that exists in a state of privation or corruption. Therefore, evil must be caused, though it cannot be caused by evil itself (since evil is not a thing) but rather only by what is good—never as an end in itself (since everything that exists is necessarily ordered toward the good in a teleological sense). Thus, evil is caused accidentally, as the byproduct of some good thing acting toward good ends. In this way, God can be the cause of natural evil such that God causes the world to exist and function as its nature requires, and as a byproduct of its natural operations (always ordered to the good), evil can and does result. Further, moral evil is caused by those creatures who have a defect of the will and act in pursuit of the good, though defectively, such that evil follows. Thus, God cannot be the cause of moral evil since God's will is necessarily perfect. Hence, God cannot cause evil directly (as an end in itself) and cannot cause evil on account of some defect in the divine essence that would result in moral evil. Therefore, all evil must necessarily be explained by the good it inhabits and affects in a privative sense as well as the causes of that evil as the accidental byproduct of some good thing acting (as teleologically directed) toward the good.

In consideration of the nature of God and the nature of evil (as from a position of a Thomistic natural theology), I have argued that the evidential problem of evil commits an illicit category mistake by ascribing moral duties and obligations to God on account of his perfect goodness. As such, the evidential argument fails to establish that gratuitous evil is necessarily incompatible with the existence of God, and thus evidence of apparently gratuitous evil in the world offers no evidential support for a denial of God's existence.

Nevertheless, as I have also argued, taking the approach of a denial of God's moral goodness toward a solution to the evidential problem of evil, another potential challenge emerges, akin to what I have called the "why" question of evil. This challenge takes into account what I have argued concerning the nature of God and the nature of evil and takes on a form that is similar to traditional evidential arguments, though without the same category mistake in consideration of God as a "moral being." The new argument embraces the definition of evil as existing only in a privative sense in that which is otherwise good and caused only by other good things teleologically directed toward the good themselves—thus, all evil must necessarily be *explicable* in these terms if those evils occur in a theistic universe. Taking this into account, one may argue that some instance of evil in the world is apparently *inexplicable* in the way I have described, thus one would arguably have cause to deny that the God of classical theism exists as the cause of everything in the world if it also contains inexplicable evil in this way. Since such an argument is inherently limited to identifying some instance of evil that is only inexplicable *from a human perspective* (lacking the direct knowledge of all of the causal interactions involved in some complex instance of evil such that one could not hope to understand how that evil came about and what goods might have been involved), I have argued that the force of this objection is directed not to the existence of God *per se* but to the human act of belief and trust in God in the face of what appears by all accounts to be inexplicable evil.

Considering this new argument, the response must stay true to both the existence and nature of God, the privative nature of evil, and the perspective of the argument as limited and constrained by what humans can or should reasonably conclude concerning God and evil in the world. The solution available to the theist is simply a confidence in God and his nature in the face of evil on the basis of what can be known and demonstrated of God and his nature from a Thomistic natural theology. Thus, the response to this new argument for the theist draws not on the necessity to discover and identify the *actual* explanation of some instance of evil—rather the proper response relies on what the theist can properly know and deduce about the world and its causal operations in consideration of the existence and nature of God and the necessity of an explanation of evil on that basis. As such, so long as God's existence and attributes can be demonstrated and defended by theistic argument, and there is no obvious contradiction apparent in some evidential instance of evil (such as some sort of evil that exists without any possible cause or evil that arises as an end in itself), the new evidential argument is resolved.

An additional consideration is how the theist may rightly identify goods in the universe in relation to evil such that a *possible* explanation of evil is apparent. Here, one can recognize certain goods associated with evil in an explanatory sense, such as goods that arise in the face of evil, the good of the natural order that causes natural evil accidentally, the good of human free will that results in moral evil, and the impact of particular theistic traditions (such as Christianity) that goes to great lengths (on the basis of divine revelation) to explain the metaphysical origin, causes, and ends of evil. Finally, I have considered various possible objections to both the denial of God as a "moral being" and have anticipated objections to my own response to the new evidential argument. As I have concluded, each of these objections fail for one reason or another, and thus I believe I have successfully provided a cogent response to both the traditional evidential problem of evil, as well as the new evidential problem of evil I have proposed.

In consideration of what can be properly understood about God and his nature from a Thomistic natural theology, one can be confident that God exists, he is in fact omniscient, omnipotent, and perfectly good as classical theism affirms, and yet evil does exist in the world that may be genuinely *gratuitous*—with no morally justifying goods associated with that evil. The consistency of theism with the existence of gratuitous evil, therefore, rests on a denial of God as a "moral being" subject to moral duties and obligations in the same way that creatures are. Thus, God is under no obligation to act toward the good of creatures in any way that their suppositional natures do not inherently require—nor is God obliged to create only the world with the most good and least evil possible. Thus, the evidential problem of evil presents no challenge for the theist. Further, a new evidential argument proposed on the basis of the Thomistic approach to natural theology I have defended suggests that some instance of evil can be identified without a sufficient explanation in terms of its causes and the proper teleology involved in those causes. However, so long as a causal explanation remains at least *possible* for any proposed instance of evil, one can be confident that at least some explanation is in fact *actual* on the basis of the same approach to natural theology utilized in response to the original evidential argument. Thus, a committed belief and trust in God in the face of evil (on the basis of what can be known from a Thomistic natural theology) is sufficient to resolve the evidential problem of evil.

Bibliography

Adams, Marilyn McCord. *Christ and Horrors: The Coherence of Christology*. Cambridge: Cambridge University Press, 2006.

———. "Hell and the Justice of God." *Religious Studies* 4 (1975) 433–47.

———. "Horrendous Evils and the Goodness of God." In *The Problem of Evil*, edited by Marilyn McCord Adams and Robert Merrihew Adams, 209–21. Oxford: Oxford University Press, 1990.

———. *Horrendous Evils and the Goodness of God*. Ithaca, NY: Cornell University Press, 1999.

———. "The Problem of Hell: A Problem of Evil for Christians." In *Reasoned Faith: Essays in Philosophical Theology in Honor of Norman Kretzmann*. Ithaca, NY: Cornell University Press, 1993.

———., and Robert Merrihew Adams, eds. *The Problem of Evil*. Oxford: Oxford University Press, 1990.

Adams, Robert M. "Plantinga on the Problem of Evil." In *Alvin Plantinga*, edited by James E. Tomberlin and Peter van Inwagen, 225–55. Dordrecht, Netherlands: D. Reidel, 1985.

Allen, Diogenes. *Traces of God*. Cambridge: Cowley, 1981.

———. "Natural Evil and the Love of God." *Religious Studies* 16 (1980) 439–56.

Alston, William P. "The Inductive Argument from Evil and the Human Cognitive Condition." *Philosophical Perspectives* 5: "Philosophy of Religion" (1991) 29–67.

———. "Theism as a Theory and the Problem of Evil." *Topoi* 2 (1995) 135–48.

Aquinas, Thomas. *De Ente et Essentia*. Translated by Joseph Kenny. https://isidore.co/aquinas/DeEnte&Essentia.htm.

———. *De Spiritualibus Creaturis*. Translated by Mary C. Fitzpatrick and John J. Wellmuth. https://isidore.co/aquinas/QDdeSpirCreat.htm.

———. *Expositio in Symbolum Apostolorum*. Translated by Joseph B. Collins. https://isidore.co/aquinas/Creed.htm.

———. *Expositio Libri Peryermeneias*. Translated by Jean T. Oesterle. https://isidore.co/aquinas/PeriHermeneias.htm.

———. *Expositio Super Iob ad Litteram*. Translated by Brian Mulladay. https://isidore.co/aquinas/SSJob.htm#014.

———. *On Evil*. Translated by Richard Regan. Edited by Brian Davies. Oxford: Oxford University Press, 2003.

———. *Quaestiones Disputatae de Potentia*. Translated by the English Dominican Fathers. https://isidore.co/aquinas/QDdePotentia.htm.

———. *Questiones Disputatae de Veritate*. Translated by Robert W. Mulligan. https://isidore.co/aquinas/QDdeVer.htm.

———. *Summa Contra Gentiles: Book One*. Translated by Anton C. Pegis. https://isidore.co/aquinas/ContraGentiles.htm.

———. *Summa Theologica*. Translated by Fathers of the English Dominican Province. https://isidore.co/aquinas/summa/index.html.

———. *Super ad Romanos*. Translated by Fr. Fabian R. Larcher. Edited by the Aquinas Institute. https://aquinas.cc/la/en/~Rom.

———. *Expositio in Symbolum Apostolorum*. Translated by Joseph B. Collins. New York: 1939. https://isidore.co/aquinas/Creed.htm.

Augustine. *City of God*. Translated by Marcus Dods. Peabody, MA: Hendrickson, 2009.

———. *Enchiridion*. Translated by Albert C. Outler. http://www.tertullian.org/fathers/augustine_enchiridion_02_trans.htm#C3.

———. *On the Free Choice of the Will, On Grace and Free Choice, and Other Writings*. Edited and translated by Peter King. Cambridge University Press, 2010.

Berger, Robert L. "Nazi Science—The Dachau Hypothermia Experiments." *New England Journal of Medicine* 20 (1990) 1435–40.

Billings, Todd. "Theodicy as a 'Lived Question': Moving Beyond a Theoretical Approach to Theodicy." *Journal for Christian Theological Research* 2 (2000) 33–54.

Boethius. *The Consolation of Philosophy of Boethius*. Translated by H. R. James. https://www.gutenberg.org/cache/epub/14328/pg14328-images.html.

Ayer, A. J. *Language, Truth, and Logic*. New York: Dover, 1952.

Blanchette, Kyle, and Jerry L. Walls. "God and Hell Reconciled." In *God and Evil: The Case for God in a World Filled with Pain*, edited by Chad Meister and James K. Dew Jr., 243–58. Downers Grove, IL: IVP, 2013.

Bonner, Gerald. *Freedom and Necessity: St. Augustine's Teaching on Divine Power and Human Freedom*. Washington, DC: Catholic University of America Press, 2007.

Boyd, Gregory A. *God at War: The Bible and Spiritual Conflict*. Downers Grove, IL: InterVarsity, 1997.

———. *Satan and the Problem of Evil: Constructing a Trinitarian Warfare Theodicy*. Downers Grove, IL: IVP Academic, 2001.

Brown, Michael L. *Job: The Faith to Challenge God*. Peabody, MA: Hendrickson Academic, 2019.

Burrell, David. *Analogy and Philosophical Language*. Eugene, OR: Wipf & Stock, 2016.

Butler, Joshua Ryan. *The Skeletons in God's Closet*. Nashville: W Publishing Group, 2014.

Cary, Phillip. "A Classic View." In *God and the Problem of Evil: Five Views*, edited by Chad Meister and James K. Dew Jr., 13–36. Downers Grove, IL: IVP Academic, 2017.

Copan, Paul. "Evil and Primeval Sin: How Evil Emerged in a Very Good Creation." In *God and Evil: The Case for God in a World Filled with Pain*, edited by Chad Meister and James K. Dew, 109–23. Downers Grove, IL: IVP, 2013.

Cornman, James W., Keith Lehrer, and George S. Pappas. *Philosophical Problems and Arguments: An Introduction*. 4th ed. Indianapolis: Hackett, 1992.

Davies, Brian. *An Introduction to the Philosophy of Religion*. 3rd ed. Oxford: Oxford University Press, 2004.

———. *Philosophy of Religion: A Guide and Anthology*. Oxford University Press, 2000.

———. *The Reality of God and the Problem of Evil*. London: Continuum, 2006.

———. *Thomas Aquinas on God and Evil*. Oxford: Oxford University Press, 2011.

———. *Thomas Aquinas's Summa Theologiae: A Guide and Commentary*. Oxford: Oxford University Press, 2014.

———. *The Thought of Thomas Aquinas*. Oxford: Clarendon Press, 1992.

———., and Eleanor Stump, ed. *The Oxford Handbook of Aquinas*. Oxford: Oxford University Press, 2012.

Davis, Stephen T., ed. *Encountering Evil: Live Options in Theodicy*. Louisville: Westminster/John Knox Press, 2001.

DeWeese, Garry. "Natural Evil: A 'Free Process' Defense." In *God and Evil: The Case for God in a World Filled with Pain*, edited by Chad Meister and James K. Dew Jr., 53–64. Downers Grove, IL: IVP, 2013.

Dolezal, James E. *God Without Parts: Divine Simplicity and the Metaphysics of God's Absoluteness*. Eugene, OR: Pickwick, 2011.

Draper, Paul. "Pain and Pleasure: An Evidential Problem for Theists." *Nous* 3 (1989) 331–50.

———. "Probabilistic Arguments from Evil." *Religious Studies* 3 (1992) 303–17.

———. "The Problem of Evil." In *The Oxford Handbook of Philosophical Theology*, edited by Thomas P. Flint and Michael C. Rea, 332–51. Oxford: Oxford University Press, 2009.

———. "The Skeptical Theist." In *The Evidential Argument from Evil*, edited by Daniel Howard-Snyder, 175–92. Bloomington, IN: Indiana University Press, 1996.

Eagleton, Terry. *On Evil*. New Haven: Yale University Press, 2010.

Earl, Dennis. "Divine Intimacy and the Problem of Horrendous Evil." *International Journal for Philosophy of Religion* 1 (2011) 17–28.

Ehrman, Bart D. *God's Problem: How the Bible Fails to Answer Our Most Important Question—Why We Suffer*. New York: Harper One, 2008.

Elders, Leo. *The Philosophical Theology of St. Thomas Aquinas*. Leiden, Netherlands: Brill, 1990.

Erickson, Millard J. *Christian Theology*. 2nd ed. Grand Rapids: Baker, 2001.

Farley, Wendy. *Tragic Vision and Divine Compassion: A Contemporary Theodicy*. Louisville: Westminster/John Knox, 1990.

Feser, Edward. *Aquinas*. London: Oneworld, 2013.

———. *The Last Superstition: A Refutation of the New Atheism*. South Bend, IN: St. Augustine's, 2008.

———. *Philosophy of Mind: A Beginner's Guide*. Oxford: Oneworld, 2006.

Fiddes, Paul S. "Christianity, Atonement, and Evil." In *The Cambridge Companion to the Problem of Evil*, edited by Chad Meister and Paul K. Moser, 210–29. New York: Cambridge University Press, 2017.

Fitzpatrick, F. J. "The Onus of Proof in Arguments About the Problem of Evil." *Religious Studies* 17 (1981) 19–38.

Ganssle, Gregory E. "Evil as Evidence for Christianity." In *God and Evil: The Case for God in a World Filled with Pain*, edited by Chad Meister and James K. Dew Jr., 214–26. Downers Grove, IL: IVP, 2013.

———., and Yena Lee. "Evidential Problems of Evil." In *God and Evil: The Case for God in a World Filled with Pain*, edited by Chad Meister and James K. Dew Jr., 15–25. Downers Grove, IL: IVP, 2013.

Garcia, Laura "Moral Perfection." In *The Oxford Handbook of Philosophical Theology*, edited by Thomas P. Flint and Michael C. Rea, 217–40. Oxford: Oxford University Press, 2013.

Geach, P. T. "Good and Evil." *Analysis* 2 (1956) 33–42.
Geisler, Norman L. *God and Philosophy*. London: Yale University Press, 2002.
———. *If God, Why Evil?* Minneapolis: Bethany House, 2011.
———. *The Roots of Evil*. 3rd ed. Matthews, NC: Bastion, 2013.
———. *Systematic Theology, Volume Two: God and Creation*. Minneapolis: Bethany House, 2003.
———., and Winfried Corduan. *Philosophy of Religion*. 2nd ed. Grand Rapids: Baker, 1988.
Geivett, R. Douglas. "Augustine and the Problem of Evil." In *God and Evil: The Case for God in a World Filled with Pain*, edited by Chad Meister and James K. Dew Jr., 65–79. Downers Grove, IL: IVP, 2013.
Gilson, Etienne. *Being and Some Philosophers*. 2nd ed. Toronto: Pontifical Institute of Mediaeval Studies, 1952.
———. *The Christian Philosophy of St. Thomas Aquinas*. Translated by L. K. Shook. 1956; Notre Dame: University of Notre Dame Press, 2013.
———. *God and Philosophy*. 2nd ed. New Haven: Yale University Press, 2002.
———. *Methodical Realism*. Translated by Philip Trower. 1935; San Francisco: Ignatius, 1990.
Hanink, James G., ed. *Aquinas & Maritain on Evil: Mystery and Metaphysics*. Washington, DC: Catholic University of America Press, 2013.
Hasker, William. "The Open Theist Response." In *God and the Problem of Evil: Five Views*, edited by Chad Meister and James K. Dew Jr., 151–62. Downers Grove, IL: IVP Academic, 2017.
———. *God, Time, and Foreknowledge*. Ithaca, NY: Cornell University, 2019.
———. *Providence, Evil, and the Openness of God*. New York: Rutledge, 2004.
Helm, Paul. *The Providence of God: Contours of Christian Theology*. Downers Grove, IL: InterVarsity, 1993.
Helseth, Paul Kloss. "On Divine Ambivalence: Open Theism and the Problem of Particular Evils." *Journal of the Evangelical Theological Society* 3 (2001) 493–511.
Hernandez, Jill Graper. "Leibniz and the Best of All Possible Worlds." In *God and Evil: The Case for God in a World Filled with Pain*, edited by Chad Meister and James K. Dew Jr., 94–108. Downers Grove, IL: IVP, 2013.
Hick, John. *Evil and the God of Love*. 1966; New York: Palgrave Macmillan, 2010.
———. "God, Evil, and Mystery." *Religious Studies* 2 (1968) 539–46.
———. "Richard Swinburne, Providence and the Problem of Evil." *International Journal for Philosophy of Religion* 47 (2000) 57–61.
———. "Soul-making and Suffering." In *The Problem of Evil*, edited by Marilyn McCord Adams and Robert Merrihew Adams, 168–88. Oxford: Oxford University Press, 1990.
Holland, R. F. *Against Empiricism: On Education, Epistemology, and Value*. Totowa, NJ: Barnes & Noble, 1980.
Holloway, Maurice. *An Introduction to Natural Theology*. New York: Appleton-Century-Crofts, 1959.
Howard-Snyder, Daniel. "The Argument from Inscrutable Evil." In *The Evidential Argument from Evil*, edited by Daniel Howard-Snyder, 286–310. Bloomington, IN: Indiana University Press, 1996.
———, ed. *The Evidential Argument from Evil*. Bloomington, IN: Indiana University Press, 1996.

Hume, David. *Dialogues Concerning Natural Religion.* 2nd ed. Edited by Richard H. Hopkins. Indianapolis: Hackett, 1998.

Irwin, Terence. *Aristotle's First Principles.* Oxford: Oxford University Press, 1988.

Kellenberger, James. *God's Goodness and God's Evil.* Lanham, MD: Lexington, 2017.

Kenny, Anthony. *Aquinas on Being.* Oxford: Oxford University Press, 2002.

———. "Divine Foreknowledge and Human Freedom." In *Readings in the Philosophy of Religion: An Analytic Approach*, edited by Baruch A. Brody, 403–13. Englewood Cliffs, NJ: 1974.

———. *What Is Faith?: Essays in the Philosophy of Religion.* Oxford: Oxford University Press, 1992.

Kerr, Gavin. *Aquinas's Way to God: The Proof in* De Ente et Essentia. Oxford: Oxford University Press, 2015.

Klubertanz, George P. *St. Thomas Aquinas on Analogy: A Textual Analysis and Systematic Synthesis.* Eugene, OR: Wipf & Stock, 1960.

Kreeft, Peter. *Making Sense Out of Suffering.* Cincinnati: Servant, 1983.

Kretzmann, Norman, Anthony Kenny, Jan Pinborg, and Eleonore Stump. "Thomas Aquinas on Human Action." In *The Cambridge History of Later Medieval Philosophy*, 642–54. Cambridge: Cambridge University Press, 1982.

Larrimore, Mark, ed. *The Problem of Evil: A Reader.* Malden, MA: Blackwell, 2001.

Leibniz, Gottfried Wilhelm. *Theodicy.* Whithorn, UK: Anados, 2019.

Leon, Felipe. "A Perfectly Good Personal Foundation: Some Reasons for Doubt." In *Is God the Best Explanation of Things?: A Dialogue.* London: Palgrave Macmillan, 2019.

Lewis, C. S. *The Problem of Pain.* San Francisco: Harper, 2001.

Little, Bruce A. *A Creation-Order Theodicy: God and Gratuitous Evil.* Lanham, MD: University Press of America, 2005.

———. "God and Gratuitous Evil." In *God and Evil: The Case for God in a World Filled with Pain*, edited by Chad Meister and James K. Dew Jr., 38–52. Downers Grove, IL: IVP, 2013.

———. *God, Why This Evil?* Lanham, MD: Hamilton, 2010.

Long, Steven A. "God, Freedom, and the Permission of Evil." In *Aquinas and Maritain on Evil.* Edited by James G. Hanink. Washington, DC: Catholic University of America Press, 2013.

———. "On the Natural Knowledge of the Real Distinction of Essence and Existence." *Nova et Vetera* 1 (2003) 75–108.

Macdonald, Paul A., Jr. "Hell, the Problem of Evil, and the Perfection of the Universe." *American Catholic Philosophical Quarterly* 4 (2015) 603–28.

MacDonald, Scott, ed. *Being and Goodness.* Ithaca, NY: Cornell University Press, 1991.

Mackie, J. L. "Evil and Omnipotence." *Mind* 254 (1955) 200–212.

MacPherson, Anthony. *The Redeemed Good Defense: The Great Controversy as a Theodicy Response to the Evidential Problem of Evil.* Eugene, OR: Wipf & Stock, 2021.

MacQuarrie, John. *God-Talk: Examination of the Language and Logic of Theology.* New York: Harper & Row, 1967.

Martin, Edward N. "Planting a Rawlsian Garden: Proper Function, the Problem of Evil, and 'Thinking Behind the Veil.'" In *Tough-Minded Christianity*, edited by William Dembski and Thomas Schirrmacher, 558–96. Nashville: B&H, 2008.

Martin, Michael. "Is Evil Evidence Against the Existence of God?" In *The Problem of Evil: Selected Readings*. Edited by Michael L. Peterson. 1st ed. Notre Dame: University of Notre Dame Press, 1992.

Mavrodes, George I. "Some Puzzles Concerning Omnipotence." *Philosophical Review* 72 (1963) 221–23.

McCabe, Herbert. *God and Evil in the Theology of St. Thomas Aquinas*. Edited by Brian Davies. London: Continuum, 2010.

McCloskey, H. J. "Evil and the Problem of Evil." *Sophia* 5 (1966) 14–19.

———. "The Problem of Evil." *Journal of Bible and Religion* 3 (1962) 187–97.

McCluskey, Colleen. "Intellective Appetite and the Freedom of Human Action." *Thomist* 66 (2002) 434–42.

Moreland, J. P., and William Lane Craig. *Philosophical Foundations for a Christian Worldview*. Downers Grove, IL: IVP Academic, 2017.

Moreno, *Undue Risk: Secret State Experiments on Humans*. New York: Routledge, 2001.

Morris, Thomas V. *Our Idea of God: An Introduction to Philosophical Theology*. Downers Grove, IL: InterVarsity, 1991.

Moskop, John C. *Divine Omniscience and Human Freedom: Thomas Aquinas and Charles Hartshorne*. Macon, GA: Mercer University Press, 1984.

Murray, Michael J. "Theodicy." In *The Oxford Handbook of Philosophical Theology*, edited by Thomas P. Flint and Michael C. Rea, 352–73. Oxford: Oxford University Press, 2009.

O'Connor, David. *God and Inscrutable Evil: In Defense of Theism and Atheism*. Lanham, MD: Rowman & Littlefield, 1998.

Oppy, Graham. "Logical Problems of Evil and Free Will Defenses." In *The Cambridge Companion to the Problem of Evil*, edited by Chad Meister and Paul K. Moser, 45–64. New York: Cambridge University Press, 2017.

Owens, Joseph. "Aquinas' Distinction at *De Ente et Essentia* 4.119–23." *Mediaevil Studies* 48 (1986) 264–87.

———. *An Elementary Christian Metaphysics*. Houston: Center for Thomistic Studies, 1985.

———. "Quiddity and Real Distinction in St. Thomas Aquinas." *Mediaevil Studies* 27 (1965) 1–22.

Peckham, John C. *Theodicy of Love: Cosmic Conflict and the Problem of Evil*. Grand Rapids: Baker Academic, 2018.

Penelhum, Terence. "Divine Goodness and the Problem of Evil." *Religious Studies* 1 (1966) 95–107.

Peterson, Michael L. "Christian Theism and the Problem of Evil." *Journal of the Evangelical Theological Society* 1 (1978) 35–46.

———. *Evil and the Christian God*. Grand Rapids: Baker, 1982.

———. *God and Evil: An Introduction to the Issues*. Boulder, CO: Westview, 1998.

Phillips, D. Z. *The Problem of Evil and the Problem of God*. Minneapolis: Augsburg Fortress, 2005.

———. "Theism without Theodicy." In *Encountering Evil: Live Options in Theodicy*. Edited by Stephen T. Davis. Louisville: Westminster John Knox, 2001.

Pike, Nelson. "Hume on Evil." *Philosophical Review* 72 (1963) 180–97.

———. "Omnipotence and God's Ability to Sin." *American Philosophical Quarterly* 6 (1969) 208–16.

Pilsner, Joseph. *The Specification of Human Actions in St. Thomas Aquinas*. Oxford: Oxford University Press, 2006.

Plantinga, Alvin. "Ad Walls." *Philosophy and Phenomenological Research* 3 (1991) 621–24.

———. "On Being Evidentially Challenged." In *The Evidential Argument from Evil*, edited by Daniel Howard-Snyder, 244–61. Bloomington, IN: Indiana University Press, 1996.

———. *Does God Have a Nature?* Milwaukee: Marquette University Press, 1980.

———. "Epistemic Probability and Evil." In *The Evidential Argument from Evil*, edited by Daniel Howard-Snyder, 69–96. Bloomington, IN: Indiana University Press, 1996.

———. *God, Freedom, and Evil*. Grand Rapids: Eerdmans, 1977.

———. *God and Other Minds: A Study of the Rational Justification of Belief in God*. Ithaca, NY: Cornell University Press, 1967.

———. *The Nature of Necessity*. Oxford: Clarendon, 1974.

———. "On Ockham's Way Out." *Faith and Philosophy* 3 (1986) 235–69.

Poe, Harry Lee, and J. Stanley Mattson, ed. *What God Knows: Time, Eternity, and Divine Knowledge*. Waco, TX: Baylor University Press, 2005.

Quinn, Philip L. "God, Moral Perfection, and Possible Worlds." In *The Problem of Evil: Selected Readings*, 2nd ed., edited by Michael L. Peterson, 428–43. Notre Dame: University of Notre Dame Press, 2017.

Reichenbach, Bruce. *Evil and a Good God*. New York: Fordham University Press, 1982.

Rice, Richard. *Suffering and the Search for Meaning: Contemporary Responses to the Problem of Pain*. Downers Grove, IL: IVP Academic, 2014.

Rocca, Gregory P. *Speaking the Incomprehensible God: Thomas Aquinas on the Interplay of Positive and Negative Theology*. Washington, DC: Catholic University of America Press, 2004.

Rowe, William L. "Augustine on Foreknowledge and Free Will." *Review of Metaphysics* 18 (1964) 356–63.

———. "Divine Power, Goodness, and Knowledge." In *The Oxford Handbook of Philosophy of Religion*, edited by William J. Wainwright, 15–34. New York: Oxford University Press, 2005.

———. "The Evidential Argument from Evil: A Second Look." In *The Evidential Argument from Evil* by Daniel Howard-Snyder, 262–85. Bloomington: Indiana University Press, 1996.

———. "Evil and the Theistic Hypothesis: A Response to Wykstra." *International Journal for Philosophy of Religion* 16 (1984) 95–100.

———, ed. *God and the Problem of Evil*. Malden, MA: Blackwell, 2001.

———. *Philosophy of Religion: An Introduction*. 4th ed. Belmont, CA: Wadsworth, 2007.

———. "The Problem of Evil and Some Varieties of Atheism." *American Philosophical Quarterly* 4 (1979) 335–41.

———. "Ruminations About Evil." *Philosophical Perspectives* 5 (1991) 69–88.

Russell, Bertrand. *Why I Am Not a Christian*. New York: Simon & Schuster, 1957.

Russell, Bruce. "Defenseless." In *The Evidential Argument from Evil* by Daniel Howard-Snyder, 196–205. Bloomington, IN: Indiana University Press, 1996.

Sanders, John. "God, Evil, and Relational Risk." In *The Problem of Evil*, edited by Michael L. Peterson, 327–43. Notre Dame: University of Notre Dame Press, 2017.

———. *The God Who Risks: A Theology of Providence*. Downers Grove, IL: InterVarsity, 1998.

Savage, C. Wade. "The Paradox of the Stone." *Philosophical Review* 76 (1967) 74–79.

Schellenberg, J. L. "Stalemate and Strategy: Rethinking the Evidential Argument from Evil." *American Philosophical Quarterly* 4 (2000) 405–19.

Schlesinger, G. "The Problem of Evil and the Problem of Suffering." *American Philosophical Quarterly* 3 (1964) 244–47.

Scott, Mark S. M. *Pathways in Theodicy: An Introduction to the Problem of Evil*. Minneapolis: Fortress, 2014.

Scott, Michael. *Religious Language*. New York: Palgrave Macmillan, 2013.

Sehon, Scott. "The Problem of Evil: Skeptical Theism Leads to Moral Paralysis." *International Journal of the Philosophy of Religion* 67 (2010) 67–80.

Shanley, Brian. "Eternal Knowledge of the Temporal in Aquinas." *American Catholic Philosophical Quarterly* 71 (1997) 197–224.

———. *The Thomist Tradition*. London: Kluwer Academic, 2002.

Smith, George H. *Atheism: The Case Against God*. New York: Prometheus, 1989.

Soelle, Dorothy. *Suffering*. London: Darton, Longman, & Todd, 1975.

Spiegel, James S. "Hell and the Problem of Eternal Evil." *Toronto Journal of Theology* 2 (2015) 239–48.

Stackhouse, John G. *Can God Be Trusted? Faith and the Challenge of Evil*. Downers Grove, IL: IVP, 2009.

Staley, Kevin M. "Aquinas: Compatibilist or Libertarian?" *Saint Anselm Journal* 2 (2005) 73–79.

Sterba, James P. *Is a Good God Logically Possible?* Cham, Switzerland: Palgrave Macmillan, 2019.

Steuer, Axel D. "The Epistemic Status of Theistic Belief." *Journal of the American Academy of Religion* 2 (1987) 235–56.

Stump, Eleanor, and Norman Kretzmann. "Eternity and God's Knowledge: A Reply to Shanley." *American Catholic Philosophical Quarterly* 72 (1998) 439–45.

Stump, Eleanor. *Aquinas*. London: Routledge, 2009.

———. "Aquinas on the Sufferings of Job." In *The Evidential Argument from Evil*, edited by Daniel Howard-Snyder, 49–68. Bloomington, IN: Indiana University Press, 1996.

———. "The Problem of Suffering: A Thomistic Approach." In *The Problem of Evil: Eight Views in Dialogue*. Edited by N. N. Trakakis. Oxford: Oxford University Press, 2018.

———. *Wandering in the Darkness: Narrative and the Problem of Suffering*. Oxford: Oxford University Press, 2010.

Surin, Kenneth. *Theology and the Problem of Evil*. Eugene, OR: Wipf & Stock, 2004.

Swinburne, Richard. *The Coherence of Theism*. 2nd ed. Oxford: Oxford University Press, 2016.

———. *The Existence of God*. 2nd ed. Oxford: Oxford University Press, 2004.

———. "Knowledge from Experience and the Problem of Evil." In *The Rationality of Religious Belief: Essays in Honour of Basil Mitchell*, edited by William J. Abraham and Steven W. Holtzer, 141–67. Oxford: Clarendon, 1987.

———. "Natural Evils and Moral Choice." In *The Problem of Evil: Selected Readings*, 2nd ed., edited by Michael L. Peterson, 444–58. Notre Dame: University of Notre Dame Press, 2017.

———. *Providence and the Problem of Evil.* Oxford: Clarendon, 1998.

———. "Some Major Strands of Theodicy." In *The Evidential Argument from Evil*, edited by Daniel Howard-Snyder, 30–48. Bloomington: Indiana University Press, 1996.

———. "A Theodicy of Heaven and Hell." In *The Existence and Nature of God*, edited by Alfred J. Freddoso, 35–54. Notre Dame: University of Notre Dame Press, 1983.

Tilley, Terrence W. *The Evils of Theodicy.* Eugene, OR: Wipf and Stock, 2000.

Tinker, Melvin. "Purpose in Pain?: Teleology and the Problem of Evil." *Themelios* 3 (1991) 15–18.

Torrell, Jean-Pierre. *Saint Thomas Aquinas: The Person and His Work.* Washington, DC: Catholic University Press of America, 1996.

Trakakis, N. N. "Anti-Theodicy." In *The Cambridge Companion to the Problem of* Evil, edited by Chad Meister and Paul K. Moser, 124–46. New York: Cambridge University Press, 2017.

———. *The God Beyond Belief: In Defence of William Rowe's Evidential Argument from Evil.* Dordrecht, Netherlands: Springer, 2007.

———. "Rowe's New Evidential Argument from Evil: Problems and Prospects." *Sophia* 1 (2006) 57–77.

Twetten, David. "How Save Aquinas's '*Intellectus Essentiae* Argument' for the Real Distinction between Essence and *Esse*?" *Roczniki Filozoficzne: Annals of Philosophy* 4 (2019) 129–43.

van Inwagen, Peter. "Ontological Arguments." *Nous* 11 (1977) 375–95.

———. *The Problem of Evil: The Gifford Lectures Delivered in the University of Saint Andrews in 2003.* Oxford: Clarendon Press, 2006.

———. "Problem of Evil, the Problem of Air, and the Problem of Silence." *Philosophical Perspectives* 5 (1991) 135–65.

Vanhoozer, Kevin J. *Faith Speaking Understanding: Performing the Drama of Doctrine.* Louisville: Westminster John Knox, 2005.

Vitale, Vince R. *Non-Identity Theodicy: A Grace-Based Response to the Problem of Evil.* Oxford: Oxford University Press, 2020.

Walls, Jerry L. "A Fable of Foreknowledge and Freedom." *Philosophy* 239 (Jan 1987) 67–75.

———. "Why Plantinga Must Move from Defense to Theodicy." *Philosophy and Phenomenological Research* 2 (1991) 375–78.

Weingartner, Paul. *Theodicy—From a Logical Point of View.* Berlin: Peter Lang, 2021.

Wetzel, James. "Can Theodicy Be Avoided? The Claim of Unredeemed Evil." *Religious Studies* 25 (1989) 1–13.

Wilhelmsen, Frederick D. *Man's Knowledge of Reality: An Introduction to Thomistic Epistemology.* Brooklyn: Angelica, 2021.

Wippel, John F. *The Metaphysical Thought of Thomas Aquinas: From Finite Being to Uncreated Being.* Washington, DC: Catholic University Press of America, 2000.

Wittgenstein, Ludwig. *Tractatus Logico-Philosophicus.* London: Kegan Paul, Trench, Trubner, 1922.

Wright, N. T. *Evil and the Justice of God.* Downers Grove, IL: IVP, 2006.

Wykstra, Stephen J. "The Humean Obstacle to Evidential Arguments from Suffering: On Avoiding the Evils of 'Appearance.'" *International Journal for Philosophy of Religion* 16 (1984) 73–93.

———. "Rowe's Noseeum Arguments from Evil." In *The Evidential Argument from Evil*. Edited by Daniel Howard-Snyder, 126–50. Bloomington, IN: Indiana University Press, 1996.

Zaibert, Leo. "Beyond Bad: Punishment Theory Meets the Problem of Evil." *Midwest Studies in Philosophy* 1 (2012) 93–111.

Zagzebski, Linda Trinkaus. *The Dilemma of Freedom and Foreknowledge*. New York: Oxford University Press, 1991.

———., and Timothy D. Miller, eds. *Readings in Philosophy of Religion: Ancient to Contemporary*. Malden, MA: Wiley-Blackwell, 2009.

Subject Index

Name Index

www.ingramcontent.com/pod-product-compliance
Lightning Source LLC
LaVergne TN
LVHW020540100826
845148LV00010B/1548
9798385262823